BELLY LAUGHS FOR ALL!

Adult Version Volume 3

ROBERTA CAVA

Belly Laughs for All!
Adult Version
Volume 3
Roberta Cava

Published by Cava Consulting
105 / 3 Township Drive,
Burleigh Heads, 4220, Queensland, Australia
info@dealingwithdifficultpeople.info

Discover other titles by Roberta Cava at
www.dealingwithdifficultpeople.info

National Library of Australia
Cataloguing-in-publication data:

ISBN: 97809923579-0-0

BOOKS BY ROBERTA CAVA

Dealing with Difficult People

(22 publishers – in 16 languages)

Dealing with Difficult Situations – at Work and at Home

Dealing with Difficult Spouses and Children

Dealing with Difficult Relatives and In-Laws

Dealing with Domestic Violence and Child Abuse

Dealing with School Bullying

Dealing with Workplace Bullying

What am I going to do with the rest of my life?

Before tying the knot – Questions couples Must ask each other Before they marry!

How Women can advance in business

Survival Skills for Supervisors and Managers

Easy Come – Hard to go – The Art of Hiring, Disciplining and Firing Employees

Human Resources at its best!

Time and Stress – Today's silent killers

Take Command of your Future – Make things Happen

Human Resources Policies and Procedures

Employee Handbook

Belly laughs for All! - Volumes 1-4

Wisdom of the World! - The happy, sad and wise things in life!

That Something Special

BELLY LAUGHS FOR ALL!

Adult Version

Volume 3

Table of Contents

INTRODUCTION

This book is unlike any others I have written. Most of my books relate to how to deal with difficult people and situations. I had been feeling very depressed after writing my last three books - which focused around bullying - at home, at school and at work. This was a lovely change from that disturbing and depressing research.

I had collected jokes for years and enjoyed reading them whenever I felt down-in-the-dumps. This is what stimulated me to write a book on humour. It was soon evident that I had too many jokes for just one volume, hence wrote Volumes 1 to 4. They discuss humour in different areas, so there's no repetition. I also realised that the books were meant for adult audiences and **are not suitable for children.**

I hope you enjoy this volume enough to want to obtain the other three volumes.

COUPLES

Grounds for divorce

A judge was interviewing a woman regarding her pending divorce and asked, *'What are the grounds for your divorce?'*

She replied, *'About four acres and a nice little home in the middle of the property with a stream running by.'*

'No,' he said, *'I mean what is the foundation of this case?'*

'It is made of concrete, brick and mortar,' she responded.

'I mean,' he continued, *'what are your relations like?'*

'I have an aunt and uncle living here in town and so do my husband's parents.'

He said, *'Do you have a real grudge?'*

'No,' she replied, *'we have a two-car carport and have never really needed one.'*

'Please,' he tried again, *'is there any infidelity in your marriage?'*

'Yes, both my son and daughter have stereo sets. We don't necessarily like the music, but the answer to your questions is yes.'

'Ma'am, does your husband ever beat you up?'

'Yes,' she responded, *'about twice a week he gets up earlier than I do.'*

Finally, in frustration, the judge asked, *'Lady, why do you want a divorce?'*

'Oh, I don't want a divorce,' she replied. *'I've never wanted a divorce. My husband does. He said he can't communicate with me!'*

True Love

He: *'Whenever I get mad at you, you never seem to get upset. How do you manage to control your temper?'*
She: *'I just go and clean the toilet.'*
He: *'How does that help?'*
She: *'I use your toothbrush.'*

No Pain

A married couple went to the hospital to have their baby delivered. Upon their arrival, the doctor said that the hospital was testing an amazing new high-tech machine that would transfer a portion of the mother's labour pain to the baby's father. He asked if they were interested. Both said they were very much in favour of it.

The doctor set the pain transfer to 10% for starters, explaining that even 10% was probably more pain than the father had ever experienced before. But as the labour progressed, the husband felt fine and asked the doctor to go ahead and kick it up a notch. The doctor then adjusted the machine to 20% pain transfer. The husband was still feeling fine. The doctor then checked the husband's blood pressure and was amazed at how well he was doing.

At this point they decided to try for 50%. The husband continued to feel quite well. Since the pain transfer was obviously helping the wife considerably, the husband encouraged the doctor to transfer ALL the pain to him.

The wife delivered a healthy baby with virtually no pain and the husband had experienced none. She and her husband were ecstatic. When they got home they found the milkman dead on the porch.

And then the Fight Started:

My wife and I were watching Who wants to be a Millionaire while we were in bed. I turned to her and said, *'Do you want to have sex?'*

'No,' she answered.

I then said, *'Is that your final answer?'* She didn't even look at me this time, simply saying *'Yes.'*

So I said, *'Then I'd like to phone a friend.'*

And then the fight started ...

I asked my wife, *'Where do you want to go for our anniversary?'*

It warmed my heart to see her face melt in sweet appreciation. *'Somewhere I haven't been in a long time!'* she said.

So I suggested, *'How about the kitchen?'*

And then the fight started ...

Saturday morning I got up early, quietly dressed, made my lunch, grabbed the dog and slipped quietly into the garage. I hooked up the boat up to the truck and proceeded to back out into a torrential downpour. The wind was blowing 50 mph, so I pulled back into the garage, turned on the radio and discovered that the weather would be bad all day. I went back into the house, quietly undressed and slipped back into bed. I cuddled up to my wife's back, now with a different anticipation and whispered, *'The weather out there is terrible.'*

My loving wife of ten years replied, *'Can you believe my stupid husband is out fishing in that?'*

And then the fight started ...

A man and a woman were asleep like two innocent babies. Suddenly, at 3 o'clock in the morning, a loud noise came from outside. The woman, bewildered, jumped up from the bed and yelled at the man *'Holy Shit! That must be my husband!'*

So the man jumped out of the bed; scared and naked jumped out the window. He smashed himself on the ground, ran through a thorn bush and to his car as fast as he could go. A few minutes later he returned and went up to the bedroom and screamed at the woman, *'I am your husband!'*

The woman yelled back, *'Yeah, then why were you running?'*

And then the fight started ...

I tried to talk my wife into buying a case of Miller Light for $14.95. Instead, she bought a jar of cold cream for $7.95. I told her the beer would make her look better to me at night than the cold cream.

And then the fight started ...

A woman was standing nude, looking in the bedroom mirror. She was not happy with what she saw and said to her husband, *'I feel horrible; I look old, fat and ugly. I really need you to pay me a compliment.'*

The husband replies, *'Your eyesight's damn near perfect.'*

And then the fight started ...

I took my wife to a restaurant. The waiter, for some reason, took my order first.

'I'll have the strip steak, medium rare, please.'

He said, *'Aren't you worried about the mad cow?'*

'Nah, she can order for herself.'

And then the fight started ...

My wife and I were sitting at a table at my high school reunion and I kept staring at a drunken lady swigging her drink as she sat alone at a nearby table.

My wife asked, *'Do you know her?'*

'Yes,' I sighed, *'she's my old girlfriend. I understand she took to drinking right after we split up those many years ago and I hear she hasn't been sober since.'*

'My God!' said my wife, *'who would think a person could go on celebrating that long?'*

And then the fight started ...

After retiring, I went to the Social Security office to apply for Social Security. The woman behind the counter asked me for my driver's license to verify my age. I looked in my pockets and realised I had left my wallet at home. I told the woman that I was very sorry, but I would have to go home and come back later.

The woman said, *'Unbutton your shirt.'* So I opened my shirt revealing my curly silver hair.

She said, *'That silver hair on your chest is proof enough for me'*

And she processed my Social Security application.

When I got home, I excitedly told my wife about my experience at the Social Security office.

She said, *'You should have dropped your pants. You might have gotten disability, too.'*

And then the fight started ...

My wife sat down on the couch next to me as I was flipping channels.

She asked, *'What's on TV?'*

I said, *'Dust.'*

And then the fight started ...

My wife was hinting about what she wanted for our upcoming anniversary. She said, *'I want something shiny that goes from 0 to 150 in about 3 seconds.'*

I bought her a bathroom scale.

And then the fight started ...

The Magic Penis

A businessman was preparing to go on a long business trip, so he thought he'd buy his wife something to keep her occupied. He went to a sex shop and explained his situation. The man there said, *'Well, I don't know that I have anything that will keep her occupied for so many weeks, except ... 'The Magic Penis!'*

The husband said, *'The what'?*

The man repeated, *'The Magic Penis,' and pulled out what seemed to be an ordinary dildo.*

The husband laughed and said, *'It looks like a dildo!'*

The man then pointed to the door and said, *' Magic Penis, door!'*

The penis rose out of its box, darted over to the door and started pounding away at the keyhole. The whole door shook wildly with vibrations, so much so, that a crack began to form down the middle. Then the man said, *'Magic Penis, return to box!'* and the penis stopped and returned to the box.

The husband bought it and took it home to his wife. After the husband had been gone a few days, the wife remembered the Magic Penis. She undressed, opened the box and said: *'Magic Penis, my vagina.'*

The penis shot to her crotch. It was absolutely incredible. After three mind shattering orgasms, she became very exhausted and decided she'd had enough. She tried to pull it out, but it was stuck. Her husband had neglected to tell her how to turn it off so she put her clothes on, got in her car and started for the closest hospital.

On the way, another incredibly intense orgasm made her swerve all over the road. A Police Officer saw this and immediately pulled her over. He asked for her license and then asked how much she'd had to drink.

Gasping and twitching, the woman said, *'I haven't had anything to drink officer. You see, I've got this Magic Penis thing stuck in my crotch and it won't stop screwing me.'*

The officer looked at her for a second, shook his head and replied, *'Yeah right ... Magic Penis, my A$$ ...!!!*

The rest, as they say, is history.

Friendship among Women:

A woman didn't come home one night. The next morning she told her husband that she had slept over at a friend's house. The man called his wife's 10 best friends. None of them knew anything about where she was.

Friendship among Men:

A man didn't come home one night. The next morning he told his wife that he had slept over at a friend's house. The woman called her husband's 10 best friends. Eight confirmed that he had slept over and two said he was still there.

Lotto Tickets

One day, the wife comes home with a spectacular diamond ring.

'Where did you get that ring?' her husband asks.

'Well,' she replies, *'my boss and I played the lotto and we won, so I bought it with my share of the winnings.'*

A week later, his wife comes home with a long shiny fur coat.

'Where did you get that coat?' her husband asks.

She *replies 'My boss and I played the lotto and we won again, so I bought it with my share of the winnings.'*

Another week later, his wife comes home, driving a flaming red Ferrari, You guessed it: Her share of the lotto winnings.

That night, the wife asks her husband to run her a nice warm bath while she gets undressed. When she entered the bathroom, she finds that there is barely enough water in the bath to cover the bath plug.

'What's this?' she asks her husband.

'Well,' he replies, *'We don't want to get your lotto ticket wet, do we??'*

Romantic Poetry?

These are entries to a Washington Post competition asking for a two-line rhyme with the *most romantic* first line and the *least romantic* second line:

1. My darling, my lover, my beautiful wife, marrying you has screwed up my life.
2. I see your face when I am dreaming, that's why I always wake up screaming.
3. Kind, intelligent, loving and hot, this describes everything you are not.
4. Love may be beautiful, love may be bliss, but I only slept with you 'cause I was pissed.
5. I thought that I could love no other, that is, until I met your brother.
6. Roses are red, violets are blue, sugar is sweet and so are you, but the roses are wilting, the violets are dead, the sugar bowl's empty and so is your head.
7. I want to feel your sweet embrace, but don't take that paper bag off your face.
8. I love your smile, your face and your eyes, damn; I'm good at telling lies!
9. My love, you take my breath away, what have you stepped in to smell this way?
10. What inspired this amorous rhyme? Two parts vodka, one part lime.

Who said poetry is boring?

Story about getting even

One December day we found an old straggly cat at our door. She was a sorry sight. Starving, dirty, smelled terrible, skinny and hair all matted down. We felt sorry for her so we put her in a carrier and took her to the vet. We didn't know what to call her so we named her 'Pussycat.'

The vet decided to keep her for a day or so. He said he would let us know when we could come and get her. My husband (the complainer) said, *'Okay, but don't forget to wash her, she stinks.'* He reminded the vet that it was his wife that wanted the dirty cat, not him.

My husband and my Vet don't see eye to eye. The vet calls my husband 'El-Cheap-O' and my husband calls the vet 'El-Charge-O.' They love to hate each other and constantly 'snipe' at one another, with my husband getting in the last word on this particular occasion. The next day my husband had an appointment with his doctor, who is located in the same building, next door to the vet.

The MD's waiting room was full of people waiting to see the doctor. A side door opened and the vet leaned in - he had obviously seen my husband arrive. He looked straight at my husband and in a loud voice said, *'Your wife's pussy doesn't stink any more. We washed and shaved it and now she smells like a rose. Oh and, by the way, I think she's pregnant. God only knows who the father is!'* Then he closed the door.

Now THAT, my friends, is getting even!

The Postman

One Monday morning the Postman is riding his bike on his usual route, delivering the post. As he approaches one of the homes he noticed that both cars were still in the driveway. Next thing, Derek, the homeowner, comes out with a load of empty beer and wine bottles for the recycling bin.

'Wow Derek, looks like you had one hell of a party last night,' the Postman comments.

Derek, in obvious pain, replies *'Actually we had it Saturday night. This is the first time I have felt like moving since 4:00 am Sunday morning. We had about fifteen couples from around the neighbourhood over for some fun and games and it got a bit wild. We all got so drunk around midnight that we started playing Who am I?'*

The Postman thinks a moment and says, *'How do you play Who am I?'*

'Well, all the blokes go in the bedroom and we come out one at a time with a sheet covering us, with only our 'family jewels'

showing through a hole in the sheet, then the women try to guess who it is.'

The Postman laughs and says, *'Sounds like fun. I'm sorry I missed that.'*

'Probably a good thing you did,' Derek responded. *'Your name came up seven times ...'*

Poker night

Two couples were playing poker one evening. Jim accidentally dropped some cards on the floor. When he bent down under the table to pick them up, he noticed Bob's wife, Sue, wasn't wearing any underwear under her dress! Shocked by this, Jim hit his head on the table as he tried to sit up again and emerged red-faced.

Later, Jim went to the kitchen to get some refreshments. Bob's wife followed and asked, *'Did you see anything that you like under there?'*

Surprised by her boldness, Jim admitted that, well indeed he did. She said, *'Well, you can have it but it will cost you $500.'*

After taking a minute or two to assess the financial and moral costs of this offer, Jim confirmed that he was interested. Sue told him that since her husband Bob worked Friday afternoons and Jim didn't, Jim should be at her house around 2 pm Friday afternoon.

When Friday rolled around, Jim showed up at Bob's house at 2 pm sharp and after paying Sue the agreed sum of $500 - they went to the bedroom and closed their transaction, as agreed. Afterwards, Jim quickly dressed and left.

As usual, Bob came home from work at 6 pm. Upon arriving home, Bob asked his wife: *'Did Jim come by the house this afternoon?'*

With a lump in her throat Sue answered *'Why yes, he did stop by for a few minutes this afternoon.'* Her heart nearly skipped a beat when her husband curtly asked, *'And did he give you $500?'*

Sue, using her best poker face replied, *'Well, yes, in fact he did give me $500.'*

With a satisfied look on his face, Bob surprised his wife by saying, *'He came by the office this morning and borrowed $500 from me. He promised he'd stop by our house this afternoon on his way home and pay me back.'*

Now THAT, my friends, is a poker player.

The geography of a woman

- Between 18 and 22, a woman is like Africa, half discovered, half wild, fertile and naturally beautiful!
- Between 23 and 30, a woman is like Europe, well developed and open to trade, especially for someone with cash.
- Between 31 and 35, a woman is like Spain, very hot, relaxed and convinced of her own beauty.
- Between 36 and 40, a woman is like Greece, gently aging but still a warm and desirable place to visit.
- Between 41 and 50, a woman is like Great Britain, with a glorious and all conquering past.
- Between 51 and 60, a woman is like Russia, has been through war and doesn't make the same mistakes twice, takes care of business.
- Between 61 and 70, a woman is like Canada, self-preserving, but open to meeting new people.
- After 70, she becomes Tibet, wildly beautiful, with a mysterious past and the wisdom of the ages ... only those with an adventurous spirit and a thirst for spiritual knowledge visit there.

Mean old man

An old man and woman were married for many years and they grew to hate each other. When they had a confrontation, screaming and yelling could be heard deep into the night.

The old man would shout, *'When I die, I will dig my way up and out of the grave and come back and haunt you for the rest of your life!'*

Neighbours feared him. They believed he practiced black magic, because of the many strange occurrences that took place in their neighbourhood. The old man liked the fact that he was feared. To everyone's relief, he died of a heart attack when he was 98.

His wife had a closed casket at the wake. After the burial, she went straight to the local bar and began to party, as if there was no tomorrow. Her neighbours, concerned for her safety, asked, *'Aren't you afraid that he may indeed be able to dig his way up and out of the grave and come back to haunt you for the rest of your life?'*

The wife put down her drink and said, *'Let him dig. I had the old bastard buried upside down ...'*

The nude runner

A woman was having a daytime affair while her husband was at work. One hot and lusty day she was in bed with her boyfriend when, to her horror, she heard her husband's car pull into the driveway.

'Oh my God - Hurry! Grab your clothes and jump out the window. My husband's home early!'

'I can't jump out the window. It's raining out there!'

'If my husband catches us in here, he'll kill us both!' she replied. *'He's got a hot temper and a gun, so the rain is the least of your problems!'*

So the boyfriend scoots out of bed, grabs his clothes and jumps out the window! As he ran down the street in the pouring rain, he quickly discovered he had run right into the middle of the town's annual marathon, so he started running along beside the others, about 100 of them. Being naked, with his clothes tucked under his arm, he tried to blend in as best he could. After a little while a small group of runners who had been watching him with some curiosity, jogged closer.

'Do you always run in the nude?' one asked.

'Oh yes!' he replied, gasping in air. *'It feels so wonderfully free!'*

Another runner moved a long side. *'Do you always run carrying your clothes with you under your arm?'*

'Oh yes' our friend answered breathlessly. *'That way I can get dressed right at the end of the run and get in my car to go home!'*

Then a third runner cast his eyes a little lower and queried, *'Do you always wear a condom when you run?'*

'Nope ... just when it's raining.'

Marriage Humour

Wife: *'What are you doing?'*
Husband: *'Nothing.'*
Wife: *'Nothing? You've been reading our marriage certificate for an hour.'*
Husband: 'I was looking for the expiration date.'

Wife: *'Do you want dinner?'*
Husband: *'Sure. What are my choices?'*
Wife: *'Yes and no.'*

Wife: *'You always carry my photo in your wallet. Why?'*

Husband: *'When there is a problem, no matter how great, I look at your picture and the problem disappears.'*
Wife: *'You see how miraculous and powerful I am for you?'*
Husband: *'Yes. I see your picture and ask myself what other problem can there be greater than this one!'*

Stress Reliever Girl: *'When we get married, I want to share all your worries, troubles and lighten your burden.'*
Boy: *'It's very kind of you darling, but I don't have any worries or troubles.'*
Girl: *'Well, that's because we aren't married yet.'*

A newly married man asked his wife, *'Would you have married me if my father hadn't left me a fortune?'*
'Honey,' the woman replied sweetly, *'I'd have married you, no matter who left you a fortune!'*

Girl to her boyfriend: *'One kiss and I'll be yours forever.'*
The guy replies: *'Thanks for the early warning.'*

A wife asked her husband: *'What do you like most in me, my pretty face or my sexy body?'*
He looked at her from head to toe and replied: 'I like your sense of humour!'

A man was sitting reading his newspaper when his wife hit him on the head with a frying pan.

'What was that for?' the man asked.

The wife replied *'That was for the piece of paper with the name Jenny on it that I found in your pants pocket'.*

The man then said *'When I was at the races last week Jenny was the name of the horse I bet on'*

The wife apologised and went on with the housework. Three days later the man is watching TV when his wife bashes him on the head with an even bigger frying pan, knocking him unconscious. Upon re-gaining consciousness the man asked why she had hit again. His wife replied. *'Your horse phoned'*

Husband asks, *'Do you know the meaning of WIFE? It is: Without Information Fighting Every time'*
Wife replies, *'No, it means: 'With Idiot For Ever!'*

- Women and cats will do as they please and men and dogs should relax and get used to the idea.
- No man is truly married until he understands every word his wife is not saying.
- What is the definition of Mistress? Someone between the Mister and the mattress.
- What's the difference between stress, tension and panic? Stress is when wife is pregnant. Tension is when girlfriend is pregnant. Panic is when both are pregnant.

A woman asks man who is travelling with six children, *'Are all these kids yours?'*

The man replies, *'No, I work in a condom factory and these are customer complaints.'*

Toilet paper

Fresh from my shower, I stand in front of the mirror complaining to my husband that my breasts are too small. Instead of characteristically telling me it's not so, he uncharacteristically comes up with a suggestion.

'If you want your breasts to grow, then every day take a piece of toilet paper and rub it between them for a few seconds.'

Willing to try anything, I fetch a piece of toilet paper and stand in front of the mirror, rubbing it between my breasts.

'How long will this take?' I asked.

'They will grow larger over a period of years,' my husband replies.

I stopped. *'Do you really think rubbing a piece of toilet paper between my breasts every day will make my breasts larger over the years?'*

Without missing a beat he says, *'Worked for your arse, didn't it?'*

He's still alive and with a great deal of therapy, he may even walk again, although he will probably continue to take his meals through a straw.

Stupid, stupid man!

Complete and Finished

No English dictionary has been able to explain the difference between the two words Complete and Finished, in a way that's easy to understand.

Some people say there is no difference between Complete and Finished. I beg to differ because, there is!

When you marry the right woman, you are *'Complete.'*

And when you marry the wrong one, you *are 'Finished!'*

And when the right one catches you with the wrong one, you are ... *'Completely Finished!!'*

Happiness

To be happy with a man, you must understand him a lot and love him a little.
To be happy with a woman, you must love her a lot and not try to understand her at all.

Longevity

Married men live longer than single men do, but married men are a lot more willing to die.

Man comes home, finds his wife with his friend in bed. He shoots his friend and kills him.

Wife says *'If you behave like this, you will lose ALL your friends!'*

Romance Mathematics

Smart man + smart woman = romance
Smart man + dumb woman = affair
Dumb man + smart woman = marriage
Dumb man + dumb woman = pregnancy

No Speak English

A Russian woman married a Canadian gentleman and they lived happily ever after in Toronto. The poor lady was not very proficient in English, but did manage to communicate with her husband. The real problem arose whenever she had to shop for groceries.

One day, she went to the butcher and wanted to buy chicken legs. She didn't know how to put forward her request, so, in desperation, clucked like a chicken and lifted up her skirt to show her thighs. Her butcher got the message and gave her the chicken legs.

Next day she needed to get chicken breasts, again she didn't know how to say it, so she clucked like a chicken and unbuttoned her blouse to show the butcher her breasts. The butcher understood again and gave her some chicken breasts.

On the third day, the poor lady needed to buy sausages. Unable to find a way to communicate this, she brought her husband to the store.

What were you thinking? Her husband speaks English!
I worry about you sometimes!

The Curtains

Paddy met Mick in the street and Mick said: *'Paddy will you draw your bedroom curtains before making love to your wife in the future?'*

'Why?' Paddy asked.

'Because,' said Mick *'all the street was laughing when they saw you making love yesterday'*

Paddy replies *'Silly buggers, the laughs on them. I wasn't home yesterday!!'*

Dining out

A man and woman were having dinner in a fine restaurant. They were gazing lovingly at each other and holding hands. Their waitress, taking another order at a table a few steps away, suddenly noticed the man slowly sliding down his chair and under the table, but the woman acted unconcerned.

The waitress watched as the man slid all the way down his chair and out of sight under the table. Still, the woman appeared calm and unruffled apparently unaware her dining companion had disappeared.

The waitress went over to the table and said to the woman, *'Pardon me, ma'am, but I think your husband just slid under the table.'*

The woman calmly looked up at her and said, *'No, he didn't. He just walked in.'*

Jumping On the Bed

A fiftyish woman was at home happily jumping on her bed and squealing with delight. Her husband watches her for a while and asks, *'Do you have any idea how ridiculous you look? What's the matter with you?'*

The woman continues to bounce on the bed and says, *'I don't care, I just came from having a mammogram and the doctor says I have the breasts of an 18 year-old.'*

The husband said, *'What did he say about your 60 year old ass?'*

'Your name never came up,' she replied.

(Men ... some of them just never know when to shut up, do they?)

I'm dead

An older couple is lying in bed one morning. They had just awakened from a good night's sleep. He takes her hand and she responds, *'Don't touch me.'*

'Why not?' he asked.

She answered, *'Because I'm dead.'*

The husband asked, *'What are you talking about? We're both lying here in bed together and talking to one another!'*

She said, *'No, I'm definitely dead.'*

He insisted, *'You are not dead. What in the world makes you think you're dead?'*

'Because I woke up this morning and nothing hurts.'

No justice

- I spent $10,000 on a boob job for the wife. She was delighted.
- I spent another $8,000 on a nose job for her. She was ecstatic.
- I spent $7,000 on liposuction for her and she was over the moon.
- I spent $75 on a blow job for myself and she goes mental.

Women!

The Mule

An old hillbilly farmer had a wife who nagged him unmercifully. From morning until night she was always complaining about something. The only time he got any relief was when he was out plowing with his old mule. He tried to plow a lot.

One day, when he was out ploughing, his wife brought him lunch in the field. He drove the old mule into the shade, sat down on a stump and began to eat his lunch.

Immediately, his wife began nagging him again. Complain, nag, complain, nag - it just went on and on. All of a sudden, the old mule lashed out with both hind feet, caught her smack in the back of the head. Killed her dead on the spot.

At the funeral several days later, the minister noticed something rather odd. When a woman mourner would approach the old farmer, he would listen for a minute and then nod his head in agreement; but when a man mourner approached him, he would listen for a minute and then shake his head in disagreement. This was so consistent, the minister decided to ask the old farmer about it.

So after the funeral, the minister spoke to the old farmer and asked him why he nodded his head and agreed with the women, but always shook his head and disagreed with all the men.

The old farmer said, *'Well, the women would come up and say something about how nice my wife looked or how pretty her dress was, so I'd nod my head in agreement.'*

'And what about the men?' the minister asked.

'They wanted to know if the mule was for sale.'

To be 8 again!

A man was sitting on the edge of the bed, watching his wife, who was looking at herself in the mirror. Since her birthday was not far off he asked what she'd like to have for her birthday.

'I'd like to be eight again,' she replied, still looking in the mirror.

On the morning of her birthday, he arose early, made her a nice big bowl of Coco Pops and then took her to Adventure World theme park. What a day! He put her on every ride in the park; the Death Slide, the Wall of Fear, the Screaming Roller Coaster, everything there was.

Five hours later they staggered out of the theme park. Her head was reeling and her stomach felt upside down. He then took her to a McDonald's where he ordered her a Happy Meal with extra fries and a chocolate shake.

Then it was off to a movie, popcorn, a soda pop and her favourite candy, M&M's. What a fabulous adventure!

Finally she wobbled home with her husband and collapsed into bed exhausted.

He leaned over his wife with a big smile and lovingly asked, *'Well dear, what was it like being eight again?'*

Her eyes slowly opened and her expression suddenly changed.

'I meant my dress size, you Retard!!!!'

The moral of the story: Even when a man is listening, he is gonna get it wrong.

Voted Best Joke in Ireland

John O'Reilly hoisted his beer and said, *'Here's to spending the rest of me life, between the legs of me wife!'*

That won him the top prize at the pub for the best toast of the night!

He went home and told his wife, Mary, *'I won the prize for the Best toast of the night'*

She said, *'Aye, did ye now. And what was your toast?'*

John said, *'Here's to spending the rest of me life, sitting in church beside me wife.'*

'Oh, that is very nice indeed, John!' Mary said.

The next day, Mary ran into one of John's drinking buddies on the street corner.

The man chuckled leeringly and said, *'John won the prize the other night at the pub with a toast about you, Mary.'*

She said, *'Aye, he told me and I was a bit surprised myself. You know, he's only been there twice in the last four years. Once he fell asleep and the other time I had to pull him by the ears to make him come.'*

Magic Sandals

A married couple were on holiday in Jamaica. They were touring around the market-place looking at the goods and such, when they passed a small sandal shop. From inside they heard the shopkeeper with a Jamaican accent say, *'You foreigners! Come in. Come into my humble shop.'*

So the married couple walked in. The Jamaican said to them, *'I 'ave some special sandals I tink you would be interested in. Dey makes you wild at sex.'*

Well, the wife was really interested in buying the sandals after what the man claimed, but her husband felt he really didn't need them, being the Sex God that he was.

The husband asked the man, *'How could sandals make you a sex freak?'*

The Jamaican replied, *'Just try dem on, Mon.'*

Well, the husband, after some badgering from his wife, finally gave in and tried them on. As soon as he slipped them onto his feet, he got this wild look in his eyes, something his wife hadn't seen before!!

In the blink of an eye, the husband grabbed the Jamaican, bent him over the table, yanked down his pants, ripped down his own pants and grabbed a firm hold of the Jamaican's thighs.

The Jamaican began screaming: *'You got dem on de wrong feet!'*

Make up your mind!

I was in my back yard trying to fly a kite. I threw the kite up in the air, the wind would catch it for a few seconds and then it would come crashing back down to earth. I tried this a few more times with no success.

All the while, Karen is watching from the kitchen window, muttering to herself how men need to be told how to do everything. She opens the window and yelled to me, '*You need a piece of tail.'*
I turned with a confused look on my face and said, *'Make up your mind. Last night, you told me to go fly a kite.'*

Frank Feldman

A man walks out to the street and manages to catch a passing taxi. He gets into the taxi and the cabbie say, *'Perfect timing. You're just like Frank.'*

Passenger: *'Who?'*

Cabbie: *'Frank Feldman. He's a guy who did everything right all the time. Like my coming along when you needed a cab, things happened like that to Frank Feldman, every single time.'*

Passenger: *'There are always a few clouds over everybody.'*

Cabbie: *'Not Frank Feldman. He was a terrific athlete. He could have won the Grand-Slam at tennis. He could golf with the pros. He sang like an opera baritone and danced like a Broadway star and you should have heard him play the piano. He was an amazing guy.'*

Passenger: *'Sounds like he was something really special.'*

Cabbie: *'There's more ... He had a memory like a computer, could remember everybody's birthday. He knew all about wine, which foods to order and which fork to eat them with. He could fix anything. Not like me. I change a fuse and the whole street blacks out. But Frank Feldman, he could do everything right.'*

Passenger: '*Wow, some guy then.'*

Cabbie: *'He always knew the quickest way to go in traffic and avoid traffic jams. Not like me, I always seem to get stuck in them. But Frank, he never made a mistake and he really knew how to treat a woman and make her feel good. He would never answer her back negatively even if she was in the wrong; and his clothing was always immaculate, shoes highly polished too. He was the perfect man! He never made a mistake. No one could ever measure up to Frank Feldman'*

Passenger: *'An amazing fellow. How did you meet him?'*

Cabbie: *'Well, I never actually met Frank. He died and I married his damned widow.'*

Sex in the Dark

There was this couple that had been married for 20 years. Every time they made love, the husband always insisted on shutting off the light. Well, after 20 years the wife felt this was ridiculous.

She figures she would break him of this crazy habit. So one night, while they were in the middle of a wild, screaming, romantic session, she turned on the lights. She looked down and saw her husband was holding a battery-operated leisure device ... a vibrator! It was soft, wonderful and larger than a real one. She went completely ballistic.

'You impotent bastard,' She screamed at him, *'How could you be lying to me all of these years? You better explain yourself!'*

The husband looks her straight in the eyes and says calmly: *'I'll explain the toy ... You explain the kids.'*

Man of the house

A husband had just finished reading a new book entitled, *'You Can Be THE Man of Your House.'*

He stormed to his wife in the kitchen and announced, *'From now on, you need to know that I am the man of this house and my word is Law. You will prepare me a gourmet meal tonight and when I'm done eating my meal, you will serve me a scrumptious dessert. After dinner, you are going to go upstairs with me and we will have the kind of sex that I want!*

'Afterwards, you are going to draw me a bath so I can relax. You will wash my back and towel me dry and bring me my robe. Then, you will massage my feet and hands. Then tomorrow, guess who's going to dress me and comb my hair?'

The wife replied, *'The funeral director would be my first guess.'*

Sharing

The old man placed an order for one hamburger, French fries and a drink. He unwrapped the plain hamburger and carefully cut it in half, placing one half in front of his wife.

He then carefully counted out the French fries, dividing them into two piles and neatly placed one pile in front of his wife.

He took a sip of the drink; his wife took a sip and then set the cup down between them. As he began to eat his few bites of hamburger, the people around them were looking over and whispering.

Obviously they were thinking, *'That poor old couple - all they can afford is one meal for the two of them.'*

As the man began to eat his fries a young man came to the table and politely offered to buy another meal for the old couple. The old man said that they were just fine - they were used to sharing everything.

People closer to the table noticed the little old lady hadn't eaten a bite. She sat there watching her husband eat and occasionally taking turns sipping the drink.

Again, the young man came over and begged them to let him buy another meal for them. This time the old woman said *'No, thank you; we are used to sharing everything.'*

Finally, as the old man finished and was wiping his face neatly with the napkin, the young man again came over to the little old lady who had yet to eat a single bite of food and asked, *'What is it you are waiting for?'*

She quietly whispered, *'The teeth!'*

Men do remember anniversaries

A woman woke up during the night to find that her husband was not in their bed. She put on her dressing gown and went downstairs to look for him. She finds him sitting at the kitchen table with a hot cup of coffee in front of him. He appears to be in deep thought, just staring at the wall. She watches as he wipes a tear from his eye and takes a sip of his coffee.

'What's the matter, dear?' she whispers as she steps into the room, *'Why are you down here at this time of night?'*

The husband looks up from his coffee, *'I am just remembering when we first met 20 years ago and started dating. You were only 16. Do you remember back then?'* he says solemnly.

The wife is touched to tears thinking that her husband is so caring, so sensitive. *'Yes, I do'* she replies.

The husband pauses. The words were not coming easily. *'Do you remember when your father caught us in the back seat of my car?'*

'Yes, I remember!' said the wife, lowering herself into a chair beside him.

The husband continues. *'Do you remember when he shoved the shotgun in my face and said, 'Either you marry my daughter or I will send you to jail for 20 years?'*

'I remember that too,' she replies softly.

He wipes another tear from his cheek and says ... *'I would have been released today.'*

Christmas visit

A man in Scotland calls his son in London the day before Christmas Eve and says, *'I hate to ruin your day but I have to tell you that your mother and I are divorcing; forty-five years of misery is enough.'*

'Dad, what are you talking about?' the son screams.

'We can't stand the sight of each other any longer,' the father says. *'We're sick of each other and I'm sick of talking about this, so you call your sister in Leeds and tell her.'*

Frantically, the son calls his sister, who explodes on the phone, *'Like hell they're getting divorced,'* she shouts, *'I'll take care of this.'*

She calls Scotland immediately and screams at her father, *'You are NOT getting divorced. Don't do a single thing until I get there. I'm calling my brother back and we'll both be there tomorrow. Until then, don't do a thing, DO YOU HEAR ME?'* and hangs up.

The old man hangs up his phone and turns to his wife. *'Done! They're coming for Christmas - and they're paying their own way.'*

Kinds of Sex

Smurf Sex: This kind of sex happens when you first meet someone and you both have sex until you are blue in the face.

Kitchen Sex: This is when you have been with your partner for a short time and you are so needy you will have sex anywhere, even in the kitchen.

Religious Sex: Which means you get Nun in the morning, Nun in the afternoon and Nun at night. (Very Popular)

Bedroom Sex: This is when you have been with your partner for a long time. Your sex has gotten routine and you usually have sex only in your bedroom.

Hallway Sex: This is when you have been with your partner for too long. When you pass each other in the hallway you both say *' F**k you.'*

Courtroom Sex: This is when you cannot stand your wife any more. She takes you to court and screws you in front of everyone.

Pension Sex: You get a little each month, but not enough to live on.

Loud sex: A wife went in to see a therapist and said, *'I've got a big problem, doctor. Every time we're in bed and my husband climaxes, he lets out this ear splitting yell.'*

'My dear,' the shrink said, *'that's completely natural. I don't see what the problem is.'*

'The problem is,' she complained, *'it wakes me up!'*

Quiet sex: Tired of a listless sex life, the man came right out and asked his wife during a recent lovemaking session, *'How come you never tell me when you have an orgasm?'*

She glanced at him and replied, *'You're never home!'*

Morning Sex: She was standing in the kitchen, preparing our usual soft-boiled eggs and toast for breakfast, wearing only the 'T' shirt that she normally slept in. As I walked in, almost awake, she turned to me and said softly, *'You've got to make love to me this very moment!'*

My eyes lit up and I thought, *'I am either still dreaming or this is going to be my lucky day!'*

Not wanting to lose the moment, I embraced her and then gave it my all; right there on the kitchen, table. Afterwards she said, *'Thanks,'* and returned to the stove, her T-shirt still around her neck. Happy, but a little puzzled, I asked, *'What was that all about?'*

She explained, *'The egg timer's broken.'*

Wedding anniversary sex: A husband and his wife had a bitter quarrel on the day of their 40th wedding anniversary. The husband yelled, *'When you die, I'm getting you a headstone that reads:*

'Here lies my wife - Cold as ever'

'Yeah,' she replied, 'When you die, I'm getting you a headstone that reads:

'Here lies my husband - Stiff at last.'

Women's humorous sex: My husband came home with a tube of KY jelly and said, *'This will make you happy tonight.*

'He was right. When he went out of the bedroom, I squirted it all over the doorknobs. He couldn't get back in.'

And; last, but not least,

Elderly sex: One night, an 87 year-old woman came home from Bingo and found her 92-year-old husband in bed with another woman. She became violent and ended up pushing him off the balcony of their 20th floor, assisted living apartment, killing him instantly.

Brought before the court on the charge of murder, the judge asked her if she had anything to say in her defence.

She began coolly, *'Yes, your honour. I figured that at 92, if he could have sex ... he could also fly.'*

Which of the above fits your sex life?

Global facts about sex

At any given moment:
79,000,000 people are engaged in sex right now
58,000,000 are kissing
37,000,000 are relaxing after having sex
1 elderly person is reading this
You hang in there, Sunshine!

A few good one-liners to make you smile.

- My husband and I divorced over religious differences. He thought he was God and I didn't.
- I don't suffer from insanity; I enjoy every minute of it.
- Some people are alive only because it's illegal to kill them.

- I used to have a handle on life, but it broke.
- Don't take life too seriously; No one gets out alive.
- You're just jealous because the voices only talk to me
- Beauty is in the eye of the beer holder.
- I'm not a complete idiot - Some parts are just missing.
- I'm out of my mind. Back in five minutes.
- God must love stupid people; He made so many.
- The gene pool could use a little chlorine.
- Earth is the insane asylum for the universe.
- NyQuil, the stuffy, sneezy, why-the-heck-is-the-room-spinning medicine.
- I have a degree in liberal arts. Do you want fries with that?
- Stupidity is not a handicap. Park elsewhere!
- Ham and eggs. A day's work for a chicken, a lifetime commitment for a pig.
- The trouble with life is there's no background music.
- The original point and click interface was a Smith and Wesson.
- I smile because I don't know what the heck is going on.
- Consciousness: That annoying time between naps.
- How do you prevent sagging skin? Just eat till the wrinkles fill out!
- Ever stop to think and forget to start again?
- Being 'over the hill' is much better than being under it!

- Wrinkled was not one of the things I wanted to be when I grew up.
- A hangover is the wrath of grapes.
- They call it PMS because Mad Cow Disease was already taken.
- He who dies with the most toys is nonetheless dead.

A couple is lying in bed. The man says, *'I am going to make you the happiest woman in the world.'*

The woman replies, *'I'll miss you ...'*

'It's just too hot to wear clothes today,' Jack says as he stepped out of the shower, *'Honey, what do you think the neighbours would think if I mowed the lawn like this?'*

'Probably that I married you for your money,' she replied.

Dear Lord, I pray for Wisdom to understand my man; love to forgive him; and Patience for his moods. Because, Lord, if I pray for Strength, I'll beat him to death. AMEN

Questions and answers

Q: What do you call a handcuffed man?
A: Trustworthy.

Q: What do you call an intelligent, good looking, sensitive man?
A: A rumour

Q: What does it mean when a man is in your bed gasping for breath and calling your name?
A: You did not hold the pillow down long enough.
Q: Why do men whistle when they are sitting on the toilet?
A: It helps them remember which end to wipe.

Q: How do you keep your husband from reading your e-mail?
A: Rename the email folder 'Instruction Manuals'

A friend is like a good Bra

- Hard to find
- Supportive
- Comfortable
- Always lifts you up
- Never lets you down or leaves you hanging
- And is always close to your heart!!!

The Scrotum Story

In Church the pastor asked if anyone in the congregation would like to express praise for answered prayers. A lady stood and walked to the podium.

She said, *'I have a praise to give. Two months ago, my husband, Tom, had a terrible bicycle wreck and his scrotum was completely crushed. The pain was excruciating and the doctors didn't know if they could help him.'*

You could hear a muffled gasp from the men in the congregation as they imagined the pain that poor Tom must have experienced.

'Tom was unable to hold me or the children,' she went on, 'and every move caused him terrible pain. We prayed as the doctors performed a delicate operation and it turned out they were able to piece together the crushed remnants of Tom's scrotum and wrap wire around it to hold it in place.'

Again, the men in the congregation were unnerved and squirmed uncomfortably as they imagined the horrible surgery performed on Tom.

'Now,' she announced in a quavering voice, *'thank the Lord, Tom is out of the hospital and the doctors say that with time, his scrotum should recover completely.'*

All the men sighed with relief. The pastor rose and tentatively asked if anyone else had something to say.

A man stood up and walked slowly to the podium. He said, *'I'm Tom.'*

The entire congregation held its breath.

'I just want to tell my wife that the word is sternum.'

South Auckland vasectomy

An Auckland couple had 9 children. They went to the doctor to see about getting the husband *'fixed.'* The doctor gladly started the required procedure and asked them what finally made them make the decision - why, after nine children, would they choose to do this.

The husband replied that they had read in a recent article that one out of every ten children being born in New Zealand was Chinese and they didn't want to take a chance on having a Chinese baby because neither of them could speak the language.

The New Dress

A woman stopped by, unannounced, at her son's house. She knocked on the door then immediately walked in. She was shocked to see her daughter-in-law lying on the couch, totally naked. Soft music was playing and the aroma of perfume filled the room.

'What are you doing?' she asked.

'I'm waiting for Justin to come home from work.' The daughter-in-law answered.

'But you're naked!' the mother-in-law exclaimed.

'This is my love dress,' the daughter-in-law explained.

'Love dress? But you're naked!'

'Justin loves me to wear this dress,' she explained. *'Every time he sees me in this dress, he instantly becomes romantic and ravages me for hours.'*

The mother-in-law left. When she got home she undressed, showered, put on her best perfume, dimmed the lights, put on a romantic CD and lay on the couch waiting for her husband to arrive. Finally, her husband came home. He walked in and saw her lying there so provocatively.

'What are you doing?' he asked.

'This is my love dress,' she whispered, sensually.

'Needs ironing,' he said, *'What's for dinner?'*

Proud Parents

Four friends, who hadn't seen each other in 30 years, reunited at a party. After several drinks, one of the men had to use the restroom. Those who remained talked about their kids. The first guy said, *'My son is my pride and joy. He started working at a successful company at the bottom of the barrel. He studied Economics and Business Administration and soon began to climb the corporate ladder and now he's the president of the company. He became so rich that he gave his best friend a top of the line Mercedes for his birthday.'*

The second guy said, *'Darn, that's terrific! My son is also my pride and joy. He started working for a big airline and then went to flight school to become a pilot. Eventually he became a partner in the company, where he owns the majority of its assets. He's so rich that he gave his best Friend a brand new jet for his birthday.'*

The third man said: *'Well, that's terrific! My son studied in the best universities and became an engineer. Then he started his own construction company and is now a multimillionaire. He also gave away something very nice and expensive to his best friend for his birthday, a 30,000 square foot mansion.'*

The three friends congratulated each other just as the fourth returned from the restroom and he asked: *'What are all the congratulations for?'*

One of the three said: *'We were talking about the pride we feel for the successes of our sons. What about your son?'*
The fourth man replied: *'My son is gay and makes a living dancing as a stripper at a nightclub.'*

The three friends said: *'What a shame. What a disappointment.'*

The fourth man replied: *'No, I'm not ashamed. He's my son and I love him. And he hasn't done too badly either. His birthday was two weeks ago and he received a beautiful 30,000 square foot mansion, a brand new jet and a top of the line Mercedes from his three boyfriends.'*

50th Wedding Anniversary

A couple were celebrating 50 years together. Their three kids, all very successful, agreed to a attend Sunday dinner in their parents' honour.

'Happy Anniversary, Mom and Dad,' gushed son number one, *'Sorry, I'm running late. I had an emergency at the hospital with a patient, you know how it is and I didn't have time to get you a gift.'*

'Not to worry,' said the father. *'The important thing is that we're all together today.'*

Son number two arrived and announced, *'You and Mom look great, Dad. I just flew in from Los Angeles between depositions and didn't have time to shop for you.'*

'It's nothing,' said the father. *'We're glad you were able to come.'*

Just then the daughter arrived. *'Hello and happy anniversary! I'm sorry, but my boss is sending me out of town and I was really busy packing so I didn't have time to get you anything ...'*

After they had finished dessert, the father said to the kids, *'There's something your mother and I have wanted to tell you for a long time. You see, we were very poor. Despite this, we worked very hard and we were able to send each of you to college. Throughout the years your mother and I knew that we loved each other very much, but we just never found the time to get married.'*

The three children gasped and blurted out at once, *'You mean we're all bastards?'*

'Yep,' said the father. *'And cheap ones too.'*

Exercise is good

The instructor was teaching the women how to breathe properly and was telling the men how to give the necessary assurance to their partners at this stage of the pregnancy.

She said *'Ladies, remember that exercise is good for you. Walking is especially beneficial. It strengthens the pelvic muscles and will make delivery that much easier!'*

She looked at the men in the room, *'And gentlemen, remember - you're in this together - it wouldn't hurt you to go walking with her.'*

The room suddenly got very quiet as the men absorbed this information. Then a man at the back of the room slowly raised his hand.

'Yes?' answered the teacher.

'I was just wondering. Is it all right if she carries a golf bag while we walk?'

Sex Education in the '60s

This is an actual extract from a sex education school textbook for girls, printed in the early 60's in the UK and explains why the world was much happier and peaceful then!

When retiring to the bedroom, prepare yourself for bed as promptly as possible. Whilst feminine hygiene is of the utmost importance; your tired husband does not want to queue for the bathroom, as he would have to do for his train. But remember to look your best when going to bed. Try to achieve a look that is welcoming without being obvious. If you need to apply face cream or hair rollers, wait until he is asleep as this can be shocking to a man last thing at night. [Groan.]

When it comes to the possibility of intimate relations with your husband, it is important to remember your marriage vows and in particularly your commitment to obey him.

If he feels that he needs to sleep immediately, then so be it, in all things be led by your husband's wishes; do not pressure him in any way to stimulate intimacy. Should your husband suggest congress then agree humbly all the while being mindful that a man's satisfaction is more important than a woman's. When he reaches his moment of fulfilment, a small moan from yourself is encouraging to him and quite sufficient to indicate any enjoyment that you may have had.

Should your husband suggest any of the more unusual practices, be obedient and uncomplaining but register any reluctance by remaining silent. [This explains why so many women used *'the silent treatment'* when upset about something!]

It is likely that your husband will then fall promptly asleep, so adjust your clothing, freshen up and apply your night-time face and hair care products.

You may then set the alarm so that you can arise shortly before him in the morning. This will enable you to have his morning cup of tea ready when he awakes.
[This was obviously written by a man!]

Eulogy

Three friends from the local congregation were asked, *'When you're in your casket and friends and congregation members are mourning over you, what would you like them to say?'*

Artie said: *'I would like them to say I was a wonderful husband, a fine spiritual leader and a great family man.'*

Eugene commented: *'I would like them to say I was a wonderful teacher and servant of God who made a huge difference in people's lives.*

Al said: *'I'd like them to say, 'Look, he's moving!'*

Letting him play through

A husband and wife are on the ninth green when she collapses with a heart attack. Her husband calls for help on his mobile phone\, talks for a few minutes, picks up his putter and lines up his putt. His wife raises her head off the green and stared at him.

'I'm dying over here and you're putting?'

'Don't worry dear,' says the husband calmly, *'they found a doctor on the second hole and he's coming to help you.'*

'Well, how long will it take for him to get here?' she asks feebly.

'*No time at all.'* he says. *'Everybody's already agreed to let him play through.'*

MALE JOKES

Two men talking:

'You know why women's work is never done? They don't get up early enough.'

'When you think about it, God has to be the best inventor of all time. He took a rib from Adam and made a loudspeaker!'

When my wife asked *'What's the best form of birth control after 40?'* I replied: *'Get naked!'*

My wife asked, *'Whatcha doin' today?'*

I replied: *'Nothing.'*

She said, *'That's what you did yesterday!*

I replied, *'I wasn't finished.'*

I got a new stick deodorant today. The instructions said: Remove cap and push up bottom. I can barely walk, but whenever I fart the room smells lovely.

The first testicular guard was used in cricket in 1874 and the first helmet was used in 1974. It took 100 years for men to realise that the brain is also important.

'If women are so perfect at multitasking, how come they can't have a headache and sex at the same time?'

Calling In Sick

We've all had trouble with our animals, but I don't think anyone can top this one: Calling in sick to work makes me uncomfortable. No matter how legitimate my excuse, I always get the feeling that my boss thinks I'm lying.

On one recent occasion, I had a valid reason but lied anyway, because the truth was just too darned humiliating. I simply mentioned that I had sustained a head injury and I hoped I would feel up to coming in the next day. By then, I reasoned, I could think up a doozy to explain the bandage on the top of my head. The accident occurred mainly because I had given in to my wife's wishes to adopt a cute little kitty.

Initially, the new acquisition was no problem. Then one morning, I was taking my shower after breakfast when I heard my wife, Deb, call out to me from the kitchen.

'Honey! The garbage disposal is dead again. Please come reset it.'

'You know where the button is,' I protested through the shower pitter-patter and steam. *'Reset it yourself!'*

'But I'm scared!' she persisted. *'What if it starts going and sucks me in?'* There was a meaningful pause and then, *'C'mon, it'll only take you a second.'*

So out I came, dripping wet and butt naked, hoping that my silent outraged nudity would make a statement about how I perceived her behaviour as extremely cowardly. Sighing loudly, I squatted down and stuck my head under the sink to find the button. It is the last action I remember performing.

It struck without warning and without any respect to my circumstances. No, it wasn't the hexed disposal, drawing me into its gnashing metal teeth. It was our new kitty, who discovered the fascinating dangling objects she spied hanging between my legs. She had been poised around the corner and stalked me as I reached under the sink. And, at the precise moment when I was most vulnerable, she leapt at the toys I unwittingly offered and snagged them with her needle-like claws. I lost all rational thought to control orderly bodily movements, blindly rising at a violent rate of speed, with the full weight of a kitten hanging from my masculine region.

Wild animals are sometimes faced with a 'fight or flight' syndrome. Men, in this predicament, choose only the 'flight' option. I know this from experience. I was fleeing straight up into the air when the sink and cabinet bluntly and forcefully impeded my ascent. The impact knocked me out cold. When I awoke, my wife and the paramedics stood over me.

Now there are not many things in this life worse than finding oneself lying on the kitchen floor butt naked, bleeding from your privates, in front of a group of 'been-there, done-that' paramedics. Even worse, having been fully briefed by my wife, the paramedics were all snorting loudly as they tried to conduct their work of placing dressings on my head and private parts, all the while trying to suppress their hysterical laughter ... and not succeeding.

Somehow I lived through it all. A few days later I finally made it back in to the office, where colleagues tried to coax an explanation out of me about my head injury. I kept silent, claiming it was too painful to talk about, which it was.

'What's the matter?' They all asked, *'Cat got your tongue?'*

If they only knew!

Why is it that only women laugh at this?

The Woodcutter

One day, while a woodcutter was cutting a branch of a tree above a river, his axe fell into the river. When he cried out, an angel appeared and asked, *'Why are you crying?'*

The woodcutter replied that his axe has fallen into water and he needed the axe to make his living. The angel went down into the water and reappeared with a golden axe. *'Is this your axe?'* the angel asked.

The woodcutter replied, *'No.'*

The angel again went down and came up with a silver Axe. *'Is this your axe?* 'The angel asked.

Again, the woodcutter replied, *'No.'*

The angel went down again and came up with an iron Axe. *'Is this your axe?'* the angel asked.

The woodcutter replied, *'Yes.'*

The angel was pleased with the man's honesty and gave him all three axes to keep and the woodcutter went home happy.

Some time later the woodcutter was walking with his wife along the riverbank and his wife fell into the river. When he cried out, the angel again appeared and asked him, *'Why are you crying?'*

'Oh angel, my wife has fallen into the water!'

The angel went down into the water and came up with Angelina Jolie. *'Is this your wife?'* the angel asked.

'Yes,' cried the woodcutter.

The angel was furious. *'You lied! That is an untruth!'*

The woodcutter replied, *'Oh, forgive me, my angel. It is a misunderstanding. You see, if I had said 'no' to Angelina Jolie you would have come up with Cameron Diaz. Then if I said 'no' to her, you would have come up with my wife. Had I then said 'yes,' you would have given me all three. Angel, I am a poor man and am not able to take care of all three wives, so THAT'S why I said yes to Angelina Jolie.'*

The moral of this story is: Whenever a man lies, it is for a good and honourable reason and for the benefit of others. Oh yeah ...?

Only a man would attempt this

A guy who purchased his lovely wife a pocket Tazer for their anniversary submitted this:

Last weekend I saw something at Larry's Pistol & Pawn Shop that sparked my interest. The occasion was our 15th anniversary and I was looking for a little something extra for my wife Julie. What I came across was a 100,000-volt, pocket/purse-sized Tazer.

The effects of the Tazer were supposed to be short lived, with no long term adverse affect on your assailant, allowing her adequate time to retreat to safety ...?

WAY TOO COOL! Long story short, I bought the device and brought it home ... I loaded two AAA batteries in the darn thing and pushed the button. Nothing! I was disappointed. I learned, however, that if I pushed the button and pressed it against a metal surface at the same time; I'd get the blue arc of electricity darting back and forth between the prongs.

AWESOME!!! Unfortunately, I have yet to explain to Julie what that burn spot is on the face of her microwave.

Okay, so I was home alone with this new toy, thinking to myself that it couldn't be all that bad with only two AAA batteries, right? There I sat in my recliner, my cat Gracie looking on intently (trusting little soul) while I was reading the directions and thinking that I really needed to try this thing out on a flesh and blood moving target.

I must admit I thought about zapping Gracie (for a fraction of a second) and then thought better of it. She is such a sweet cat. But, if I was going to give this thing to my wife to protect herself against a mugger, I did want some assurance that it would work as advertised. Am I wrong?

So, there I sat in a pair of shorts and a tank top with my reading glasses perched delicately on the bridge of my nose, directions in one hand and Tazer in another. The directions said that: a one-second burst would shock and disorient your assailant; a two-second burst was supposed to cause muscle spasms and a major loss of bodily control; and a three-second burst would purportedly make your assailant flop on the ground like a fish out of water.

Any burst longer than three seconds would be wasting the batteries.

All the while I'm looking at this little device measuring about five inches long, less than 3/4 of an inch in circumference (loaded with two itsy, bitsy AAA batteries); pretty cute really and thinking to myself, *'No possible way!'*

What happened next is almost beyond description, but I'll do my best.

I'm sitting there alone, Gracie looking on with her head cocked to one side so as to say, *'Don't do it stupid,'* reasoning that a one second burst from such a tiny little ole thing couldn't hurt all that bad. I decided to give myself a one second burst just for heck of it.

I touched the prongs to my naked thigh, pushed the button and ... *'Holy mother of God. Weapons of mass destruction. What the ...!!!'*

I'm pretty sure Hulk Hogan ran in through the side door, picked me up in the recliner and then body slammed us both on the carpet, over and over and over again. I vaguely recall waking up on my side in the foetal position, with tears in my eyes, body soaking wet, both nipples on fire, testicles nowhere to be found, with my left arm tucked under my body in the oddest position and tingling in my legs! The cat was making meowing sounds I had never heard before, clinging to a picture frame hanging above the fireplace, obviously in an attempt to avoid getting slammed by my body flopping all over the living room.

Note: If you ever feel compelled to 'mug' yourself with a Tazer, one note of caution: There is NO such thing as a one second burst when you zap yourself! You will not let go of that thing until it is dislodged from your hand by a violent thrashing about on the floor! A three second burst would be considered conservative!

A minute or so later (I can't be sure, as time was a relative thing at that point), I collected my wits (what little I had left), sat up and surveyed the landscape.

My bent reading glasses were on the mantel of the fireplace. The recliner was upside down and about eight feet or so from where it originally was. My triceps, right thigh and both nipples were still twitching. My face felt like it had been shot with Novocain and my bottom lip weighed 88 pounds. I had no control over the drooling. Apparently I had crapped in my shorts, but was too numb to know for sure, as my sense of smell was gone. I saw a faint smoke cloud above my head, which I believe came from my hair.

I'm still looking for my testicles and I'm offering a significant reward for their safe return!

PS: My wife can't stop laughing about my experience, loved the gift and now regularly threatens me with it!

Fly in the Toilet

When my friend’s hubby went to the men's room in the Schiphol Airport located in Amsterdam, he saw a fly and did his best to 'wash' it down the drain ... but failed. He figured the fly had super glue foot pads!! Now he knows why it was there!

In Amsterdam, the tile under Schiphol's urinals would pass inspection in an operating room, but nobody notices. What everybody does notice is that each urinal has a fly in it etched into the porcelain. It improves the aim. If a man sees a fly, he aims at it!

Research found that these flies reduce spillage by 80%. It gives a guy something to think about - a perfect example of attempted pest control.

Who says you can't potty train a man?

Lee Trevino - a true story

One day, shortly after joining the PGA tour in 1965, Lee Trevino, a professional golfer and married man, was at his home in Dallas, Texas mowing his front lawn, as he always did.

A lady driving by in a big, shiny Cadillac stopped in front of his house, lowered the window and asked, *'Excuse me, do you speak English?'*

Lee responded, *'Yes Ma'am, I do.'*

The lady then asked, *'What do you charge to do yard work?'*

Lee said, *'Well, the lady in this house lets me sleep with her.'*

The lady hurriedly put the car into gear and sped off.

Trivia

Well, I lost the Trivia Contest during our church pot-luck dinner last night by 1 point! Not only did I get the last question wrong, but was immediately asked to leave. The question was: *'Where do women have the curliest hair?'*

Apparently the correct answer is *Fiji Islands*

The Importance of a Second Opinion!

The doctor said, *'Joe, the good news is, I can cure your headaches. The bad news is that it will require castration. You have a very rare condition, which causes your testicles to press on your spine and the pressure creates one hell of a headache. The only way to relieve the pressure is to remove the testicles.'*

Joe was shocked and depressed. He wondered if he had anything to live for. He had no choice but to go under the knife. When he left the hospital, he was without a headache for the first time in 20 years, but he felt like he was missing an important part of himself.

As he walked down the street, he realised that he felt like a different person. He could make a new beginning and live a new life. He saw a men's clothing store and thought, *'That's what I need ... A new suit.'*

He entered the shop and told the salesman, *'I'd like a new suit.'* The elderly tailor eyed him briefly and said, *'Let's see ... Size 44 long.'*

Joe laughed, *'That's right. How did you know?'*

'Been in the business 60 years!' the tailor said.

Joe tried on the suit it fit perfectly. As Joe admired himself in the mirror, the salesman asked, *'How about a new shirt?'*

Joe thought for a moment and then said, *'Sure.'*

The salesman eyed Joe and said, *'Let's see, 34 sleeves and 16-1/2 neck.'*

Joe was surprised, *'That's right, how did you know?'*

'Been in the business 60 years.'

Joe tried on the shirt and it fit perfectly. Joe walked comfortably around the shop and the salesman asked, *'How about some new underwear?'*

Joe thought for a moment and said, *'Sure.'*

The salesman said, *'Let's see ... Size 36.'*

Joe laughed, *'Ah ha! I got you! I've worn a size 34 since I was 18 years old.'*

The salesman shook his head, *'You can't wear a size 34. A size 34 would press your testicles up against the base of your spine and give you one hell of a headache.'*

Jenny Craig for men

A guy calls a company and orders their 5-day, 10 lb. weight loss program.

The next day, there's a knock on the door and there stands before him a voluptuous, athletic, 19 year old babe dressed in nothing but a pair of Nike running shoes and a sign around her neck. She introduces herself as a representative of the weight loss company. The sign reads, *'If you can catch me, you can have me.'* Without a second thought, he takes off after her. A few miles later huffing and puffing, he finally gives up. The same girl shows up for the next four days and the same thing happens. On the fifth day, he weighs himself and is delighted to find he has lost 10 lbs. as promised.

He calls the company and orders their 5-day/20 pound program. The next day there's a knock at the door and there stands the most stunning, beautiful, sexy woman he has ever seen in his life. She is wearing nothing but Reebok running shoes and a sign around her neck that reads, *'If you catch me you can have me.'* Well, he's out the door after her like a shot. This girl is in excellent shape and he does his best, but no such luck. So for the next four days, the same routine happens with him gradually getting in better and better shape. Much to his delight on the fifth day when he weighs himself, he discovers that he has lost another 20 lbs. as promised.

He decides to go for broke and calls the company to order the 7-day/50 pound program. *'Are you sure?'* asks the representative on the phone ... *'This is our most rigorous program.'*

'Absolutely,' he replies, *'I haven't felt this good in years.'* The next day there's a knock at the door; and when he opens it he finds a huge muscular guy standing there wearing nothing but pink running shoes and a sign around his neck that reads, *'If I catch you, you're mine.'* He lost 63 pounds that week.

The wisdom of Larry the cable guy

1. A day without sunshine is like night.
2. On the other hand, you have different fingers.
3. 42.7 percent of all statistics are made up on the spot.
4. 99 percent of lawyers give the rest a bad name.
5. Remember, half the people you know are below average.
6. He who laughs last, thinks slowest.
7. Depression is merely anger without enthusiasm.
8. The early bird may get the worm, but the second mouse gets the cheese in the trap.
9. Support bacteria. They're the only culture some people have.
10. A clear conscience is usually the sign of a bad memory.
11. Change is inevitable, except from vending machines.
12. If you think nobody cares, try missing a couple of payments.
13. Okay, so what's the speed of dark?
14. When everything is coming your way, you're in the wrong lane.
15. Hard work pays off in the future. Laziness pays off now.
16. How much deeper would the ocean be without sponges?
17. Eagles may soar, but weasels don't get sucked into jet engines.
18. What happens if you get scared half to death, twice?
19. Why do psychics have to ask you your name?
20. Inside every older person is a younger person wondering, *'What the heck happened?'*
21. Just remember - if the world didn't suck, we would all fall off.
22. Light travels faster than sound. That's why some people appear bright until you hear them speak.
23. Life isn't like a box of chocolates. It's more like a jar of jalapenos. What you do today, might burn your butt tomorrow.

Men's Rules:

We always hear 'the rules' from the female side. Now here are the rules from the male side. These are our rules: Please note ... these are all numbered '1' on purpose!

1. Learn to work the toilet seat. You're a big girl. If it's up, put it down. We need it up, you need it down. You don't hear us complaining about you leaving it down.
1. Saturday = sports. It's like the full moon or the changing of the tides. Let it be
1. Shopping is NOT a sport. And no, we are never going to think of it that way.
1. Crying is blackmail
1. Ask for what you want. Let us be clear on this one: Subtle hints do not work! Strong hints do not work! Obvious hints do not work! JUST SAY IT!
1. 'Yes' and 'No' are perfectly acceptable answers to almost every question.
1. Come to us with a problem only if you want help solving it. That's what we do. Sympathy is what your girlfriends are for.
1. A headache that lasts for 17 months is a problem. See a doctor.
1. Anything we said 6 months ago is inadmissible in an argument. In fact, all comments become null and void after 7 days.
1. If you think you're fat, you probably are. Don't ask us.
1. If something we said can be interpreted two ways and one of the ways makes you sad or angry, we meant the other one.
1. You can either ask us to do something or tell us how you want it done. Not both. If you already know best how to do it, just do it yourself.
1. Whenever possible, please say whatever you have to say during commercials.
1. Christopher Columbus did not need directions and neither do we.
1. ALL men see in only 16 colours, like Windows default settings. Peach, for example, is a fruit, not a colour. Pumpkin is also a fruit. We have no idea what mauve is.
1. If it itches, it will be scratched. We do that.
1. If we ask what is wrong and you say 'nothing,' we will act like nothing's wrong. We know you are lying, but it is just not worth the hassle.
1. If you ask a question you don't want an answer to, expect an answer you don't want to hear.

1. When we have to go somewhere, absolutely anything you wear is fine. Really.
1. Don't ask us what we're thinking about unless you are prepared to discuss such topics as: Sex, Sports or Cars.
1. You have enough clothes.
1. You have too many shoes.
1. I am in shape. Round is a shape.

Thank you for reading this; Yes, I know, I have to sleep on the couch tonight, but did you know men really don't mind that; it's like camping.

Manners

A man was sunbathing naked at a private beach. For the sake of civility and to keep it from getting sunburned, he had a hat over his privates.

A woman walks past and says, snickering, *'If you were a gentleman you'd lift your hat.'*

He raised an eyebrow and replied, *'If you weren't so ugly it would lift itself.'*

What is Stress?

You pick up a hitchhiker, a beautiful girl. Suddenly she faints inside your car and you take her to hospital. Now that's stressful. But at the hospital, they say she is pregnant and congratulate you that you are going to be a father.

You say that you are not the father, but the girl says you are. This is getting very stressful. So then you request a DNA test to prove that you are not the father. After the tests are completed, the doctor says that you are infertile and probably have been since birth. You are extremely stressed but relieved.

On your way back home, you think about your three kids at home. Now that's stress!!

A real woman is a man's best friend.

- She will never stand him up and never let him down.
- She will reassure him when he feels insecure and comfort him after a bad day.
- She will inspire him to do things he never thought he could do; to live without fear and forget regret.

- She will enable him to express his deepest emotions and give in to his most intimate desires.
- She will make sure he always feels as though he's the most handsome man in the room and will enable him to be the most confident, sexy, seductive and invincible ...

No, ... wait ... Sorry. I'm thinking of whiskey. It's whiskey that does all that shit. Never mind.

Eating Out

A group of 40 year-old buddies discuss and discuss where they should meet for dinner.

Finally it is agreed upon that they should meet at the Gausthof zum Lowen restaurant because the waitresses there have low cut blouses and nice breasts.

10 years later, at 50 years of age, the group meets and once again they discuss and discuss where they should meet. Finally it is agreed upon that they should meet at the Gausthof zum Lowen because the food there is very good and the wine selection is good also.

10 years later at 60 years of age, the group meets and once again they discuss and discuss where they should meet. Finally it is agreed upon that they should meet at the Gausthof zum Lowen because they can eat there in peace and quiet and the restaurant is smoke free.

10 years later, at 70 years of age, the group meets and once again they discuss and discuss where they should meet. Finally it is agreed upon that they should meet at the Gausthof zum Lowen because the restaurant is wheel chair accessible and they even have an elevator.

10 years later, at 80 years of age, the group meets and once again they discuss and discuss where they should meet. Finally it is agreed upon that they should meet at the Gausthof zum Lowen because that would be a great idea as they have never been there before.

Ear rings

A man is at work one day, when he notices that his co-worker is wearing an earring. This man knows his co-worker to be a normally conservative fellow and is curious about his sudden change in 'fashion sense.'

The man walked up to him and said, *'I didn't know you were into earrings.'*

'Don't make such a big deal out of this, it's only an earring,' he replies sheepishly.

His friend falls silent for a few minutes, but then his curiosity prods him to say, *'So how long have you been wearing one?'*

'Ever since my wife found it in my truck ...'

[I always wondered how this trend got started.]

Trade Places

A man was sick and tired of going to work every day while his wife stayed home. He wanted her to see what he went through so he prayed:

'Dear Lord:
I go to work every day and put in 8 hours while my wife merely stays at home. I want her to know what I go through. So, please allow her body to switch with mine for a day.

God, in his infinite wisdom, granted the man's wish. The next morning, sure enough, the man awoke as a woman ... He arose, cooked breakfast for his mate, awakened the kids, set out their school clothes, fed them breakfast, packed their lunches, drove them to school, came home and picked up the dry cleaning, took it to the cleaners and stopped at the bank to make a deposit, went grocery shopping, then drove home to put away the groceries, paid the bills and balanced the check book.

He cleaned the cat's litter box and bathed the dog, then, it was already 1 pm and he hurried to make the beds, do the laundry, vacuum, dust and sweep and mop the kitchen floor. He ran to the school to pick up the kids and got into an argument with them on the way home.

Set out milk and cookies and got the kids organised to do their homework. Then, set up the ironing board and watched TV while he did the ironing. At 4:30 he began peeling potatoes and washing vegetables for salad, breaded the pork chops and snapped fresh beans for supper.

After supper, he cleaned the kitchen, ran the dishwasher, folded laundry, bathed the kids and put them to bed.

At 9 pm he was exhausted and, though his daily chores weren't finished, he went to bed where he was expected to make love, which he managed to get through without complaint.

The next morning, he awoke and immediately knelt by the bed and said: *Lord, I don't know what I was thinking. I was so wrong to envy my wife's being able to stay home all day. Please, Oh! Please, let us trade back. Amen!'*

The Lord, in his infinite wisdom, replied: *'My son, I feel you have learned your lesson and I will be happy to change things back to the way they were. You'll just have to wait nine months, though. You got pregnant last night.'*

Depressed

Fred lost one of his arms in an accident. He became very depressed because he had loved to play guitar and a lot of things that took two arms. One day he could not stand it any more. He decided to commit suicide. He went to the top of a tall building to jump off. He was standing on the ledge looking down and saw this man on the pavement below skipping along whistling and kicking up his heels. Looking closer, he noticed this man didn't have any arms at all!

Fred started thinking, *'What am I doing up here feeling sorry for myself. I still have one good arm to do things with. There goes a man with no arms skipping down the sidewalk happy and going on with his life.'* He hurried down and caught the man with no arms. He told him how glad he was to see him because he had lost one of his arms and felt ugly, useless and was going to kill himself. Fred thanked him again for saving his life and he now knew he could make it with one arm if that guy could do it with no arms.

The man with no arms began dancing and whistling and kicking up his heels again.

Fred asked *'Why are you so happy anyway?'*

He said *'I'm not happy; my arse is itchy.'*

Apartment for Rent

A businessman met a beautiful girl and agreed to spend the night with her for $500. They did their thing and, before he left, he told her that he did not have any cash with him, but he would have his secretary write a check and mail it to her, calling the payment *'Rent for Apartment.'*

On the way to the office, he regretted what he had done, realising that the whole event had not been worth the price. So he had his secretary send a check for $250 and enclose the following typed note:

Dear Madam:

Enclosed find a check for $250 for rent of your apartment. I am not sending the amount agreed upon, because when I rented the place, I was under the impression that:

#1 - it had never been occupied;
#2 - there was plenty of heat; and
#3 - it was small enough to make me feel cosy and at home.

However, I found out that:

#1 - it had been previously occupied,
#2 - there wasn't any heat and
#3 - it was entirely too large.'

Upon receipt of the note, the girl immediately returned the check for $250 with the following note:

Dear Sir:

#1 - I cannot understand how you could expect a beautiful apartment to remain unoccupied indefinitely.
#2 - As for the heat, there is plenty of it, if you know how to turn it on.
#3 - Regarding the space, the apartment is indeed of regular size, but if you don't have enough furniture to fill it, please do not blame the management. So, Please send the rent in full or we will be forced to contact your present landlady ...

Financial Plan

Dan was a single guy living at home with his father and working in the family business. When he found out he was going to inherit a fortune when his sickly father died, he decided he needed a wife with which to share his fortune.

One evening at an investment meeting he spotted the most beautiful woman he had ever seen. Her natural beauty took his breath away.

'I may look like just an ordinary man,' he said to her, *'but in just a few years, my father will die and I'll inherit $65 million.'*

Impressed, the woman obtained his business card and three days later, she became his stepmother.

Women are so much better at financial planning than men.

How to get home

A farmer stopped by the local mechanics shop to have his truck fixed. They couldn't do it while he waited, so he said he didn't live far and would just walk home.

On the way home he stopped at the hardware Store and bought a bucket and a gallon of paint. He then stopped by the feed store and picked up a couple of chickens and a goose. However, struggling outside the store he now had a problem - how to carry his entire purchases home.

While he was scratching his head he was approached by a little old lady who told him she was lost. She asked, *'Can you tell me how to get to 1603 Mockingbird Lane?'*

The farmer said, *'Well, as a matter of fact, my farm is very close to that house I would walk you there but I can't carry this lot.'*

The old lady suggested, *'Why don't you put the can of paint in the bucket. Carry the bucket in one hand, put a chicken under each arm and carry the goose in your other hand?'*

'Why thank you very much,' he said and proceeded to walk the old girl home.

On the way he says *'Let's take my short cut and go down this alley. We'll be there in no time.'*

The little old lady looked him over cautiously then said, *'I am a lonely widow without a husband to defend me. How do I know that when we get in the alley you won't hold me up against the wall, pull up my skirt and have your way with me?'*

The farmer said, *'Holy smokes lady! I'm carrying a bucket, a gallon of paint, two chickens and a goose. How in the world could I possibly hold you up against the wall and do that?'*

The old lady replied, *'Set the goose down, cover him with the bucket, put the paint on top of the bucket and I'll hold the chickens'*

About Dads

A man knows when he is growing old when he starts looking like his father.

FEMALES

A woman's Job

She'd been taught 'housework is a woman' job'. But one evening Jenny arrived home from work to find the children bathed, one load of laundry in the washer and another in the dryer. Dinner was on the stove and the table set. She was astonished!!

Turned out that Ralph had read an article that said, *'Wives who work full-time and then had to do their own housework were too tired to have sex'.*

The night went very well. The next day, she told her office friends all about it. *'We had a great dinner. Ralph even cleaned up the kitchen. He helped the kids do their homework, folded all the laundry and put it away. I really enjoyed the evening.'*

'But what about afterward?' asked her friends.

'Oh, that ... Ralph was too tired.'

God is Good

Good Housekeeping Tip

Always keep several get well cards on display ... so if unexpected visitors arrive, they'll think you've been sick and haven't been able to clean the house

Hey - why did no one tell me this earlier!!! I should have figured it out sooner. It's the shampoo I use in the shower. When I wash my hair, the shampoo runs down my whole body. Printed very clearly on the shampoo label it reads, '*For extra volume and body.'*

I have gotten rid of the shampoo and I am going to start using Palmolive Dish detergent. Its label reads, *'Dissolves fat that is otherwise difficult to remove.'*

Problem solved! Geeze! It sure pays to read the label!

Best Menopausal Question Ever:

Question: How many Menopausal women does it take to change a light bulb?

Woman's Answer: One! ONLY ONE!!!! And do you know WHY? Because no one else in this house knows HOW to change a bloody light bulb! They don't even know that the bulb is BURNED OUT!! They would sit in the dark for THREE DAYS before they figured it out.

And, once they figured it out, they wouldn't be able to find the #&%!* light bulbs despite the fact that they've been in the SAME

DAMNED CABINET for the past 17 YEARS! But if they did, by some miracle of God, actually find them, 2 DAYS LATER, the chair they dragged to stand on to change the STUPID light bulb would STILL BE IN THE SAME SPOT!!!!! AND UNDERNEATH IT WOULD BE THE WRAPPER THE FREAKING LIGHT BULBS CAME IN!!! BECAUSE NO ONE EVER PICKS UP OR CARRIES OUT THE GARBAGE!!!! IT'S A WONDER WE HAVEN'T ALL SUFFOCATED FROM THE PILES OF GARBAGE THAT ARE A FOOT DEEP THROUGHOUT THE ENTIRE HOUSE!! IT WOULD TAKE AN ARMY TO CLEAN THIS PLACE! AND DON'T EVEN GET ME STARTED ON WHO CHANGES THE TOILET PAPER ROLL!!

I'm sorry. What was the question?

What kind of man attracts a woman?

A study conducted by UCLA's Department of Psychiatry has revealed that the kind of face a woman finds attractive on a man can differ depending on where she is in her menstrual cycle.

For example: If she is ovulating, she is attracted to men with rugged and masculine features. However, if she is menstruating or menopausal, she tends to be more attracted to a man with duct tape over his mouth and a spear lodged in his chest while he is on fire.
No further studies are expected.

Bitches to the end!

The doctor, after an examination, sighed and said, *'I've got some bad news. You have cancer and you'd best put your affairs in order ...'*

The woman was shocked, but managed to compose herself and walk into the waiting room where her daughter had been waiting.

'Well, daughter, we women celebrate when things are good and we celebrate when things don't go so well. In this case, things aren't well. I have cancer. So, let's head to the club and have a martini.'

After 3 or 4 martinis, the two were feeling a little less sombre. There were some laughs and more martinis. They were eventually approached by some of the woman's old friends, who were curious as to what the two were celebrating. The woman told her friends they were drinking to her impending end, *'I've been diagnosed with AIDS.'*

The friends were aghast, gave the woman their condolences and beat a hasty retreat. After the friends left, the woman's daughter leaned over and whispered, *'Mom, I thought you said you were dying of cancer and you just told your friends you were dying of AIDS! Why did you do that?'*

'Because I don't want any of those bitches sleeping with your father after I'm gone.'

And THAT, my friends, is what is called, '*Putting your affairs in order.'*

Beware of that underwear dust!!!

One evening a Husband, thinking he was being funny, said to his wife, *'Perhaps we should start washing your clothes in 'Slim Fast'. Maybe it would take a few inches off of your butt!'*

His wife was not amused and decided that she simply couldn't let such a comment go unrewarded. The next morning the husband took a pair of underwear out of his drawer. *'What the Hell is this?'* he said to himself as a little 'dust' cloud appeared when he shook them out.

'April,' he hollered into the bathroom, *'Why did you put Talcum Powder in my underwear?'*

She replied with a snicker. *'It's not talcum powder; it's 'Miracle Grow!!!'*

You guys just never learn: do not tick off a woman.

9 Words Women Use

1. *Fine*: This is the word women use to end an argument when they are right and you need to shut up.
2. *Five minutes*: If she is getting dressed, this means a half hour. Five minutes is only five minutes if you have just been given five more minutes to watch the game before helping around the house.
3. *Nothing*: This is the calm before the storm. This means something and you should be on your toes. Arguments that begin with nothing usually end using the word *'fine.'*
4. *Go ahead*: This is a dare, not permission. Don't do it!
5. *Loud sigh*: This is actually a word, but is a non-verbal statement often misunderstood by men. A loud sigh means she thinks you are an idiot and wonders why she is wasting her time standing there and arguing with you about nothing. (Refer back to #3 for the meaning of nothing.)
6. *That's Okay*: This is one of the most dangerous statements a woman can make to a man. That's okay means she wants to think long and hard before deciding how and when you will pay for your mistake.
7. *Thanks*: A woman is thanking you, do not question or faint. Just *say 'You're welcome.'* (I want to add in a clause here - This is

true, unless she says, *'Thanks a lot'* - that is PURE sarcasm and she is not thanking you at all. DO NOT say *'You're welcome'* ... that will bring on a *'whatever'*).

8. *Whatever*: Is a woman's way of saying f*** you!
9. *Don't worry about it, I got it:* Another dangerous statement, meaning this is something that a woman has told a man to do several times, but is now doing it herself. This will later result in the man asking *'What's wrong?'* For the woman's response, refer to #3.

Eleven People On a rope

Eleven people were hanging on a rope, under a helicopter; ten men and one woman. The rope was not strong enough to carry them all, so they decided that one had to leave, because otherwise they were all going to fall.

They weren't able to choose that person, until the woman gave a very touching speech. She said that she would voluntarily let go of the rope, because, as a woman, she was used to giving up everything for her husband and kids or for men in general and was used to always making sacrifices with little in return.

As soon as she finished her speech, all the men started clapping.

A woman's poem:

Before I lay me down to sleep,
I pray for a man who's not a creep,
One who's handsome, smart and strong.
One who loves to listen long,
One who thinks before he speaks,
One who'll call, not wait for weeks.
I pray he's rich and self-employed,
And when I spend, won't be annoyed.
Pull out my chair and hold my hand.
Massage my feet and help me stand.
Oh send a king to make me queen.
A man who loves to cook and clean.
I pray this man will love no other.
And relish visits with my mother.

Kinda brings a tear to your eye doesn't it

A man's poem:

I pray for a deaf-mute gymnast nymphomaniac with big tits who owns a bar on a golf course and loves to send me fishing and drinking. This doesn't rhyme and I don't give a shit.

Thin vs. Fat

Recently, in a large city in Australia, a poster featuring a young, thin and tan woman appeared in the window of a gym. It said, *'This summer, do you want to be a mermaid or a whale?'*

A middle-aged woman, whose physical characteristics did not match those of the woman on the poster, responded publicly to the question posed by the gym.

Broccoli Casserole

A woman goes to her boyfriend's parents' house for Christmas dinner. This is to be her first time meeting the family and she is very nervous.

They all sit down and begin eating a fine meal. The woman is beginning to feel a little discomfort, thanks to her nervousness and the broccoli casserole. The gas pains are almost making her eyes water. Left with no other choice, she decides to relieve herself a bit and lets out a dainty fart.

It wasn't loud, but everyone at the table heard the poof. Before she even had a chance to be embarrassed, her boyfriend's father looked over at the dog that had been snoozing under the woman's chair and said in a rather stern voice, *'Skippy!'*

The woman thought, *'This is great!'* and a big smile came across her face. A couple of minutes later, she was beginning to feel the pain again. This time, she didn't even hesitate. She let a much louder and longer rrrrrip.

The father again looked at the dog and yelled, *'Skippy!'*

Once again the woman smiled and thought *'Yes!'* A few minutes later the woman had to let another rip. This time she didn't even think about it. She let a fart rip that rivalled a train whistle blowing.

Once again, the father looked at the dog with disgust and yelled, *'Skippy, get away from her, before she shits on you!'*

How to clean the house

1. Make a new file in your PC.
2. Call it '*Housework.*'
3. Send to the *Recycle Bin.*

4. Then, empty the *Recycle Bin.*
5. You will be asked, '*Are you sure you want to delete Housework permanently*?'
6. Firmly click mouse with your answer, *'Yes.'*
7. Now, are you feeling better?

To Whom It May Concern,

Whales are always surrounded by friends (dolphins, sea lions, curious humans.) They have an active sex life, get pregnant and have adorable baby whales. They have a wonderful time with dolphins stuffing themselves with shrimp. They play and swim in the seas, seeing wonderful places like Patagonia, the Bering Sea and the coral reefs of Polynesia.

Whales are wonderful singers and have even recorded CDs. They are incredible creatures and virtually have no predators other than humans. They are loved, protected and admired by almost everyone in the world.

Mermaids don't exist. If they did exist, they would be lining up outside the offices of Argentinean psychoanalysts due to identity crisis. Fish or human? They don't have a sex life because there are no Manmaids. They kill ordinary men who get close to them, not to mention how could they have sex? Just look at them ... where is IT? Therefore, they don't have kids either. Not to mention, who wants to get close to a girl who smells like a fish store?

The choice is perfectly clear to me: I want to be a whale.

P.S. We are in an age when media puts into our heads the idea that only skinny people are beautiful, but I prefer to enjoy an ice cream with my kids, a good dinner with a man who makes me shiver and a glass of wine with my friends. With time, we gain weight because we accumulate so much information and wisdom in our heads that when there is no more room, it distributes out to the rest of our bodies. So we aren't heavy, we are enormously cultured, educated and happy. Beginning today, when I look at my butt in the mirror I will think, '*Good grief, look at how smart I am!'*

The Knob

A woman visited a plastic surgeon who told her about a new procedure called 'The Knob,' where a small knob is placed at the top of the woman's head and could be turned to tighten up her skin and produce the effect of a brand new face-lift. Of course, the woman wanted 'The Knob.'

Over the course of the years, the woman tightened the knob and the effects were wonderful, the woman remained young looking and vibrant. After fifteen years, the woman returned to the surgeon with two problems.

'All these years, everything has been working just fine. I've had to turn the knob many times and I've always loved the results. But now I've developed two annoying problems: First, I have these terrible bags under my eyes and the knob won't get rid of them.'

The doctor looked at her closely and said, *'Those aren't bags, those are your breasts.'*

She said, *'Well, I guess there's no point in asking about the goatee.'*

Christmas shopping

A woman was in town on a Christmas shopping trip. She began her day finding the most perfect shoes in the first shop and a beautiful dress on sale the second. In the third shop everything had just been reduced to five dollars when her mobile phone rang. It was a female doctor notifying her that her husband had just been in a terrible accident and was in a critical condition in the ICU.

The woman told the doctor to inform her husband where she was and that she'd be there as soon as possible. As she hung up she realised she was leaving what was shaping up to be her best day ever in the shops. She decided to go into a couple of more shops before heading to the hospital. She ended up shopping for the rest of the morning, finishing her trip with a cup of coffee and a beautiful cream slice, complimentary from the last shop! She was jubilant.

Then she remembered her husband. Feeling guilty, she dashed to the hospital. She saw the doctor in the corridor and asked about her husband's condition. The lady doctor glared at her and shouted, *'You went ahead and finished your shopping trip didn't you! I hope you're proud of yourself! While you were out for the past four hours enjoying yourself in town, your husband has been languishing in the Intensive Care Unit! It's just as well you went ahead and finished, because it will more than likely be the last shopping trip you ever take! For the rest of his life he will require round the clock care. And you'll now be his carer!'*

The woman was feeling so guilty she broke down and sobbed.

The lady doctor then chuckled and said, *'I'm just pulling your leg. He's dead. Now, what did you buy?'*

Serious Warning to Women:

You've heard about people who have been abducted and had their kidneys removed by black-market organ thieves. My thighs were stolen from me during the night a few years ago. I went to sleep and woke up with someone else's thighs. It was just that quick. The replacements had the texture of cooked oatmeal. Whose thighs were these and what happened to mine? I spent the entire summer looking for my thighs. Finally, hurt and angry, I resigned myself to living out my life in jeans. And then the thieves struck again.

My butt was next. I knew it was the same gang, because they took pains to match my new rear-end to the thighs they had stuck me with earlier. But my new butt was attached at least three inches lower than my original! I realised I'd have to give up my jeans in favour of long skirts.

Two years ago I realised my arms had been switched. One morning I was fixing my hair and was horrified to see the flesh of my upper arm swing to and fro with the motion of the hairbrush. This was really getting scary - my body was being replaced one section at a time. What could they do to me next?

When my poor neck suddenly disappeared and was replaced with a turkey neck, I decided to tell my story. Women of the world; wake up and smell the coffee! Those 'plastic' surgeons are using REAL replacement body parts - stolen from you and me! The next time someone you know has something 'lifted', look again - was it lifted from you?

This is not a hoax! This is happening to women everywhere every night. Warn your friends!

P. S. Last year I thought someone had stolen my Boobs. I was lying in bed and they were gone! But when I jumped out of bed, I was relieved to see that they had just been hiding in my armpits as I slept. Now I keep them hidden in my waistband.

These same thieves come in my closet and shrink my clothes! How do they do it??

A new Woolworths supermarket has just opened near us!

It has an automatic water mister to keep the produce fresh. Just before it goes on, you hear the distant sound of thunder and the smell of fresh rain.

When you pass the milk cases, you hear cows mooing and you experience the scent of fresh cut hay.

In the meat department there is the aroma of charcoal grilled steaks and snags.

In the liquor department, the fresh, clean, crisp smell of tapped Cascade Lite.

When you approach the egg case, you hear hens cluck and cackle and the air is filled with the pleasing aroma of bacon and eggs frying.

The bread department features the tantalising smell of fresh baked bread and cookies.

I don't buy toilet paper there anymore.

Why females should avoid a girls night out after they are married

The other night I was invited out for a night with the 'girls.' I told my husband that I would be home by midnight, *'I promise!'*

Well, the hours passed and the margaritas went down way too easily. Around 3 am, a bit loaded, I headed for home. Just as I got in the door, the cuckoo clock in the hallway started up and cuckooed three times. Quickly, realising my husband would probably wake up, I cuckooed another nine times.

I was really proud of myself for coming up with such a quick-witted solution, in order to escape a possible conflict with him. (Even when totally smashed ... three cuckoos plus nine cuckoos totals equals twelve cuckoos - Midnight!)

The next morning my husband asked me what time I got in, I told him *'Midnight'* ... He didn't seem pissed off in the least.
Whew, I got away with that one! Then he said *'We need a new cuckoo clock.'*

When I asked him why, he said, *'Well, last night our clock cuckooed three times, then said 'Oh shit.' Cuckooed 4 more times, cleared its throat, cuckooed another three times, giggled, cuckooed twice more and then tripped over the coffee table and farted.'*

Curtain Rods - Priceless!

She spent the first day packing her belongings into boxes, crates and suitcases. On the second day, she had the movers come and collect her things. On the third day, she sat down for the last time at their beautiful dining room table by candle-light, put on some soft background music and feasted on a pound of shrimp, a jar of caviar and a bottle of spring-water.

When she had finished, she went into each and every room and deposited a few half-eaten shrimp shells dipped in caviar into the hollow of the curtain rods. She then cleaned up the kitchen and left.

When the husband returned with his new girlfriend, all was bliss for the first few days. Then slowly, the house began to smell.

They tried everything; cleaning, mopping and airing the place out. Vents were checked for dead rodents and carpets were steam cleaned. Air fresheners were hung everywhere. Exterminators were brought in to set off gas canisters, during which they had to move out for a few days and in the end they even paid to replace the expensive wool carpeting. Nothing worked.

People stopped coming over to visit. Repairmen refused to work in the house. The maid quit. Finally, they could not take the stench any longer and decided to move.

A month later, even though they had cut their price in half, they could not find a buyer for their stinky house. Word got out and eventually even the local realtors refused to return their calls.

Finally, they had to borrow a huge sum of money from the bank to purchase a new place. The ex-wife called the man and asked how things were going. He told her the saga of the rotting house. She listened politely and said that she missed her old home terribly and would be willing to reduce her divorce settlement in exchange for getting the house back.

Knowing his ex-wife had no idea how bad the smell was, he agreed on a price that was about 1/10th of what the house had been worth, but only if she were to sign the papers that very day. She agreed and within the hour his lawyers delivered the paperwork.

A week later the man and his girlfriend stood smiling as they watched the moving company pack everything to take to their new home ... And to spite the ex-wife; they even took the curtain rods!!!!!!

I love a happy ending, don't you?

Black robbers (A True Story)

On a recent weekend in Atlantic City, a woman won a bucketful of quarters at a slot machine. She took a break from the slots for dinner with her husband in the hotel dining room. But first she wanted to stash the quarters in her room. *'I'll be right back and we'll go to eat'* she told her husband and carried the coin-laden bucket to the elevator.

As she was about to walk into the elevator she noticed two men already aboard. Both were Black. One of them was very tall and had an intimidating figure. The woman froze. Her first thought was: *'These two are going to rob me.'*

Her next thought was: *'Don't be a bigot; they look like perfectly nice gentlemen.'* But racial stereotypes are powerful and fear immobilised her. Avoiding eye contact, she turned around stiffly and faced the elevator doors as they closed.

A second passed and then another second and then another. Her fear increased! The elevator didn't move. Panic consumed her. *'My God'* she thought, *'I'm trapped and about to be robbed!'* Her heart plummeted. Perspiration poured from every pore.

Then one of the men said, *'Hit the floor.'*

Instinct told her to do what they told her. The bucket of quarters flew upwards as she threw out her arms and collapsed on the elevator floor. A shower of coins rained down on her.

'Take my money and spare me', she prayed.

More seconds passed. She heard one of the men say politely, *'Ma'am, if you'll just tell us what floor you're going to, we'll push the button.'*

The one who said it had a little trouble getting the words out. He was trying mightily to hold in a belly laugh. The woman lifted her head and looked up at the two men. They reached down to help her up.

Confused, she struggled to her feet. *'When I told my friend here to hit the floor,'* said the average sized one, *'I meant that he should hit the elevator button for our floor. I didn't mean for you to hit the floor, ma'am.'*

He spoke genially. He bit his lip. It was obvious he was having a hard time not laughing.

The woman thought: *'My God, what a spectacle I've made of myself.'* She was too humiliated to speak.

The three of them gathered up the strewn quarters and refilled her bucket. When the elevator arrived at her floor they then insisted on walking her to her room. She seemed a little unsteady on her feet and they were afraid she might not make it down the corridor. At her door they bid her a good evening.

As she slipped into her room she could hear them roaring with laughter as they walked back to the elevator. The woman brushed herself off. She pulled herself together and went downstairs for dinner with her husband.

The next morning flowers were delivered to her room; a dozen roses. Attached to EACH rose was a crisp one hundred-dollar bill.

The card said: *'Thanks for the best laugh we've had in years.'* It was signed: Eddie Murphy and Michael Jordan.

Four Worms and the lesson to be learned!

A minister decided that a visual demonstration would add emphasis to his Sunday sermon. Four worms were placed into four separate jars. The first worm was put into a container of alcohol. The second worm was put into a container of cigarette smoke. The third worm was put into a container of chocolate syrup. The fourth worm was put into a container of good clean soil.

At the conclusion of the sermon, the Minister reported the following results:

- The first worm in alcohol - Dead
- The second worm in cigarette smoke - Dead
- Third worm in chocolate syrup - Dead
- Fourth worm in good clean soil - Alive.

So the Minister asked the congregation - *'What did you learn from this demonstration?'*

Marlene was sitting in the back, quickly raised her hand and said, *'As long as you drink, smoke and eat chocolate, you won't have worms!'*

That pretty much ended the service.

Crap

Whatever you give a woman, she will make greater. If you give her sperm, she'll give you a baby. If you give her a house, she'll give you a home. If you give her groceries, she'll give you a meal. If you give her a smile, she'll give you her heart. She multiplies and enlarges what is given to her.

So, if you give her any crap, be ready to receive a ton of shit.

Dear diary

Dear diary - day 1

All packed for the cruise ship - all my nicest dresses, swimsuits, short sets. Really, really exciting. Our local Women's Guild decided on this 'all-girls' trip. It will be my first one, - and I can't wait!

Dear diary - day 2

Entire day at sea - beautiful. Saw whales and dolphins. Met the Captain today - seems like a very nice man.

Dear diary - day 3

At the pool today. Did some shuffleboard and hit golf balls off the deck. Captain invited me to join him at his table for dinner. Felt honoured and had a wonderful time. He is very attractive and attentive.

Dear diary - day 4

Won $800.00 in the ship's casino. Captain asked me to have dinner with him in his own cabin. Had a scrumptious meal complete with caviar and champagne. He asked me to stay the night, but I declined. Told him I could not be unfaithful to my husband.

Dear diary - day 5

Pool again today. Got sunburned and I went inside to drink at piano-bar, stayed there for rest of day. Captain saw me, bought me several large drinks. Really is quite charming. Again asked me to visit his cabin for the night. Again I declined. He told me, if I did not let him have his way with me, he would sink the ship. I was shocked.

Dear diary - day 6

Today I saved 1,600 lives. Twice.

Men vs. Women regarding jokes

When a man expects a woman to have a sense of humour, it does not mean she tells him jokes - it means that she laughs at his!

There's definitely a gender difference between what men and women consider funny. When it comes to comedy, research tells us there is a significant difference between how the brains of men and women react when confronted with a joke.

As men and women lay inside an MRI machine their brain activity was examined as the subjects looked at comics and pressed one of two buttons to show whether they found the information funny. Women were found to be faster than men at deciding if a cartoon was not funny. They were also more likely to use more of their brains to process and react to the comedy. So women seem to be all business when it comes to humour and focus on the alleged comedy. They decide quickly if it works for them then move on.

When women found cartoons to be funny, there was an increased activity in their reward centre. If the joke wasn't funny, there was no activity in the reward centre.

In Men the reward centre of men remained stable when a cartoon was amusing and actually declined when exposed to jokes they didn't consider funny. These differences between genders, is a result of expectations. The women were generally sceptical and didn't expect the jokes to be funny. When they were, they laughed setting off a reward in their brains. Men expected to be amused so when they weren't they experienced disappointment.

SINGLES

First Date

If you didn't see this on the Tonight show, I hope you're sitting down when you read it. This is probably the funniest date story ever, first date or not!!! We have all had bad dates but this takes the cake.
Jay Leno went into the audience to find the most embarrassing first date that a woman ever had. The winner described her worst first date experience. There was absolutely no question as to why her tale took the prize!

She said it was midwinter ... snowing and quite cold ... and the guy had taken her skiing in the mountains outside Salt Lake City, Utah. It was a day trip (not overnight). They were strangers, after all and truly had never met before. The outing was fun but relatively uneventful until they were headed home late that afternoon.

They were driving back down the mountain, when she gradually began to realise that she should not have had that extra latte. They were about an hour away from anywhere from a rest room and in the middle of nowhere! Her companion suggested she try to hold it, which she did for a while.

Unfortunately, because of the heavy snow and slow going, there came a point where she told him that he had better stop and let her go beside the road or it would be the front seat of his car.

They stopped and she quickly crawled out beside the car, yanked her pants down and started. In the deep snow she didn't have good footing, so she let her butt rest against the rear fender to steady herself.

Her companion stood on the side of the car watching for traffic and indeed was a real gentleman and refrained from peeking. All she could think about was the relief she felt despite the rather embarrassing nature of the situation.

Upon finishing however, she soon became aware of another sensation. As she bent to pull up her pants, the young lady discovered her buttocks were firmly glued against the car's fender.

Thoughts of tongues frozen to poles immediately came to mind as she attempted to disengage her flesh from the icy metal. It was quickly apparent that she had a brand new problem due to the extreme cold.

Horrified by her plight and yet aware of the humour of the moment, she answered her date's concerns about *'What is taking so long'* with a reply that indeed, she was *'Freezing her butt off'* and in need of some assistance!

He came around the car as she tried to cover herself with her sweater and then, as she looked imploringly into his eyes, he burst out laughing. She too, got the giggles and when they finally managed to compose themselves, they assessed her dilemma.

Obviously, as hysterical as the situation was, they also were faced with a real problem. Both agreed it would take something hot to free her chilly cheeks from the grip of the icy metal!

Thinking about what had gotten her into the predicament in the first place, both quickly realised that there was only one way to get her free.

So, as she looked the other way, her first-time date proceeded to unzip his pants and pee her butt off the fender. As the audience screamed in laughter, she took the Tonight Show prize hands down. Or perhaps that should be *'pants down.'* And you thought your first date was embarrassing.

Oh and how did the first date turn out? He became her husband and was sitting next to her on the Leno show.

Birth Control

The mother of a 17-year-old girl was concerned that her daughter was having sex. Worried the girl might become pregnant and adversely impact the family's status, she consulted the family doctor. The doctor told her that teenagers today were very wilful and any attempt to stop the girl would probably result in rebellion. He then told her to arrange for her daughter to be put on birth control and until then, talk to her and give her a box of condoms.

Later that evening, as her daughter was preparing for a date, the woman told her about the situation and handed her a box of condoms.

The girl burst out laughing and reached over to hug her mother, saying, *'Oh Mom! You don't have to worry about that! I'm dating Susan!'*

Irish Virginity Test Kit

Paddy, one of the little people, is planning to marry, he is, he is. So he goes to visit the king of the little people and asks him how he could tell if his bride-to-be is still a virgin.

The king says, *'Aye Paddy, to be sure, all Irish humans use three things for what they call a Do-it-Yourself VirginityTest Kit ... A can of red paint; a can of blue paint and a shovel'*

Paddy asks, *'Aye and to be sure, what do I do with these things oh King?'*

The king of the fairies replies, *'Before ye climb into bed on your wedding night, you paint one of your balls red and the other blue. If she says, That's the strangest pair of balls I ever did see ...! You hit her with the shovel.'*

Debutante Ball

A US Navy cruiser anchored in Mississippi for a week's shore leave. The first evening, the ship's Captain received the following note from the wife of a wealthy plantation owner:

'Dear Captain,
Thursday will be my daughter Melinda's Debutante Ball. I would like you to send four well-mannered, handsome, unmarried officers in their formal dress uniforms to attend the dance. They should arrive promptly at 8:00 pm for an evening of polite Southern conversation. They should be excellent dancers, as they will be the escorts of refined young ladies. One last point: No Jews please.'

Sending a written message by his own yeoman, the captain replied:

'Madam
'Thank you for your invitation. In order to present the widest possible knowledge base for polite conversation, I am sending four of my best and most prized officers, all unmarried.

One is a lieutenant commander and a graduate of Annapolis with an additional Masters degree from MIT in fluid technologies and ship design. He is a current Chairman at a Toastmaster's Chapter.

The second is a Lieutenant, a helicopter pilot and a graduate of Northwestern University in Chicago, with a BSC in Aeronautical Engineering. He has a Masters Degree and PhD in Aeronautical and Mechanical Engineering and is also an astronaut candidate.

The third officer is also a lieutenant, with degrees in both computer systems and information technology from SMU and he is awaiting notification on his Doctoral Dissertation from Cal Tech.

The fourth officer, also a lieutenant commander, is our ship's doctor, with an undergraduate degree from the University of Georgia and his medical degree is from the University of North Carolina. We are very proud of him, as he is also a senior fellow in Trauma Surgery at Bethesda.'

Upon receiving this letter, Melinda's mother was quite excited and looked forward to Thursday with pleasure. Her daughter would be escorted by four handsome and highly-qualified naval officers; and the other women in her social circle would be insanely jealous.

At precisely 8 pm on Thursday, Melinda's mother answered a knock on the door, to find, in smart dress uniform, four handsome, smiling officers … all Black.

Her mouth fell open, but pulling herself together, she stammered, *'There must be some mistake.'*

'No, Madam,' said the first officer. *'Captain Goldberg never makes mistakes.'*

Scratching

A man was lying in bed with his new girlfriend. After having great sex, she spent the next hour just scratching his nuts - something she seemed to love to do.

As he was enjoying it, he turned and asked her, *'Why do you love doing that?*

'Because,' she replied, *'I really miss mine.'*

First Time with a Condom

I recall my first time with a condom. I was sixteen or so. I went in to buy a packet of condoms at the pharmacy. There was this beautiful woman assistant behind the counter and she could see that I was new at it. She handed me the package and asked if I knew how to wear one.

I honestly answered, *'No, this is my first time.'*

So she unwrapped the package, took one out and slipped it over her thumb. She cautioned me to make sure it was on, tight and secure. I apparently still looked confused, so she looked all around the store to see if it was empty. It was empty

'Just a minute,' she said and walked to the door and locked it. Taking my hand, she led me into the back room, unbuttoned her blouse and removed it. She unhooked her bra and laid it aside.

'Do these excite you?' she asked.

Well, I was so dumb-struck that all I could do was nod my head. She then said it was time to slip the condom on. As I was slipping it on, she dropped her skirt, removed her panties and lay down on a desk.

'Well, come on', she said, *'We don't have much time.'*

So I climbed on her. It was so wonderful, that unfortunately, I could no longer hold back and KAPOW, I was done within a few minutes.

She looked at me with a bit of a frown. *'Did you put that condom on?'* she asked

I said, *'I sure did,'* and held up my thumb to show her.

She fainted.

Gift from the Bride

All eyes were on the radiant bride as her father escorted her down the aisle. They reached the altar and the waiting groom; the bride kissed her father and placed something in his hand.

The guests in the front pews responded with ripples of laughter, even the priest smiled broadly. As her father gave her away in marriage, the bride gave him back his credit card.

Romantic Poetry - Not

These are entries to a Washington post competition asking for a two-line rhyme with the most romantic first line and the least romantic second line:

1. My darling, my lover, my beautiful wife: Marrying you has screwed up my life.
2. My love, you take my breath away. What have you stepped in to smell this way?
3. Kind, intelligent, loving and hot; this describes everything you are not.
4. Love may be beautiful, love may be bliss, but I only slept with you 'cause I was pissed.
5. I thought that I could love no other - that is until I met your brother.
6. Roses are red, violets are blue, sugar is sweet and so are you. But the roses are wilting, the violets are dead, the sugar bowl's empty and so is your head.
7. I want to feel your sweet embrace; but don't take that paper bag off your face.
8. I love your smile, your face and your eyes. Damn, I'm good at telling lies!
9. I see your face when I am dreaming. That's why I always wake up screaming.
10. My feelings for you no words can tell, except for maybe *'Go to hell.'*

11. What inspired this amorous rhyme? Two parts vodka, one part lime.

Who said poetry is boring?

How to stop people from bugging you about getting married

Old aunts used to come up to me at weddings, poking me in the ribs and cackling, telling me, *'You're next.'* They stopped after I started doing the same thing to them at funerals.

Buddies

Jack decided to go skiing with his buddy, Bob. So they loaded up Jack's minivan and headed north. After driving for a few hours, they got caught in a terrible blizzard. So they pulled into a nearby farm and asked the attractive lady who answered the door if they could spend the night.

'I realise it's terrible weather out there and I have this huge house all to myself, but I'm recently widowed,' she explained. *'I'm afraid the neighbours will talk if I let you stay in my house.'*

'Don't worry,' Jack said. *'We'll be happy to sleep in the barn. And if the weather breaks, we'll be gone at first light.'*

The lady agreed and the two men found their way to the barn and settled in for the night. Come morning, the weather had cleared and they got on their way. They enjoyed a great weekend of skiing. But about nine months later, Jack got an unexpected letter from an attorney. It took him a few minutes to figure it out, but he finally determined that it was from the attorney of that attractive widow he had met on the ski weekend.

After their meeting Jack dropped in on his friend Bob and asked, *'Bob, do you remember that good-looking widow from the farm we stayed at on our ski holiday up north about nine months ago?'*

'Yes, I do.' Said Bob.

'Did you, er, happen to get up in the middle of the night, go up to the house and pay her a visit?'

'Well, um, yes!' Bob admitted, a little embarrassed about being found out, *'I have to admit that I did.'*

'And did you happen to give her my name instead of telling her your name?'

Bob's face turned beet red and he said, *'Yeah, look, I'm sorry, buddy. I'm afraid I did. Why do you ask?'*

'She just died and left everything to me!'

[And you thought the ending would be different, didn't you? You know you smiled ... now keep that smile for the rest of the day!]

How to be a gracious bitch

Jennifer's wedding day was fast approaching. Nothing could dampen her excitement - not even her parent's nasty divorce. Her mother had found the perfect dress to wear and would be the best-dressed mother-of-the-bride ever!

A week later, Jennifer was horrified to learn that her father's new, young wife had bought the exact same dress as her mother!

Jennifer asked her father's new young wife to exchange it, but she refused. *'Absolutely not! I look like a million bucks in this dress and I'm wearing it,'* she replied.

Jennifer told her mother who graciously said, *'Never mind sweetheart. I'll get another dress. After all, it's your special day.'*

A few days later, they went shopping and did find another gorgeous dress for her mother. When they stopped for lunch, Jennifer asked her mother, *'Aren't you going to return the other dress? You really don't have another occasion where you could wear it.'*

Her mother just smiled and replied, *'Of course I do, dear ... I'm wearing it to the rehearsal dinner the night before the wedding.'*

[Now I ask you - Is there a woman out there - anywhere, who wouldn't enjoy this story?]

Shy Bride

A young Chinese couple gets married. She's a virgin. Truth be told, he's a virgin too, but she doesn't know that. On their wedding night, she cowers naked under the sheets as her husband undresses in the darkness.

He climbs into bed next to her and tries to be reassuring. *'My darring,'* he whispers, *'I know dis you firss time in da bed wit a mans and you be berry flighten. I promise you, I give you anyting you wants, I do anyting - juss anyting you wants for to make you happy wife. You juss ask me. So, whatchu want?'* he says, trying to sound experienced and worldly, which he hopes will impress her.

A thoughtful silence follows and he waits patiently (and eagerly) for her request.

She eventually shyly whispers back, *'I want we try someting I hears about from odda girls at work ... Numbaa 69 in da bed'*

More thoughtful silence, this time from him. Eventually, in a puzzled tone he asks her *'Rearry, on da wedding night you want ... Garlic Chicken wif snow peas?'*

Breasts

A sexy young woman was sitting next to a man on a plane. After a little while she said to him, *'Can you help me remove something from my breasts please?'*

The excited young man replied, *'Wow! It would be my pleasure – so what is it?'*

Her reply: *'Your eyes, you moron!'*

LAWYERS

Murder at Coles:

Tired of constantly being broke and stuck in an unhappy marriage, a young husband decided to solve both problems by taking out a large life insurance policy on his wife naming himself as the beneficiary and then arranging to have her killed. A 'friend of a friend' put him in touch with a nefarious dark-side underworld figure that went by the name of *'Artie.'*

Artie met and explained to the husband that his going price for snuffing out a spouse was $5,000. The husband said he was willing to pay that amount, but that he wouldn't have any cash on hand until he could collect his wife's insurance money. Artie insisted on being paid at least something up front, so the man opened his purse, displaying the $1 coin that rested inside. Artie sighed, rolled his eyes and reluctantly agreed to accept the $1 as down payment for the dirty deed.

A few days later, Artie followed the man's wife to the local Coles store. There, he surprised her in the produce department and proceeded to strangle her with his gloved hands. But as the poor unsuspecting woman drew her last breath and slumped to the floor, the manager of the produce department stumbled unexpectedly onto the murder scene. Unwilling to leave any living witnesses behind, old Artie had no choice but to strangle the produce manager as well. However, unknown to Artie, the entire proceedings were captured by the hidden security cameras and observed by the store's security guard, who immediately called the police.

Artie was caught and arrested before he could even leave the store. Under intense questioning at the police station, Artie revealed the whole sordid plan, including his unusual financial arrangements with the hapless husband, who was also quickly arrested.

The next day in the newspaper, the headline declared ...

[*You're going to hate me for this ...*]

Artie Chokes 2 for $1 at Coles

Oh, quit groaning! I don't write this stuff, I receive it from my other warped friends and then pass it on to you.

The reason Politicians try so hard to get re-elected is that they would *'hate'* to have to make a living under the laws they've passed.

Court Humour

Attorney: What gear were you in at the moment of the impact?
Witness: Gucci sweats and Reeboks.

Attorney: Are you sexually active?
Witness: No, I just lie there.

Attorney: This myasthenia gravis, does it affect your memory at all?
Witness: Yes.
Attorney: And in what ways does it affect your memory?
Witness: I forget.
Attorney: You forget? Can you give us an example of something you forgot?

Attorney: Do you know if your daughter has ever been involved in voodoo?
Witness: We both do.
Attorney: Voodoo?
Witness: We do.
Attorney: You do?
Witness: Yes, voodoo.

Attorney: Now doctor, isn't it true that when a person dies in his sleep, he doesn't know about it until the next morning?
Witness: Did you actually pass the bar exam?

Attorney: The youngest son, the twenty-year-old, how old is he?
Witness: He's twenty, much like your IQ.

Attorney: Were you present when your picture was taken?
Witness: Are you shitting me?

Attorney: So the date of conception (of the baby) was August 8th?
Witness: Yes.
Attorney: And what were you doing at that time?
Witness: Getting laid.

Attorney: She had three children, right?
Witness: Yes.
Attorney: How many were boys?
Witness: None.
Attorney: Were there any girls?

Witness: Your Honour, I think I need a different attorney. Can I get a new attorney?

The 10 commandments

The real reason that we can't have the Ten Commandments posted in a courthouse or Parliament is this - You cannot post 'Thou Shalt Not Steal', 'Thou Shalt Not Commit Adultery' and 'Thou Shall Not Lie' in a building full of lawyers, judges and politicians ... It creates a hostile work environment.

The Jury

In a criminal justice system based on twelve individuals not smart enough to get out of jury duty, here is a jury to be proud of:

A defendant was on trial for murder. There was strong evidence indicating guilt, but there was no corpse. In the defence's closing statement, the lawyer, knowing that his client would probably be convicted, resorted to a trick.

'Ladies and gentlemen of the jury, I have a surprise for you all,' the lawyer said as he looked at his watch. *'Within one minute, the person presumed dead in this case will walk into this courtroom.'*

He looked toward the courtroom door. The jurors, somewhat stunned, all looked on eagerly. A minute passed. Nothing happened.

Finally the lawyer said, *'Actually, I made up the previous statement. But you all looked on with anticipation. I, therefore, put it to you that you have a reasonable doubt in this case as to whether anyone was killed and I insist that you return a verdict of not guilty.'*

The jury retired to deliberate. A few minutes later, the jury returned and pronounced a verdict of guilty.

'But how?' inquired the lawyer. *'You must have had some doubt; I saw all of you stare at the door.'*

The jury foreman replied: *'Yes, we did look, but your client didn't.'*

Politics and Whiskey

A True Story ...

In 1952, Armon M. Sweat, Jr., a member of the Texas House of Representatives, was asked about his position on whiskey. What follows is his exact answer (taken from the Political Archives of Texas):

'If you mean whiskey, the devil's brew, the poison scourge, the bloody monster that defiles innocence, dethrones reason, destroys

the home, creates misery and poverty, yea, literally takes the bread from the mouths of little children; if you mean that evil drink that topples Christian men and women from the pinnacles of righteous and gracious living into the bottomless pit of degradation, shame, despair, helplessness and hopelessness, then, my friend, I am opposed to it with every fiber of my being.

However, if by whiskey you mean the oil of conversation, the philosophic wine, the elixir of life, the ale that is consumed when good fellows get together, that puts a song in their hearts and the warm glow of contentment in their eyes; if you mean Christmas cheer, the stimulating sip that puts a little spring in the step of an elderly gentleman on a frosty morning; if you mean that drink that enables man to magnify his joy and to forget life's great tragedies and heartbreaks and sorrow; if you mean that drink the sale of which pours into Texas treasuries untold millions of dollars each year, that provides tender care for our little crippled children, our blind, our deaf, our dumb, our pitifully aged and infirm, to build the finest highways, hospitals, universities and community colleges in this nation, then my friend, I am absolutely, unequivocally in favour of it.

This is my position and as always, I refuse to compromise on matters of principle.'

DOCTORS

Black Testicles

A male patient is lying in bed in the hospital, wearing an oxygen mask over his mouth and nose, still heavily sedated from a difficult four hour surgical procedure. A young student nurse appears to give him a partial sponge bath

'Nurse,' he mumbles, from behind the mask *'Are my testicles black?'*

Embarrassed, the young nurse replies, *'I don't know, Sir. I'm only here to wash your upper body.'*

He struggles to ask again, *'Nurse, are my testicles black?'*

Concerned that he may elevate his vitals from worry about his testicles, she overcomes her embarrassment and sheepishly pulls back the covers. She raises his gown, holds his penis in one hand and his testicles in the other, lifting and moving them around and around gently.

Then, she takes a close look and says, *'No sir, they aren't and I assure you, there's nothing wrong with them, Sir !!'*

The man pulls off his oxygen mask, smiles at her and says very slowly, *'Thank you very much. That was wonderful, but listen very, very closely ... Are my test results back?'*

Unfaithful Wife

A man goes to a shrink and says, *'Doctor, my wife is unfaithful to me. Every evening, she goes to Larry's bar and picks up men. In fact, she sleeps with anybody who asks her! I'm going crazy. What do you think I should do?'*

'Relax,' says the Doctor, *'take a deep breath and calm down. Now, tell me, exactly where is Larry's bar?'*

The gynecologist who became a mechanic

A gynaecologist had become fed up with malpractice insurance and HMO paperwork and was burned out. Hoping to try another career where skilful hands would be beneficial, he decided to become a mechanic. He went to the local technical college, signed up for evening classes, attended diligently and learned all he could.

When the time of the practical exam approached, the gynaecologist prepared carefully for weeks and completed the exam with tremendous skill. When the results came back, he was surprised to find that he had obtained a score of 150%. Fearing an error, he called the Instructor, saying, *'I don't want to appear ungrateful for such an outstanding result, but I wonder if there is an error in the grade?'*

The instructor said, *'During the exam, you took the engine apart perfectly, which was worth 50% of the total mark. You put the engine back together again perfectly, which is also worth 50% of the mark.'*

After a pause, the instructor added, *'and I gave you an extra 50% because you did it all through the muffler, which I've never seen done in my entire career.'*

Prostate exam

A man goes to his doctor for his physical and gets sent to the Urologist as a precaution. When he gets there, he discovers the urologist is a very pretty female doctor.

The female doctor says, *'I'm going to check your prostate today, but this new procedure is a little different from what you are probably used to. I want you to lie on your right side, bend your knees, then while I check your prostate, take a deep breath and say, '99.'*

The guy obeys and says, *'99!'*

The doctor says, *'Great. Now turn over on your left side and again, while I repeat the check, please take a deep breath and say, '99.'*

Again, the guy says, *'99.'*

The doctor said, *'Very good. Now then, I want you to lie on your back with your knees raised slightly. I'm going to check your prostate with this hand and with the other hand I'm going to hold on to your penis and your testicles, to keep them out of the way. Now take a deep breath and say, '99.'*

The guy begins, *'One ... Two ... Three ...'*

Missing part

Mr. Goldberg wakes up in the hospital, bandaged from head to foot. The doctor comes in and says, *'Ah, I see you've regained consciousness. Now, you probably won't remember, but you were in a pileup on the freeway. You're going to be okay, you'll walk again and everything, but ... something happened. I'm trying to break this gently ... but the fact is ... your penis was chopped off in the wreck and we were unable to find it.'*

Goldberg groans, but the doctor goes on, *'You've got $9,000 in insurance compensation coming to you and we have the technology* *to build you a new penis that will work as well as your old one did ... maybe even better! But the thing is; it doesn't come cheap. It's $1,000.00 per inch.'*

Goldberg perks up at this!

'So,' the doctor says, *'It's for you to decide how many inches you want. But it's something you'd better discuss with your wife. I mean, if you had a five inch one before and you decide to go for nine inches, she might be a bit put out. But if you had a nine inch one before and you decide only to invest in five inches this time, she might be disappointed. So it's important that she plays a role in helping you make the decision.'*

He agrees to talk with his wife. The doctor comes back the next day and says, *'So, have you spoken with your wife?'*

'I have,' says Mr. Goldberg.

'And has she helped you in making the decision?'

'Yes, she has,' he says.

'And what is it?' asks the doctor.

'We're getting granite countertops.'

Soiled Bed Sheets!

An extremely modest man was in the hospital for a series of tests, the last of which had left his bodily systems extremely upset. Upon making several false alarm trips to the bathroom, he decided the latest episode was another and stayed put.

He suddenly filled his bed with diarrheal and was embarrassed beyond his ability to remain rational. In a complete loss of composure he jumped out of bed, gathered up the bed sheets and threw them out of the hospital window.

A drunk was walking by the hospital when the sheets landed on him. He started yelling, cursing and swinging his arms violently trying to get the unknown things off and ended up with the soiled sheets in a tangled pile at his feet.

As the drunk stood there, unsteady on his feet, staring down at the sheets, a hospital security guard, (barely containing his laughter) and who had watched the whole incident, walked up and asked, *'What the heck is going on here?'*

The drunk, still staring down at the bed sheets in amazement, replied: *'I think I just beat the shit out of a ghost.'*

Medical Blunder

The phone rings and the lady of the house answers, *'Hello.'*

'Mrs. Sanders, please.'

'Speaking.'

'Mrs. Sanders, this is Doctor Jones at Saint Agnes Laboratory. When your husband's doctor sent his biopsy to the lab last week, a biopsy from another Mr. Sanders arrived as well. We are now uncertain which one belongs to your husband. Frankly, either way the results are not too good.'

'What do you mean?' Mrs. Sanders asks nervously.

'Well, one of the specimens tested positive for Alzheimer's and the other one tested positive for HIV. We can't tell which is which.'

'That's dreadful! Can you do the test again?' questioned Mrs. Sanders.

'Normally we can, but Medicare will only pay for these expensive tests once.'

'Well, what am I supposed to do now?'

'The Medicare Helpdesk recommend that you drop your husband off somewhere in the middle of town. If he finds his way home, don't sleep with him!'

Greenie revenge!

The chief woman 'Greenie Tree-Hugging Activist,' who was responsible for getting horses banned from National parks and State forests, was climbing a tree to have a look out over the forest when a Tawny Frogmouth Owl attacked her for invading its nesting site.

In a panic to escape, she slid down the tree, getting a great number of splinters lodged in her crotch area. In considerable pain she hurried to the nearest doctor, told him she was an environmentalist and how she got all the splinters.

The doctor listened with great patience and then told her to go into the examining room and he would see if he could help her. She waited for three hours before he reappeared.

Angry, she asked what took him so long.

'Well ...' replied the doctor, *'I had to get permits from the Environmental Protection Agency; the Forestry Service; the National Parks and Wildlife Service; the Wilderness Society and the Department of Conservation and Land Management before I could remove 'old growth timber' from a 'recreational area' ... I'm sorry but they all turned me down.'*

Two different doctors' offices

Boy, if this doesn't hit the nail on the head, I don't know what does!

Two patients limp into two different medical clinics with the same complaint. Both have trouble walking and appear to require a hip replacement.

The first patient is examined within the hour, is X-rayed the same day and has a time booked for surgery the following week.

The second sees his family doctor after waiting three weeks for an appointment, then waits eight weeks to see a specialist, then gets an X-ray, which isn't reviewed for another week. And finally has his surgery scheduled for a month from then.

Why the different treatment for the two patients?

The first is a Golden Retriever. The second is a Senior Citizen.

Next time I'm going to a vet!

Layman's medical dictionary

- Artery: A study of paintings
- Bacteria: Back door to cafeteria
- Barium: What doctors do when patients die
- Benign: What you become after eight
- Caesarean Section: A neighbourhood in Rome
- Cat scan: Searching for kitty
- Cauterise: Made eye contact with her
- Coma: A punctuation mark
- Dilate: To live long
- Fester: Quicker than someone else
- Impotent: Distinguished, well-known
- Medical Staff: A doctor's cane
- Morbid: A higher offer
- Nitrates: Cheaper than day rates
- Outpatient: A patient who has fainted
- Post-operative: A letter carrier
- Rectum: Darned near killed him
- Seizure: Roman emperor
- Terminal Illness: Getting sick at the airport
- Tumour: One plus one more
- Urine: Opposite of *'You're out'*

Health message:

1. If walking/cycling is good for your health, the postman would be immortal.
2. A whale swims all day, only eats fish, drinks water and is fat.
3. A rabbit runs and hops and only lives 15 years.

4. A tortoise doesn't run, does nothing. yet lives for 150 years.

And you tell me to exercise!

The Gloves

Next time you use a pair of rubber gloves, you're going to smile when you think of this:

A dentist noticed that his next patient, a little old lady, was nervous, so he decided to tell her a little joke as he put on his gloves.

'Do you know how they make these gloves?' he asked.

'No, I don't,' she replied.

'Well,' he spoofed, *'there's a building in Canada with a big tank of latex and workers of all hand sizes walk up to the tank, dip in their hands, let them dry, then peel off the gloves and throw them into boxes of the right size.'*

She didn't crack a smile.

'Oh, well. I tried,' he thought.

But five minutes later, during a delicate portion of the procedure, she burst out laughing.

'What's so funny?' he asked.

'I was just envisioning how condoms are made!'

Gotta watch those little old ladies! Their minds are always working!

Semen sample

Old people have problems that you haven't even considered yet!

An 85-year-old man was requested by his doctor for a sperm count as part of his physical exam. The doctor gave the man a jar and said, *'Take this jar home and bring back a semen sample tomorrow'*

The next day the 85-year-old man reappeared at the doctor's office and gave him the jar, which was as clean and empty as on the previous day.

The doctor asked what happened and the man explained, *'Well, doc, it's like this - first I tried with my right hand, but nothing. Then I tried with my left hand, but still nothing. 'Then I asked my wife for help. She tried with her right hand, then with her left, still nothing. She tried with her mouth, first with the teeth in, then with her teeth out, still nothing.*

'We even called up Arleen, the lady next door and she tried too, first with both hands, then an armpit and she even tried squeezin' it between her knees, but still nothing.'

The doctor was shocked! *'You asked your neighbour?'*

The old man replied, *'Yep, none of us could get the jar open.'*

Pain Killer

The female dentist pulls out a numbing needle to give the man a shot.

'No way! No needles I hate needles' the patient said.

The dentist starts to hook up the nitrous oxide and the man objects.

'I can't do the gas thing. The thought of having the gas mask on suffocates me!'

The dentist then asks the patient if he has any objection to taking a pill.

'No objection,' the patient says. *'I'm fine with pills.'*

The dentist then returns and says, *'Here's a Viagra.'*

The patient says, *'Wow! I didn't know Viagra worked as a pain killer!'*

'It doesn't' said the dentist, *'but it's going to give you something to hold on to when I pull your tooth.'*

Medical research

Remember this the next time you have major surgery and need a blood transfusion, this is good to know!!

Australian Medical Association researchers have found that patients needing blood transfusions may benefit from receiving chicken blood rather than human blood. It tends to make men cocky and women lay better.

Just thought you'd like to know. Okay, I'll be going to my room now.

Stress management

Just in case you are having a rough day, here is a stress management technique recommended in all the latest psychological journals. The funny thing is that it really does work and will make you smile.

1. Picture yourself lying on your tummy on a warm rock that hangs out over a crystal clear stream.
2. Picture yourself with both your hands dangling in the cool running water.
3. Birds are sweetly singing in the cool mountain air.
4. No one knows your secret place.

5. You are in total seclusion from that hectic place called the world.
6. The soothing sound of a gentle waterfall fills the air with a cascade of serenity.
7. The water is so crystal clear that you can easily make out the face of the person you are holding under the water.

There, see, it really does work. You're smiling already and your stress is gone.

Toilet seat

Charlie's wife, Lucy, had been after him for several weeks to paint the seat on their toilet. Finally, he got around to doing it while Lucy was out. After finishing, he left to take care of another matter before she returned.

Lucy came home and undressed to take a shower. Before getting in the shower, she sat on the toilet. As she tried to stand up, she realised that the not-quite-dry epoxy paint had glued her to the toilet seat.

About that time, Charlie got home and realised her predicament. They both pushed and pulled without any success whatsoever. Finally, in desperation, Charlie undid the toilet seat bolts. Lucy wrapped a sheet around herself and Charlie drove her to the hospital emergency room.

The ER Doctor got her into a position where he could figure out how to free her. Lucy tried to lighten the embarrassment of it all by saying, *'Well, Doctor, I'll bet you've never seen anything like this before.'*

The Doctor replied, *'Actually, I've seen lots of them. I just never saw one mounted and framed!'*

Female Urologist

As men age, we start seeing more and more of the medical world and its employees, which nowadays seems to have more and more women as our physicians and therapists etc. And in this case a new Urologist for me.

My family Doctor just recently referred me to a just out of medical school female urologist. I saw her yesterday and she's absolutely drop-dead gorgeous as well as unbelievably sexy.

She told me that I must stop masturbating. I asked her why and she said, *'Because I'm trying to examine you ...'*

Advice to live by:

Q: Doctor, I've heard that cardiovascular exercise can prolong life. Is this true?
A: Your heart is only good for so many beats and that's it ... don't waste them on exercise. Everything wears out eventually. Speeding up your heart will not make you live longer; that's like saying you can extend the life of your car by driving it faster. Want to live longer? Take a nap.

Q: Should I cut down on meat and eat more fruits and vegetables?
A: You must grasp logistical efficiencies. What does a cow eat? Hay and corn. And what are these? Vegetables. So a steak is nothing more than an efficient mechanism of delivering vegetables to your system. Need grain? Eat chicken. Beef is also a good source of field grass (green leafy vegetable). And a pork chop can give you 100% of your recommended daily allowance of vegetable products.

Q: Should I reduce my alcohol intake?
A: No, not at all. Wine is made from fruit. Brandy is distilled wine. That means they take the water out of the fruity bit so you get even more of the goodness that way. Beer is also made out of grain. Bottoms up!

Q: How can I calculate my body/fat ratio?
A: Well, if you have a body and you have fat, your ratio is one to one. If you have two bodies, your ratio is two to one, etc.

Q: What are some of the advantages of participating in a regular exercise program?
A: Can't think of a single one, sorry. My philosophy is: No Pain ... Good!

Q: Aren't fried foods bad for you?
A: You're not listening!!! Foods are fried these days in vegetable oil. In fact, they're permeated in it. How could getting more vegetables be bad for you?

Q: Will sit-ups help prevent me from getting a little soft around the middle?
A: Definitely not! When you exercise a muscle, it gets bigger. You should only be doing sit-ups if you want a bigger stomach.

Q: Is chocolate bad for me?
A: Are you crazy? HELLO Cocoa beans! Another vegetable!!! It's the best feel-good food around!

Q: Is swimming good for your figure?
A: If swimming is good for your figure, explain whales to me.

Q: Is getting in-shape important for my lifestyle?
A: Hey! Round' is a shape!

Well, I hope this has cleared up any misconceptions you may have had about food and diets. For those of you who watch what you eat, here's the final word on nutrition and health. It's a relief to know the truth after all those conflicting nutritional studies.

1. The Japanese eat very little fat and suffer fewer heart attacks than Americans.
2. The Mexicans eat a lot of fat and suffer fewer heart attacks than Americans.
3. The Chinese drink very little red wine and suffer fewer heart attacks than Americans.
4. The Italians drink a lot of red wine and suffer fewer heart attacks than Americans.
5. The Germans drink a lot of beer and eat lots of sausages and fats and suffer fewer heart attacks than Americans.

Conclusion: Eat and drink what you like. Speaking English is apparently what kills you.

What is the difference between Bird Flu and Swine Flu? For bird flu you need tweetment and for swine flu you need oinkment.

Check for Alzheimer's - Pretty Amazing!

You have a better chance of getting it right if you read slowly. The following was developed as a mental age assessment to determine whether you are a candidate for Alzheimer's disease:

Take your time and see if you can read each line aloud without a mistake. The average person over 40 years of age cannot do it!

1. This is this cat.
2. This is is cat.
3. This is how cat.
4. This is to cat.

5. This is keep cat.
6. This is an cat.
7. This is old cat.
8. This is fart cat.
9. This is busy cat.
10. This is for cat.
11. This is forty cat.
12. This is seconds cat.

Now go back and read the third word in each line from the top down.

Two good questions

A surgeon examined a new patient most carefully. After studying the X-rays, he turned to the man and said, *'Could you pay for an operation if I told you it was necessary?'*

The patient thought for a moment, then said to the doctor, *'Would you find one necessary if I told you I couldn't pay for it?'*

Tired Nurse

A very tired nurse walks into a bank, totally exhausted after an eighteen-hour shift. Preparing to write a cheque, she pulls a rectal thermometer out of her purse and tries to write with it.

When she realises her mistake, she looks at the flabbergasted teller and without missing a beat, she says: *'Well, that's great ... that's just great ... Some arsehole's got my pen!'*

Patient's comments

A surgeon tells us that the following comments were actually made by his patients (predominantly male) while he was performing colonoscopies:

'I usually don't do this on the first date.'

'Take it easy, Doc. You're boldly going where no man has gone before!'

'Can you hear me now?'

'Are we there yet? Are we there yet? Are we there yet?'

'You know, in some states, we're now legally married.'

'Any sign of the trapped miners, Chief?'

'You put your left hand in, you take your left hand out, you put your left and in and you shake it all about ...'

'Hey! Now I know how a Muppet feels!'

'If your hand doesn't fit, you must quit!'

'Hey Doc, let me know if you find my dignity.'

And the best one of them all ...

'Could you write a note for my wife stating that, in your considered medical opinion, my head is not up there?'

Pharmacology Lesson

In pharmacology, all drugs have two names, a trade name and a generic name. For example:

The trade name of Tylenol was a generic name of Acetaminophren.

Aleve is also called Naproxen.

Amoxil is called amoxicillin and

Advil is also called Ibuprofen.

The FDA has been looking for a generic name for Viagra. After careful consideration by a team of government experts, it recently announced that it has settled on the generic name of Mycoxafloppin. Also considered were Mycoxafailin, Mydixadrupin, Mydixrizin, Mydixadud, Dixafix and of course, Ibepokin.

EMERGENCY SERVICES

December, '09 update on Sheriff Joe Arpaio

You all remember Sheriff Joe Arpaio of Arizona, who painted the jail cells pink and made the inmates wear pink prison garb. Well ... he's at it again!

Maricopa County was spending approximately $18 million dollars a year on stray animals, like cats and dogs. Sheriff Joe offered to take the department over and the County Supervisors said okay. The animal shelters are now all staffed and operated by prisoners. They feed and care for the strays. Every animal in his care is taken out and walked twice daily. He now has prisoners who are experts in animal nutrition and behaviour. They give great classes for anyone who'd like to adopt an animal. He has literally taken stray dogs off the street, given them to the care of prisoners and had them place in dog shows.

The best part? His budget for the entire department is now under $3 million. Teresa and I adopted a Weimaraner from a Maricopa County shelter two years ago. He was neutered and current on all shots, in great health and even had a microchip inserted the day we got him. The cost: $78.00

The prisoners get the benefit of about $0.28 an hour for working, but most would work for free, just to be out of their cells for the day. Most of his budget is for utilities, building maintenance, etc. He pays the prisoners out of the fees collected for adopted animals.

I have long wondered when the rest of the country would take a look at the way he runs the jail system and copy some of his ideas. He has a huge farm, donated to the county years ago, where inmates can work and they grow most of their own fresh vegetables and food, doing all the work and harvesting by hand.

He has a pretty good sized hog farm, which provides meat and fertilizer. It fertilizes the Christmas tree nursery, where prisoners work and you can buy a living Christmas tree for $6.00 to $8.00 for the holidays and plant it later. We have six trees in our yard from the Prison.

Yup, he was re-elected last year with 83% of the vote. Now he's in trouble with the ACLU again. He painted all his buses and vehicles with a mural that has a special hotline phone number painted on it, where you can call and report suspected illegal aliens. Immigrations and Customs Enforcement wasn't doing enough in his eyes, so he had 40 deputies trained specifically for enforcing immigration laws, started up his hotline and bought four new buses just for hauling folks back to the border. He's kind of a 'Git-R Dun' kind of Sheriff.

To those of you not familiar with Joe Arpaio he is the Maricopa, Arizona county sheriff and he keeps getting elected over and over and this is one of the reasons why:

He created the 'Tent City Jail': He has jail meals down to 40 cents a serving and charges the inmates for them. He stopped smoking and porno magazines in the jails. Took away their weights. Cut off all but 'G' rated movies. He started chain gangs so the inmates could do free work on county and city projects. Then he started chain gangs for women so he wouldn't get sued for discrimination.

He took away cable TV until he found out there was a Federal Court Order that required cable TV for jails so he hooked up the cable TV again; only let in the Disney Channel and the Weather Channel. When asked why the Weather Channel he replied, *'So they will know how hot it's gonna be while they are working on my Chain Gangs.'*

He cut off coffee since it has zero nutritional value. When the inmates complained, he told them *'This isn't the Ritz/Carlton ... if you don't like it, don't come back!'*

More On The Arizona Sheriff: With temperatures being even hotter than usual in Phoenix (116 degrees just set a new record), the Associated Press reports: About 2,000 inmates living in a barbed-wire-surrounded tent encampment at the Maricopa County Jail have been given permission to strip down to their government-issued pink boxer shorts. On Wednesday, hundreds of men wearing boxers were either curled up on their bunk beds or chatted in the tents, which reached 138 degrees inside the week before. Many were also swathed in wet, pink towels as sweat collected on their chests and dripped down to their pink socks.

'It feels like we are in a furnace,' said James Zanzot, an inmate who has lived in the tents for one year. *'It's inhumane.'*

Joe Arpaio, the tough-guy sheriff who created the tent city and long ago started making his prisoners wear pink and eat bologna sandwiches, is not one bit sympathetic. He said Wednesday that he told all of the inmates: *'It's 120 degrees in Iraq and our soldiers are living in tents too and they have to wear full battle gear, but they didn't commit any crimes, so shut your mouths!'*

Way to go, Sheriff! Maybe if all prisons were like this one there would be a lot less crime and/or repeat offenders. Criminals should be punished for their crimes - not live in luxury until it's time for their parole, only to go out and commit another crime so they can get back in to live on taxpayers money and enjoy things taxpayers can't afford to have for themselves.

Pet fish

A redneck with a bucket full of live fish was approached recently by a game warden in Central Mississippi as he started to drive his boat away from a lake.

The game warden asked the man, *'May I see your fishing license please?'*

'Naw, sir,' replied the redneck. *'I don't need none of them there papers. These here are my pet fish.'*

'Pet fish?'

'Yep. Once a week, I bring these here fish o'mine down to the lake and let 'em swim 'round for a while. Then when I whistle, they swim right back into my net and I take 'em home.'

*'What a line of horse sh*t ... you're under arrest.'*

The redneck said, *'It's the truth, Mr. Gov'ment Man. I'll show ya! We do this all the time!!'*

'WE do, now, do WE?' smirked the warden. *'PROVE it!'*

The redneck released the fish into the lake and stood and waited. After a few minutes, the warden said, *'Well?'*

'Well, WHUT?' said the redneck.

The warden asked, *'When are you going to call them back?'*

'Call who back?'

'The FISH,' replied the warden!

'Whut fish?' asked the redneck.

Moral of the story: We may not be as smart as some city slickers, but we ain't as dumb as some government employees. You can say what you want about the South, but you never hear of anyone retiring and moving north.

The Fire Fighters

One dark night outside a small town near Christchurch (Little River) a fire started inside the local chemical plant and in a blink of an eye it exploded into massive flames. The alarm went out to all the fire departments for miles around.

When the volunteer fire fighters appeared on the scene, the chemical company president rushed to the fireman in charge and said, *'All our secret formulas are in the vault in the centre of the plant. They must be saved. I will give $50,000 to the fire department that brings them out intact.'*

But the roaring flames held the fire-fighters off. Soon more fire departments had to be called in as the situation became desperate. As the firemen arrived, the president shouted out that the offer was now $100,000 to the fire station who could bring out the company's secret files. From the distance, a lone siren was heard as another fire truck came into sight. It was the nearby Maori rural township volunteer fire company composed mainly of Maoris over the age of 65. To everyone's amazement, that little run-down fire engine roared right past all the newer sleek engines that were parked outside the plant. Without even slowing down it drove straight into the middle of the inferno.

Outside, the other firemen watched as the Maori old timers jumped off right in the middle of the fire and fought it back on all sides. It was a performance and effort never seen before.

Within a short time, the old timers had extinguished the fire and had saved the secret formulas. The grateful chemical company president announced that for such a superhuman feat he was upping the reward to $200,000 and walked over to personally thank each of the brave fire fighters.

The local TV news reporter rushed in to capture the event on film, asking their chief, *'What are you going to do with all that money?'*

'Well,' said Rangi, the 70-year-old fire chief, *'the first thing we gonna do is fix the brakes on that damned truck!*

Misunderstanding

The police came to my front door last night holding a picture of my wife, then asked *'Is this your wife sir?'*

Shocked I gulped and answered *'Yes.'*

He said *'I'm afraid it looks like she's been hit by a bus.'*

I said *'I know, but she has a lovely personality and she's good with the dog.'*

An actual Personals Ad in USA

To the Guy who tried to mug me in downtown Savannah night before last. Date: 2009-05-27, 1:43 a.m. E.S.T.

I was the guy wearing the black Burberry jacket that you demanded that I hand over, shortly after you pulled the knife on me and my girlfriend, threatening our lives. You also asked for my girlfriend's purse and earrings. I can only hope that you somehow come across this rather important message.

First, I'd like to apologise for your embarrassment; I didn't expect you to actually crap in your pants when I drew my pistol after you took my jacket. The evening was not that cold and I was wearing the jacket for a reason. My girlfriend had just bought me that Kimber model 1911, 45 ACP pistol for my birthday and we had picked up a shoulder holster for it that very evening. Obviously you agree that it is a very intimidating weapon when pointed at your head ... Isn't it?

I know it probably wasn't fun walking back to wherever you'd come from with that brown sludge in your pants. I'm sure it was even worse walking bare-footed since I made you leave your shoes, cell phone and wallet with me. (That prevented you from calling or running to your buddies to come help mug us again).

After I called your mother or *'Momma'* as you had her listed in your cell, I explained the entire episode of what you'd done. Then I went and filled up my gas tank as well as those of four other people in the gas station - on your credit card. The guy with the big motor home took 150 gallons and was extremely grateful!

I gave your shoes to a homeless guy with all the cash in your wallet. (That made his day!)

I then threw your wallet into the big pink *'pimp mobile'* that was parked at the curb ... after I broke the windshield and side window and keyed the entire driver's side of the car.

Later, I called a bunch of phone sex numbers from your cell phone. Ma Bell just now shut down the line, although I only used the phone for a little over a day now, so what's going on with that? Earlier, I managed to get in two threatening phone calls to the DA's office and one to the FBI, while mentioning President Obama as my possible target.

The FBI guy seemed really intense and we had a nice long chat (I guess while he traced your number etc.)

In a way, perhaps I should apologise for not killing you, but I feel this type of retribution is far more appropriate punishment for your threatened crime. I wish you well as you try to sort through some of these rather immediate pressing issues and can only hope that you have the opportunity to reflect upon and perhaps reconsider, the career path you've chosen to pursue in life. Remember, next time you might not be so lucky. Have a good day!

Thoughtfully yours, Alex

Keeping up Appearances

A Londoner parks his brand new Porsche in front of the office to show it off to his colleagues. As he's getting out of the car, a lorry comes speeding along too close to the kerb and takes off the door before zooming off.

More than a little distraught, the Londoner grabs his mobile and calls the police.

Five minutes later, the police arrive. Before the policeman has a chance to ask any questions, the man starts screaming hysterically: *'My Porsche, my beautiful silver Porsche is ruined. No matter how long it's at the panel beaters it'll simply never be the same again!'* After the man finally finishes his rant, the policeman shakes his head in disgust.

'I can't believe how materialistic you bloody Londoners are,' he says. *'You lot are so focused on your possessions that you don't notice anything else in your life.'*

'How can you say such a thing at a time like this?' sobs the Porsche owner.

The policeman replies, *'Didn't you realise that your right arm was torn off when the truck hit you.'*

The Londoner looks down in horror.

'Damn it!' he screams ... 'Where's my Rolex ...?'

New Zealand Police

A cop from the New Zealand Police was watching for speeders, but wasn't getting many. Then he discovered the problem - a twelve-year-old boy was standing up the road with a hand painted sign, which read 'RADAR TRAP AHEAD.' The officer then found a young accomplice down the road with a sign reading 'TIPS' and a bucket full of money. (And we used to just mow lawns!)

A motorist was mailed a picture of his car speeding through an automated radar post in the Manawatu with a fine of $160 included. Being cute, he sent the police department a picture of $160. The police responded with another mailed photo of handcuffs.

A young woman was pulled over for speeding. As a NZ Policeman walked to her car window, flipping open his ticket book, she said, *'I bet you are going to sell me a ticket to the Policemen's Ball.'*

He replied, *'New Zealand Policemen don't have balls.'* There was a moment of silence while she smiled and he realised what he'd just said. He then closed his book, got back in his patrol car and left.

She was laughing too hard to start her car.

Aggressive and Hostile

A police motorcycle cop stops a driver for running a red light. The guy is a real jerk and comes running back to the officer demanding to know why he is being harassed by the Gestapo! So the officer calmly tells him of the violation. The motorist instantly goes on a tirade, questioning the officer's ancestry, sexual orientation, etc., in rather explicit terms.

The tirade goes on without the officer saying anything.

When he gets done with writing the ticket he puts an *'AH'* in the lower right corner of the narrative portion of the ticket. He then hands it to the 'violator' for his signature. The guy signs the ticket angrily and when presented with his copy points to the *'AH'* and demands to know what it stands for.

The officer says, '*That's so when we go to court, I'll remember that you're an asshole!'*

Two months later they're in court. The 'violator' has such a bad driving record he is about to lose his license and has hired a lawyer to represent him. On the stand the officer testifies to seeing the man run the red light. Under cross examination the defence attorney asks; *'Officer is this a reasonable facsimile of the ticket you issued my client?'*

Officer responds, *'Yes, sir, that is the defendant's copy, his signature and mine, same number at the top.'*

Lawyer: *'Officer is there any particular marking or notation on this ticket you don't normally make?'*

'Yes, sir, in the lower right corner of the narrative there is an 'AH,' underlined.'

'What does the 'AH' stand for, officer?'

'Aggressive and hostile, Sir.'

'Aggressive and hostile?'

'Yes, Sir'

'Officer, are you sure it doesn't stand for Asshole?'

'Well, sir, you know your client better than I do!'

The Lecture

A man is stopped by the police at midnight and asked where he's going.

'I'm on the way to listen to a lecture about the effects of alcohol and drug abuse on the human body.'

The policeman asks, *'Really? And who's going to give a lecture at this time of night?'*

'My wife,' comes the reply

You have to love a good nurse

A policeman was rushed to the hospital with an inflamed appendix. The doctors operated and advised him that all was well; however, the patrolman kept feeling something pulling at the hairs in his crotch.

Worried that it might be a second surgery and the doctors hadn't told him about it, he finally got enough energy to pull his hospital gown up enough so he could look at what was making him so uncomfortable. Taped firmly across his pubic hair and private parts were three wide strips of adhesive tape, the kind that doesn't come off easily - if at all. Written on the tape in large black letters was the sentence, *'Get well soon from the nurse in the Jeep you pulled over last week.'*

Kinda brings tears to your eyes doesn't it.

Reason for Speeding

A senior citizen drove his brand new Corvette convertible out of the dealership. Taking off down the road, he floored it to 80 mph, enjoying the wind blowing through what little hair he had left.
'Amazing,' he thought as he flew down the I-45, pushing the pedal even more. Looking in his rear view mirror, he saw a state trooper behind him, lights flashing and siren blaring.

He floored it to 100 mph, then 110, then 120.

Suddenly he thought, *'What am I doing? I'm too old for this,'* and pulled over to await the trooper's arrival.

Pulling in behind him, the trooper walked up to the Corvette, looked at his watch and said, *'Sir, my shift ends in 30 minutes. Today is Friday. If you can give me a reason for speeding that I've never heard before, I'll let you go.'*

The old gentleman paused. Then said, *'Years ago, my wife ran off with a State Trooper. I thought you were bringing her back.'*

'Have a good day, sir,' replied the trooper.

Ahh! Patience!

A police officer was patrolling late at night in a well-known spot. He sees a couple in a car, with the interior light brightly glowing. The cop carefully approaches the car to get a closer look. Then he sees a young man behind the wheel, reading a computer magazine. Then he notices a young woman in the rear seat, filing her fingernails.

Puzzled by this surprising situation, the cop walks to the car and gently raps on the driver's window.

The young man lowers his window. *'Uh, yes, Officer?'*

The cop says: *'What are you doing?'*

The young man says: *'Well, Officer, I'm reading a magazine.'*

Pointing towards the young woman in the back seat the cop says: *'And her, what is she doing?'*

The young man shrugs: *'Sir, I believe she's filing her fingernails.'*

Now, the cop is totally confused. A young couple, alone, in a car, at night in a lover's lane ... And nothing obscene is happening!

The cop asks: *'What's your age, young man?'*

The young man says: *'I'm 22, sir.'*

The cop asks: *'And her ... what's her age?'*

The young man looks at his watch and replies: *'She'll be 18 in 11 minutes.'*

Traffic Camera

A man was driving when a traffic camera flashed. He thought his picture was taken for exceeding the speed limit, even though he knew he was not speeding.

Just to be sure, he went around the block and passed the same spot, driving even more slowly, but again the camera flashed. He thought this was quite funny, so he slowed down even further as he drove past the area, but the traffic camera flashed yet again. He tried a fourth time with the same result. The fifth time he was laughing when the camera flashed as he rolled past at a snail's pace.

Two weeks later, he got five traffic fine letters in the mail for driving without a seat belt.

Polk County Florida Sheriff Grady Judd

An illegal alien in Polk County Florida who got pulled over in a routine traffic stop ended up 'executing' the deputy who stopped him. The deputy was shot eight times, including once behind his right ear at close range. Another deputy was wounded and a police dog killed. A state wide manhunt ensued.

The murderer was found hiding in a wooded area with his gun. After he shot at them, SWAT team officers open fired and hit him 68 times.

Now here's the kicker: The liberal media went nuts and asked why they shot the poor undocumented immigrant 68 times.

Sheriff Grady Judd told the Orlando Sentinel: [Talk about an all-time classic answer.]

'Because that's all the ammunition we had.'

Assailant suffers injuries from a fall

[Police report - ya got ta love it!]

Orville Smith, a store manager for Best Buy in Augusta, Ga., told police he observed a male customer, later identified as Tyrone Jackson of Augusta, on surveillance cameras putting a laptop computer under his jacket. When confronted, the man became irate, knocked down an employee, drew a knife and ran for the door.

Outside on the sidewalk were four Marines collecting toys for the Toys for Tots program. Smith said the Marines stopped the man, but he stabbed one of the Marines, Cpl. Phillip Duggan, in the back; the injury did not appear to be severe.

After Police and an ambulance arrived at the scene Cpl. Duggan was transported for treatment.

The subject was also transported to the local hospital with two broken arms, a broken ankle, a broken leg, several missing teeth, possible broken ribs, multiple contusions, assorted lacerations, a broken nose and a broken jaw ... injuries he sustained when he slipped and fell off of the curb after stabbing the Marine said the police report.

AIRPLANE

Military Airplane crew

While the C-5 was turning over its engines, a female crewman gave the G.I.s on board the usual information regarding seat belts, emergency exits, etc. Finally, she said, *'Now sit back and enjoy your trip while your captain, Judith Campbell and crew take you safely to Afghanistan.'*

An old Master Sergeant sitting in the eighth row thought to himself, *'Did I hear her right? Is the captain a woman? '*

When the attendant came by he said *'Did I understand you right? Is the captain a woman?'*

'Yes!' said the attendant, *'In fact, this entire crew is female.'*

'Wow,' he said, *'I wish I had two double scotch and sodas. I don't know what to think with only women up there in the cockpit.'*

'That's another thing, Sergeant,' said the crew member, *'we no longer call it the cockpit' On this plane it's The Box Office.'*

The Nun

A nun was sitting at the airport, waiting for her flight to Chicago. She looked over in the corner and saw one of those weight machines that tells your fortune and thought to herself, *'I'll give it a try and see what it tells me.'*

She went over to the machine, stepped up on the scale and put her nickel in. Out came a card that read, *'You are a nun, you weigh 128 lbs and you are going to Chicago.'*

The nun sat back down. She told herself that the machine probably gives the same card to everyone. The more she thought about it the more curious she got so she decided to try it again she went back to the machine and again put her nickel in and out came a card that read:

'You are a nun, you weigh 128 lbs, you are going to Chicago and you are going to play a fiddle.'

The nun says to herself, *'I know that is wrong, I have never played a musical instrument even once in my life.'* She sat back down.

From out of nowhere a cowboy came over and sat down, putting his fiddle case on the seat between them. Without thinking, she opened the cowboy's case, took out the fiddle and started playing beautiful music. Surprised at what she had done, she looked over at the machine, thinking, *'This is incredible, I've got to try this again.'*

Back to the machine she went, put in another nickel and another card came out. It read, *'You are a nun, you weigh 128 lbs, you are going to Chicago and you are going to break wind.'* Now she knows the machine is wrong, as she thought to herself, *'I've never broken wind in public a single time in my life.'* But getting down off the machine she slipped and as she was straining to keep herself from falling to the floor, she broke wind.

Absolutely stunned, she sat back down and looked at the machine. She said to herself, *'This is truly remarkable. I've got to try this again.'* She went back to the machine, put in another nickel and another card came out. It read, *'You are a nun, you weigh 128 lbs, you have fiddled and farted around so long you've missed your flight to Chicago.'*

The Maintenance Crew

Remember it takes a college degree to fly a plane, but only a high school diploma to fix one; a reassurance to those of us who fly routinely in our jobs. After every flight, UPS pilots fill out a form, called a 'gripe sheet,' which tells mechanics about problems with the aircraft. The mechanics correct the problems, document their repairs on the form and then pilots review the gripe sheets before the next flight.

Never let it be said that ground crews lack a sense of humour. Here are some actual maintenance complaints submitted by UPS pilots [marked with a P] and the solutions recorded [marked with an S] by maintenance engineers.

By the way, UPS is the only major airline that has never, ever, had an accident.

P: Left inside main tire almost needs replacement.
S: Almost replaced left inside main tire.

P: Test flight Okay, except auto-land very rough.
S: Auto-land not installed on this aircraft.

P: Something loose in cockpit.
S: Something tightened in cockpit.

P: Dead bugs on windshield.
S: Live bugs on back-order.

P: Evidence of leak on right main landing gear.
S: Evidence removed.

P: Autopilot in altitude-hold mode produces a 200-feet-per-minute descent.
S: Cannot reproduce problem on ground.

P: DME volume unbelievably loud.
S: DME volume set to more believable level.

P: Friction locks cause throttle levers to stick.
S: That's what friction locks are for.

P: IFF inoperative in OFF mode.
S: IFF is always inoperative in OFF mode.

P: Suspected crack in windshield.
S: Suspect you're right.

P: Number 3 engine missing.
S: Engine found on right wing after brief search.

P: Aircraft handles funny. [I love this one!]
S: Aircraft warned to straighten up, fly right and be serious.

P: Target radar hums.
S: Reprogrammed target radar with lyrics.

P: Mouse in cockpit.
S: Cat installed.

And the best one for last:

P: Noise coming from under instrument panel. Sounds like a midget pounding on something with a hammer.
S: Took hammer away from the midget.

The Sneeze

A man and a woman were sitting beside each other in the first class section of an airplane. The woman sneezed, took out a tissue, gently wiped her nose and then visibly shuddered for ten to fifteen seconds.

The man went back to his reading.

A few minutes later, the woman sneezed again, took a tissue, wiped her nose and then shuddered violently once more.

Assuming that the woman might have a cold, the man was still curious about the shuddering. A few more minutes passed when the woman sneezed yet again. As before, she took a tissue, wiped her nose, her body shaking even more than before.

Unable to restrain his curiosity, the man turned to the woman and said, *'I couldn't help but notice that you've sneezed three times, wiped your nose and then shuddered violently. Are you okay?'*

'I am sorry if I disturbed you, I have a very rare medical condition; whenever I sneeze I have an orgasm.'

The man, more than a bit embarrassed, was still curious. *'I have never heard of that condition before'* he said. *'Are you taking anything for it?'*

The woman nodded, *'Pepper.'*

Pick-up lines

A guy sitting at a bar at Heathrow Airport noticed a really beautiful woman sitting next to him. He thought to himself: *'Wow, she's so gorgeous she must be an off duty flight attendant. But which airline does she work for?'*

Hoping to make her acquaintance, he leaned towards her and uttered the Delta slogan: *'Love to fly and it shows?'*

She gave him a blank, confused stare and he immediately thought to himself: *'Damn, she doesn't work for Delta.'*

A moment later, another slogan popped into his head. He leaned towards her again *'Something special in the air?'*

She gave him the same confused look.

He mentally kicked himself and scratched Singapore Airlines off the list. Next he tried the Thai Airways slogan: *'Smooth as Silk.'*

This time the woman turned on him, *'What the Hell do you want?'*

The man smiled, then slumped back in his chair and said, *'Ahhhhha! Air Canada.'*

Two stories both true - and worth reading

Story number one

Many years ago, Al Capone virtually owned Chicago. Capone wasn't famous for anything heroic. He was notorious for enmeshing the windy city in everything from bootlegged booze and prostitution to murder. Capone had a lawyer nicknamed 'Easy Eddie.' He was Capone's lawyer for a good reason. Eddie was very good! In fact, Eddie's skill at legal manoeuvring kept Big Al out of jail for a long time.

To show his appreciation, Capone paid him very well. Not only was the money big, but Eddie got special dividends, as well. For instance, he and his family occupied a fenced-in mansion with live-in help and all of the conveniences of the day. The estate was so large that it filled an entire Chicago City block.

Eddie lived the high life of the Chicago mob and gave little consideration to the atrocity that went on around him. Eddie did have one soft spot, however. He had a son that he loved dearly. Eddie saw to it that his young son had clothes, cars and a good education. Nothing was withheld. Price was no object. And, despite his involvement with organised crime, Eddie even tried to teach him right from wrong. Eddie wanted his son to be a better man than he was. Yet, with all his wealth and influence, there were two things he couldn't give his son; he couldn't pass on a good name or a good example.

One day, Easy Eddie reached a difficult decision. Easy Eddie wanted to rectify wrongs he had done. He decided he would go to the authorities and tell the truth about Al 'Scarface' Capone, clean up his tarnished name and offer his son some semblance of integrity. To do this, he would have to testify against The Mob and he knew that the cost would be great. But, he testified.

Within the year, Easy Eddie's life ended in a blaze of gunfire on a lonely Chicago Street. But in his eyes, he had given his son the greatest gift he had to offer, at the greatest price he could ever pay. Police removed from his pockets a rosary, a crucifix, a religious medallion and a poem clipped from a magazine. The poem read:

'The clock of life is wound but once and no man has the power to tell just when the hands will stop, at late or early hour. Now is the only time you own. Live, love, toil with a will. Place no faith in time. For the clock may soon be still.'

Story number two

World War II produced many heroes. One such man was Lieutenant Commander Butch O'Hare. He was a fighter pilot assigned to the aircraft carrier Lexington in the South Pacific. One day his entire squadron was sent on a mission. After he was airborne, he looked at his fuel gauge and realised that someone had forgotten to top off his fuel tank. He would not have enough fuel to complete his mission and get back to his ship.

His flight leader told him to return to the carrier. Reluctantly, he dropped out of formation and headed back to the fleet. As he was returning to the mother ship, he saw something that turned his blood cold; a squadron of Japanese aircraft was speeding its way toward the American fleet. The American fighters were gone on a sortie and the fleet was all but defenceless. He couldn't reach his squadron and bring them back in time to save the fleet. Nor could he warn the fleet of the approaching danger. There was only one thing to do. He must somehow divert them from the fleet.

Laying aside all thoughts of personal safety, he dove into the formation of Japanese planes. Wing-mounted 50 calibre's blazed as he charged in, attacking one surprised enemy plane and then another. Butch wove in and out of the now broken formation and fired at as many planes as possible until all his ammunition was finally spent. Undaunted, he continued the assault. He dove at the planes, trying to clip a wing or tail in hopes of damaging as many enemy planes as possible, rendering them unfit to fly. Finally, the exasperated Japanese squadron took off in another direction.

Deeply relieved, Butch O'Hare and his tattered fighter limped back to the carrier. Upon arrival, he reported in and related the event surrounding his return. The film from the gun-camera mounted on his plane told the tale. It showed the extent of Butch's daring attempt to protect his fleet. He had, in fact, destroyed five enemy aircraft. This took place on February 20, 1942 and for that action Butch became the Navy's first Ace of W.W.II and the first Naval Aviator to win the Congressional Medal of Honour.

A year later Butch was killed in aerial combat at the age of 29. His home town would not allow the memory of this WW II hero to fade and today, O'Hare Airport in Chicago is named in tribute to the courage of this great man. So, the next time you find yourself at O'Hare International, give some thought to visiting Butch's memorial displaying his statue and his Medal of Honour. It's located between Terminals 1 and 2.

So what do these two stories have to do with each other? Butch O'Hare was 'Easy Eddie's' son.

[Pretty cool, eh!]

The Contest

A lawyer and a Canadian are sitting next to each other on a long flight. The lawyer asks if the Canadian would like to play a fun game. The Canadian is tired and just wants to take a nap, so he politely declines and tries to catch a few winks.

The lawyer persists and says that the game is a lot of fun. *'I ask you a question and if you don't know the answer, you pay me only $5; you ask me one and if I don't know the answer, I will pay you $500'* he says.

This catches the Canadian's attention and to keep the lawyer quiet, he agrees to play the game. The lawyer asks the first question. *'What's the distance from the Earth to the Moon?'*

The Canadian reaches in his pocket pulls out a five-dollar bill and hands it to the lawyer without saying a word.

Now, it's the Canadian's turn. He asks the lawyer, *'What goes up a hill with three legs and comes down with four?'*

The lawyer uses his laptop and searches all references he could find on the Net. He sends e-mails to all the smart friends he knows, all to no avail. After an hour of searching he finally gives up. He wakes up the Canadian and hands him $500. The Canadian pockets the $500 and goes right back to sleep.

The lawyer is going nuts not knowing the answer. He wakes up the Canadian and asks, *'Well, so what goes up a hill with three legs and comes down with four?'*

The Canadian reaches in his pocket, hands the lawyer $5 and goes back to sleep.

CHILDREN

Two little kids are in a hospital

Two little kids are in a hospital, lying on stretchers next to each other outside the operating room. The first kid leans over and asks, *'What are you in here for?'*

The second kid says, *'I'm in here to get my tonsils out and I'm a little nervous.'*

The first kid says, *'You've got nothing to worry about. I had that done when I was four. They put you to sleep and when you wake up they give you lots of Jell-O and ice cream. It's a breeze.'*

The second kid then asks, *'What are you here for?'*

The first kid says, *'A circumcision.'*

'Whoa!' the second kid replies. *'Good luck buddy. I had that done when I was born. Couldn't walk for a year.'*

How was I born?

A little boy goes to his father and asks *'Daddy, how was I born?'*

The father answers, *'Well, son, I guess one day you will need to find out anyway! Your Mom and I first got together in a chat room on Yahoo. Then I set up a date via e-mail with your Mom and we met at a cyber-cafe. We sneaked into a secluded room, where your mother agreed to a download from my hard drive. As soon as I was ready to upload, we discovered that neither one of us had used a firewall and since it was too late to hit the delete button, nine months later a little Pop-Up appeared that said: 'You've got Male!'*

Little Boy at a nude beach

A mother and father take their 6-year old son to a nude beach. As the boy walks along the sand, he notices that many of the women have boobs bigger than his mother's, so he goes back to ask her why.

She tells her son, *'The bigger they are, the sillier the lady is.'*

The boy, pleased with the answer, goes to play in the ocean but returns to tell his mother that many of the men have larger things than his dad does.

She replies, *'The bigger they are, the dumber the man is'*

Again satisfied with her answer, the boy goes back to the ocean to play. Shortly thereafter, the boy returns and promptly tells his mother, *'Daddy is talking to the silliest lady on the beach and the longer he talks, the dumber he gets.'*

You gonna tell him?

Little boy comes down to breakfast. Since they live on a farm, his mother asks if he had done his chores.

'Not yet,' said the little boy.

His mother tells him no breakfast until he does his chores.

Well, he's a little pissed off, so he goes to feed the chickens and he kicks a chicken. He goes to feed the cows and he kicks a cow. He goes to feed the pigs and he kicks a pig. He goes back in for breakfast and his mother gives him a bowl of dry cereal.

'How come I don't get any eggs and bacon? Why don't I have any milk in my cereal?' he asks.

'Well,' his mother says, *'I saw you kick a chicken, so you don't get any eggs for a week. I saw you kick the pig, so you don't get any bacon for a week either. I saw you kick the cow so for a week you aren't getting any milk.'*

Just then, his father comes down for breakfast and kicks the cat halfway across the kitchen.

The little boy looks up at his mother with a smile and says, *'You gonna tell him or should I?'*

Power of turpentine

A little boy was sitting on the footpath with a bottle of Turpentine. He was shaking it up and watching all the bubbles. A Priest came along and asked the little boy what he had.

The little boy said, *'This is the most powerful liquid in the world; it's called Turpentine.'*

The Priest said, *'No, the most powerful liquid in the world is Holy Water. If you rub it on a pregnant woman's belly, she'll pass a healthy baby.'*

The little boy replied, *'If you rub turpentine on a cat's bum, he'll pass a Harley Davidson!'*

The Grand Daughter

A little girl ran to her Grandfather, jumped into his arms and gave him a great big hug. Then she ran her fingers along his balding head and down the side of his wrinkled face.

'Did God make you Grandad?' she asked.

'Yes honey, he made me.'

She felt her cheek and then asked, *'Did God make me too?'*

'Yes honey, he made you too.'

'Well,' she shrugged, *'Don't you think he does a better job now than he used to?'*

Education

The school inspector is assigned to the year 4 class in one of the local Brisbane state schools. He is introduced to the class by the teacher. She says to the class, *'Let's show the inspector just how clever you are by allowing him to ask you a question.'*

The inspector reasons that normally class starts with religious instruction, so he will ask a biblical question. He asks: *'Class, who broke down the walls of Jericho?'*

For a full minute there is absolute silence. The children all just stare at him blankly. Eventually, little Bruce raises his hand. The inspector excitedly points to him.

Bruce stands up and replies: *'Sir, I don't know who broke down the walls of Jericho, but I can assure you it wasn't me.'*

Of course the inspector is shocked by the answer and looks at the teacher for an explanation. Realising that he is perturbed, the teacher says: *'Well, I've known Bruce since the beginning of the year and I believe that if he says that he didn't do it, then he didn't do it.'*

The inspector is even more shocked at this and storms down to the principal's office and tells him what happened, to which the principal replies: *'I don't know the boy, but I socialise every now and then with his teacher and I believe her. If she feels that the boy is innocent, then he must be innocent.'*

The inspector can't believe what he is hearing. He grabs the phone on the principal's desk and in a rage dials Julia Gillard's telephone number and rattles the entire occurrence to her and asks her what she thinks of the education standard in the State.

The PM sighs heavily and replies: *'I don't know the boy, the teacher or the principal, but just get three quotes and have the wall fixed!!'*

Sex Education

A little girl runs out to the backyard where her father is working and asks him, *'Daddy, what's Sex?'*

'Okay,' he thinks, *'This day was bound to come and I'm not going to let my little princess learn about sex from the streets.'*

So, he sits her down and tells her all about the birds and the bees. He tells her about conception, sexual intercourse, sperms and eggs. He tells her about puberty, menstruation, erections and wet dreams.

Then she asks, *'Daddy, what is 'a couple'?'*

And he carries on, *'A couple are the two people involved in sex, but this can also be two males or two females which we call homosexual,'* and he goes on to describe masturbation oral sex, group sex, pornography, bondage and rape, paedophilia, etc.

The father finally asks, *'So why did you want to know about 'a couple' and 'Sex'?'*

'Oh, Mommy said lunch would be ready in a couple of secs ...'

Birth control

A six-year-old boy told his father he wanted to marry the little girl across the street. The father, being modern and well-schooled in handling children, hid his smile behind his hand. *'That's a serious step,'* he said. *'Have you thought it out completely?'*

'Yes,' his young son answered. *'We can spend one week in my room and the next in hers. It's right across the street, so I can run home if I get scared of the dark.'*

'How about transportation?' the father asked.

'I have my wagon and we both have our tricycles,' the little boy answered.

The boy had an answer to every question the father raised.

Finally, in exasperation, his dad asked, *'What about babies? When you're married, you're liable to have babies, you know.'*

'We've thought about that, too,' the little boy replied. *'We're not going to have babies. Every time she lays an egg, I'm going to step on it!'*

Don't mess with children.

A new teacher was trying to make use of her psychology courses. She started her class by saying, *'Everyone who thinks they're stupid, stand up!*

After a few seconds, Little Larry stood up. The teacher said, *'Do you think you're stupid, Larry?'*

'No, ma'am, but I hate to see you standing there all by yourself!'

The fundamental job of a toddler is to rule the universe.

One thing children wear out faster than shoes, is parents.

A young boy asks his Dad, *'What is the difference between confident and confidential?'*

Dad says, *'You are my son, I'm confident about that. Your friend over there is also my son, that's confidential.'*

A small boy wrote to Santa Claus, *'Send me a brother.'*
Santa wrote back, *'Send me your mother.'*

'Dear God, please send clothes for all those poor ladies in Daddy's computer ...'

Too short

A group of 3rd, 4th and 5th graders, accompanied by two female teachers, went on a field trip to the local racetrack, (Churchill Downs) to learn about thoroughbred horses and its supporting industry (bourbon) but mostly to see the horses.

When it was time to take the children to the restrooms, it was decided that the girls would go with one teacher and the boys would go with the other. The teacher assigned to the boys was waiting outside the men's room when one of the boys came out and told her that none of them could reach the high urinals.

Having no choice, she went inside, helped the boys with their pants and began hoisting the little boys up one by one, holding on to their 'wee-wees' to direct the flow away from their clothes.

As she lifted one, she couldn't help but notice that he was unusually well-endowed. Trying not to show that she was staring the teacher said, *'You must be in the 5th grade.'*

'No, ma'am,' he replied. *'I'm riding Silver Arrow in the seventh race, but I appreciate your help.'*

Little Larry

Little Larry watched, fascinated, as his mother smoothed cold cream on her face. *'Why do you do that, mommy?'* he asked.

'To make myself beautiful,' said his mother, who then began removing the cream with a tissue.

'What's the matter?' asked Little Johnny. *'Giving up?'*

The math teacher saw that little Larry wasn't paying attention in class. She called on him and said, *'Larry! What are 2 and 4 and 28 and 44?'*

Little Larry quickly replied, *'NBC, FOX, ESPN and the Cartoon Network!'*

Little Larry's kindergarten class was on a field trip to their local police station where they saw pictures tacked to a bulletin board of the ten most wanted criminals. One of the youngsters pointed to a picture and asked if it really was the photo of a wanted person.

'Yes,' said the policeman. *'The detectives want very badly to capture him'.*

Little Larry asked, *'Why didn't you keep him when you took his picture?'*

Little Larry attended a horse auction with his father. He watched as his father moved from horse to horse, running his hands up and down the horse's legs and rump and chest. After a few minutes, Johnny asked, *'Dad, why are you doing that?'*

His father replied, *'Because when I'm buying horses, I have to make sure that they are healthy and in good shape before I buy it.*

Larry, looking worried, said, *'Dad, I think the UPS guy wants to buy Mom.'*

What Is Butt Dust?

What, you ask, is 'Butt dust'? Read on and you'll discover the joy in it! These have to be original and genuine. No adult is this creative!!

- Jack (age 3) Was watching his Mom breast-feeding his new baby sister. After a while he asked: *'Mom why have you got two? Is one for hot and one for cold milk?'*
- Melanie (age 5) asked her Granny how old she was. Granny replied she was so old she didn't remember any more. Melanie said, *'If you don't remember you must look in the back of your panties. Mine say five to six.'*
- Steven (age 3) Hugged and kissed his Mom good night. *'I love you so much that when you die I'm going to bury you outside my bedroom window.'*
- Brittany (age 4) had an earache and wanted a pain killer. She tried in vain to take the lid off the bottle. Seeing her frustration, her Mom explained it was a child-proof cap and she'd have to open it for her. Eyes wide with wonder, the little girl asked: *'How does it know it's me?'*
- Susan (age 4) was drinking juice when she got the hiccups. *'Please don't give me this juice again,'* she said, *'It makes my teeth cough.*
- DJ (age 4) Stepped onto the bathroom scale and asked: *'How much do I cost?'*
- Clinton (age 5) was in his bedroom looking worried. When his Mom asked what was troubling him, he replied, *'I don't know what'll happen with this bed when I get married. How will my wife fit in it?'*

- Marc (age 4) was engrossed in a young couple that were hugging and kissing in a restaurant. Without taking his eyes off them, he asked his dad: *'Why is he whispering in her mouth?'*
- Tammy (age 4) was with her mother when they met an elderly, rather wrinkled woman her Mom knew. Tammy looked at her for a while and then asked, *'Why doesn't your skin fit your face?'* (Ouch!)
- James (age 4) was listening to a Bible story. His dad read: *'The man named Lot was warned to take his wife and flee out of the city but his wife looked back and was turned to salt.'*
  Concerned, James asked: *'What happened to the flea?'*
- The sermon I think this Mom will never forget. This particular Sunday sermon, the minister began with arms extended towards heaven and a rapturous look on his upturned face.

  'Dear Lord,' the minister began, with arms extended toward heaven and a rapturous look on his upturned face. *'Without you, we are but dust ...'* He would have continued but at that moment my very obedient daughter who was listening leaned over to me and asked quite audibly in her shrill little four year old girl voice, *'Mom, what is butt dust?'*

Plane Talk

A Canadian Member of Parliament was seated next to a little girl on the airplane leaving from Ottawa when he turned to her and said, *'Let's talk. I've heard that flights go quicker if you strike up a conversation with your fellow passenger.'*

The little girl, who had just opened her book, closed it slowly and said to the total stranger, *'What would you like to talk about?'*

'Oh, I don't know,' said the Member of Parliament. *'How about global warming or universal health care' and* he smiles smugly.

'Okay,' she said. *'Those could be interesting topics. But let me ask you a question first. A horse, a cow and a deer all eat the same stuff - grass. Yet a deer excretes little pellets, while a cow turns out a flat patty and a horse produces clumps of dried grass. Why do you suppose that is?'*

The BC MP, visibly surprised by the little girl's intelligence, thinks about it and says, *'Hmmm, I have no idea.'*

To which the little girl replies, *'Do you really feel qualified to discuss global warming or universal health care when you don't know shit?'*

Little Ralphy on math

The teacher asks her class, *'If there are five birds sitting on a fence and you shoot one of them, how many will be left?'*

She calls on little Ralphy.

He replies, *'None, they will all fly away with the first gunshot.'*

The teacher replies, *'The correct answer is 4, but I like your thinking.'*

Then little Ralphy says, *'I have a question for you. There are three women sitting on a bench having ice cream: One is delicately licking the triple scoop of ice cream. The second is gobbling down the top and sucking the cone. The third is biting off the top of the ice cream. Which one is married?'*

The teacher, blushing a great deal, replied, *'Well, I suppose the one that's gobbled down the top and sucked the cone.'*

To which Little Ralphy sides of the replied, *'The correct answer is 'the one with the wedding ring on,' but I like your thinking.'*

Little Ralphy on math (Part 2)

Little Ralphy returns from school and says he got an 'F' in arithmetic.

'Why?' asks the father?

'The teacher asked 'How much is 2x3.'

'I said '6,' replies Ralphy.

'But that's right!' says his dad.

'Yeah, but then she asked me 'How much is 3x2?'

'What's the f....n. difference?' asks the father.

'That's what I said!'

Little Ralphy on getting older

Little Ralphy was sitting on a park bench munching on one candy bar after another. After the sixth one a man on the bench across from him said, *'Son, you know eating all that candy isn't good for you. It will give you acne, rot your teeth and make you fat.'*

Little Ralphy replied, *'My grandfather lived to be 107 years old.'*

The man asked, *'Did your grandfather eat six candy bars at a time?'*

Little Ralphy answered, *'No, he minded his own f.....n. business.'*

Little Ralphy on English

Little Ralphy goes to school and the teacher says, *'Today we are going to learn multi-syllable words, class. Does anybody have an example of a multi-syllable word?'*

Ralphy says, *'Mas-tur-bate.'*

Miss Rogers smiles and says, *'Wow, little Ralphy, that's a mouthful.'*

Little Ralphy says, *'No, Miss Rogers, you're thinking of a blowjob.'*

Little Ralphy on grammar

Little Ralphy was sitting in class one day. All of a sudden, he needed to go to the toilet. He yelled out, *'Miss Jones, I need to take a piss!'*

The teacher replied, *'Now, Ralphy, that is NOT the proper word to use in this situation. The correct word you want to use is 'urinate. Please use the word 'ur-i-nate' in a sentence correctly and I will allow you to go.'*

Little Ralphy thinks for a bit and then says, *'You're an eight, but if you had bigger tits, you'd be a TEN!'*

Little Ralphy on grammar (Part 2)

One day, during lessons on proper grammar, the teacher asked for a show of hands from those who could use the word *'beautiful'* in the same sentence twice.

First, she called on little Suzie, who responded with, *'My father bought my mother a beautiful dress and she looked beautiful in it.'*
'Very good, Suzie,' replied the teacher. She then called on little Michael.

'My mummy planned a beautiful banquet and it turned out beautifully.'

She said, *'Excellent, Michael!'*

Then the teacher reluctantly called on little Ralphy.

'Last night at the dinner table, my sister told my father that she was pregnant and he said 'Beautiful, just f...... beautiful!'

Difference between Grandfathers and Grandmothers

This is funny even if you are not a grandparent.

A friend, who worked away from home all week, always made a special effort with his family on the weekends. Every Sunday morning he would take his 7-year old granddaughter out for a drive in the car for some bonding time - just him and his granddaughter.

One particular Sunday however, he had a bad cold and really didn't feel like being up at all. Luckily, his wife came to the rescue and said that she would take their granddaughter out.

When they returned, the little girl anxiously ran upstairs to see her Grandfather.

'Well, did you enjoy your ride with grandma?'

'Oh yes, Papa' the girl replied, *'and do you know what? We didn't see a single asshole, dumb bastard, dipshit or horse's ass anywhere we went today!'*

Almost brings a tear to your eye, doesn't it?

The Cowboy Boots

[Anyone who has ever dressed a child will love this one!)]
Did you hear about the Texas teacher who was helping one of her kindergarten students put on his cowboy boots? He asked for help and she could see why. Even with her pulling and him pushing, the little boots still didn't want to go on. By the time they got the second boot on, she had worked up a sweat.

She almost cried when the little boy said, *'Teacher, they're on the wrong feet.'* She looked and sure enough, they were. It wasn't any easier pulling the boots off than it was putting them on. She managed to keep her cool as together they worked to get the boots back on, this time on the right feet.

He then announced, *'These aren't my boots.'*

She bit her tongue rather than get right in his face and scream, *'Why didn't you say so?'* like she wanted to. Once again, she struggled to help him pull the ill-fitting boots off his little feet. No sooner had they gotten the boots off when he said, *'They're my brother's boots. My mom made me wear 'em.'*

Now she didn't know if she should laugh or cry. But, she mustered up what grace and courage she had left to wrestle the boots on his feet again.

Helping him into his coat, she asked, *'Now, where are your mittens?'*

He said, *'I stuffed 'em in the toes of my boots.'*

She will be eligible for parole in three years!

Proverbs

A first grade school teacher had twenty-six students in her class. She presented each child in her classroom the first half of a well-known proverb and asked them to come up with the remainder of the proverb. It's hard to believe these were actually done by first graders.

Their insight may surprise you. While reading, keep in mind that these are first-graders, 6-year-olds, because the last one is a classic!

1. Don't change horses: until they stop running.
2. Strike when the: bug is close.
3. It's always darkest before: Daylight Saving time.
4. Never underestimate the power of: termites.
5. You can lead a horse to water but: how?
6. Don't bite the hand that: looks dirty.
7. No news is: impossible.
8. A miss is as good as a: Mr.
9. You can't teach an old dog new: math
10. If you lie down with dogs, you'll: stink in the morning.
11. Love all, trust: me.
12. The pen is mightier than the: pigs.
13. An idle mind is: the best way to relax.
14. Where there's smoke, there's: pollution.
15. Happy the bride who: gets all the presents.
16. A penny saved is: not much.
17. Two's company, three's: the Musketeers.
18. Don't put off till tomorrow what: you put on to go to bed.
19. Laugh and the whole world laughs with you, cry and: you have to blow your nose.
20. There are none so blind as: Stevie Wonder.
21. Children should be seen and not spanked or grounded.
22. If at first you don't succeed; get new batteries.
23. You get out of something only what you: see in the picture on the box.
24. When the blind lead the blind: get out of the way.
25. A bird in the hand: is going to poop on you.

And the winner and last one:

26. Better late than: pregnant.

Bless Him

A little three year old boy is sitting on the toilet. His mother thinks he has been in there too long, so she goes in to see what's up. The little boy is sitting on the toilet reading a book, but about every 10 seconds or so he puts the book down, grips onto to the toilet seat with his left hand and hits himself on top of the head with his right hand.

His mother says: *'Billy, are you all right? You've been in here for a while.'*

Billy says: *'I'm fine, Mommy ... I just haven't done it yet.'*

Mother says: *'Okay, you can stay here a few more minutes. But, Billy, why are you hitting yourself on the head?'*

Billy says: *'Works for tomato sauce!'*

Bible Class

Can you imagine yourself to be the nun that is sitting at her desk grading these papers all the while trying to keep a straight face and maintain her composure!

Pay special attention to the wording and spelling. If you know the bible even a little, you'll find this hilarious! It comes from a catholic elementary school test. Kids were asked questions about the old and new testaments. The following statements about the bible were written by children. They have not been retouched or corrected. Incorrect spelling has been left in.

1. In the beginning, which occurred near the start, there was nothing but God, darkness and some gas. The Bible says, 'The Lord thy God is one, but I think He must be a lot older than that. Anyway, God said, 'Give me a light!' and someone did. Then God made the world.
2. He split the Adam and made Eve. Adam and Eve were naked, but they weren't embarrassed because mirrors hadn't been invented yet. Adam and Eve disobeyed God by eating one bad apple, so they were driven from the Garden of Eden. Not sure what they were driven in though, because they didn't have cars.
3. Adam and Eve had a son, Cain, who hated his brother as long as he was Abel. Pretty soon all of the early people died off, except for Methuselah, who lived to be like a million or something.
4. One of the next important people was Noah, who was a good guy, but one of his kids was kind of a Ham. Noah built a large boat and put his family and some animals on it. He asked some other people to join him, but they said they would have to take a rain check.
5. After Noah came Abraham, Isaac and Jacob. Jacob was more famous than his brother, Esau, because Esau sold Jacob his birthmark in exchange for some pot roast. Jacob had a son named Joseph who wore a really loud sports coat.

6. Another important Bible guy is Moses, whose real name was Charlton Heston. Moses led the Israel Lights out of Egypt and away from the evil Pharaoh after God sent ten plagues on Pharaoh's people. These plagues included frogs, mice, lice, bowels and no cable. God fed the Israel Lights every day with manicotti.
7. Then he gave them His Top Ten Commandments. These include don't lie, cheat, smoke, dance or covet your neighbor's stuff. Oh, yeah, I just thought of one more: Humour thy father and thy mother. One of Moses' best helpers was Joshua who was the first Bible guy to use spies. Joshua fought the battle of Geritol and the fence fell over on the town.
8. After Joshua came, David he got to be king by killing a giant with a slingshot. He had a son named Solomon who had about 300 wives and 500 porcupines. My teacher says he was wise, but that doesn't sound very wise to me.
9. After Solomon there were a bunch of major league prophets. One of these was Jonah, who was swallowed by a big whale and then barfed upon the shore. There were also some minor league prophets, but I guess we don't have to worry about them.
10. After the Old Testament came the New Testament. Jesus is the star of the New Testament. He was born in Bethlehem in a barn. (I wish I had been born in a barn, too, because my Mom is always saying to me, *'Close the door! Were you born in a barn?'* It would be nice to say, *'As a matter of fact, I was.'*)
11. During His life, Jesus had many arguments with sinners like the Pharisites and the Republicans. Jesus also had twelve opossums. The worst one was Judas Asparagus. Judas was so evil that they named a terrible vegetable after him.
12. Jesus was a great man. He healed many leopards and even preached to some Germans on the Mount. But the Republicans and all those guys put Jesus on trial before Pontius the Pilot. Pilot didn't stick up for Jesus. He just washed his hands instead.
13. Any way, Jesus died for our sins, then came back to life again. He went up to Heaven but will be back at the end of the Aluminum. His return is foretold in the book of Revolution.

Revenge

A little boy about 12 years old is walking down the street dragging a flattened frog on a string behind him. He came up to the doorstep of 'a house of ill repute' and knocked on the door. When the Madam answered it, she saw the little boy and asked what he wanted.

He said, *'I want to have sex with one of the women inside. I have the money to buy it and I'm not leaving until I get it.'*

The Madam figured, why not, so she told him to come in. Once in, she told him to pick any of the girls he liked. He asked, *'Do any of the girls have any diseases?'*

Of course the Madam said *'No.'*

The boy said, *'I heard all the men talking about having to get shots after making love with Amber - THAT'S the girl I want.'*

Since the little boy was so adamant and had the money to pay for it, the Madam told him to go to the first room on the right. He headed down the hall dragging the squashed frog behind him. Ten minutes later he came back, still dragging the frog, paid the Madam and headed out the door.

The Madam stopped him and asked, *'Why did you pick the only girl in the place with a disease, instead of one of the others?'*

He said, *'Well, if you must know, tonight when I get home, my parents are going out to a restaurant to eat, leaving me at home with a baby-sitter. After they leave, my baby-sitter will have sex with me because she just happens to be very fond of cute little boys. She will then get the disease that I just caught. When Mom and Dad get back, Dad will take the baby-sitter home. On the way, he'll give her one in the car and he'll catch the disease.*

Then when Dad gets home from the baby-sitter's, he and Mom will go to bed and have sex and Mom will catch it.

In the morning when Dad goes to work, the Milkman will deliver the milk, have a quickie with Mom and catch the disease and HE'S the prick who ran over my FROG!'

Big Words

The school teacher asks her class to name things that end with 'tor' that eat things.

The first little boy says, *'Alligator."*

'Very good, that's a big word.'

The second boy says, *'Predator.'*

'Yes, that's another big word. Well done.'

The third boy says, *'Vibrator, Miss.'*

After nearly falling off her chair, she says, *'That is a big word, but it doesn't eat anything.'*

'Well my mum has one and she says it eats batteries like there's no tomorrow!'

Needless to say, the teacher had to work hard not to crack up.

Children writing about the ocean

1. This is a picture of an octopus. It has eight testicles. [Kelly, age 6]
2. Oysters' balls are called pearls. [Jerry, age 6]
3. If you are surrounded by ocean you are an Island. If you don't have ocean all round you, you are incontinent. [Wayne, age 7]
4. Sharks are ugly and mean and have big teeth, just like Emily Richardson. She's not my friend any more. [Kylie, age 6]
5. A dolphin breaths through an asshole on the top of its head. [Billy, age 8]
6. My uncle goes out in his boat with 2 other men and a woman and pots and comes back with crabs. [Millie, age 6]
7. When ships had sails, they used to use the trade winds to cross the ocean. Sometimes when the wind didn't blow the sailors would whistle to make the wind come. My brother said they would have been better off eating beans. [William, age 7]
8. Mermaids live in the ocean. I like mermaids. They are beautiful and I like their shiny tails, but how on earth do mermaids get pregnant? Like, really? [Helen, age 6]
9. I'm not going to write about the ocean. My baby brother is always crying, my Dad keeps yelling at my Mom and my big sister has just got pregnant, so I can't think what to write. [Amy, age 6]
10. Some fish are dangerous. Jellyfish can sting. Electric eels can give you a shock. They have to live in caves under the sea where I think they have to plug themselves into chargers. [Christopher, age 7]
11. When you go swimming in the ocean, it is very cold and it makes my willy small. [Kevin, age 6]
12. Divers have to be safe when they go under the water. Divers can't go down alone, so they have to go down on each other. [Becky, age 8]
13. On vacation my Mom went water skiing. She fell off when she was going very fast. She says she won't do it again because water fired right up her fanny. [Julie, age 7]
14. The ocean is made up of water and fish. Why the fish don't drown, I don't know. [Bobby, age 6]
15. My dad was a sailor on the ocean. He knows all about the ocean. What he doesn't know is why he quit being a sailor and married my mom. [James, age 7]

Daddy's Cup of Tea

One day my mother was out and my dad was in charge of me. I was maybe 2 1/2 years old. Someone had given me a little 'tea set' as a gift and it was one of my favourite toys.

Daddy was in the living room engrossed in the evening news when I brought Daddy a little cup of 'tea' which was just water. After several cups of tea and lots of praise for such yummy tea, my Mom came home.

My Dad made her wait in the living room to watch me bring him a cup of tea, because it was *'just the cutest thing!'* My Mom waited and sure enough, here I come down the hall with a cup of tea for Daddy and she watches him drink it up.

Then she says, (as only a mother would know) *'Did it ever occur to you that the only place she can reach to get water is the toilet?'*

What is a grandparent?

[Taken from papers written by a class of 8-year-olds]

1. She was in the bathroom, putting on her makeup, under the watchful eyes of her young granddaughter, as she'd done many times before. After she applied her lipstick and started to leave, the little one said, *'But Gramma, you forgot to kiss the toilet paper good-bye!'* I will probably never put lipstick on again without thinking about kissing the toilet paper good-bye.
2. My young grandson called the other day to wish me Happy Birthday. He asked me how old I was and I told him, 62. My grandson was quiet for a moment and then he asked, *'Did you start at 1?'*
3. After putting her grandchildren to bed, a grandmother changed into old slacks and a droopy blouse and proceeded to wash her hair. As she heard the children getting more and more rambunctious, her patience grew thin. Finally, she threw a towel around her head and stormed into their room, putting them back to bed with stern warnings. As she left the room, she heard the three-year-old say with a trembling voice, *'Who was THAT?'*
4. A grandmother was telling her little granddaughter what her own childhood was like: *'We used to skate outside on a pond I had a swing made from a tire; it hung from a tree in our front yard. We rode our pony. We picked wild raspberries in the woods.'* The little girl was wide-eyed, taking this all in. At last she said, *'I sure wish I'd gotten to know you sooner!'*

5. My grandson was visiting one day when he asked, *'Grandma, do you know how you and God are alike?'*

   I mentally polished my halo and I said, *'No, how are we alike?'*

   'You're both old,' he replied.

6. A little girl was diligently pounding away on her grandfather's word processor. She told him she was writing a story.

   'What's it about?' he asked.

   'I don't know,' she replied. *'I can't read.'*

7. I didn't know if my granddaughter had learned her colours yet, so I decided to test her. I would point out something and ask what colour it was. She would tell me and was always correct. It was fun for me, so I continued. At last, she headed for the door, saying, *'Grandma, I think you should try to figure out some of these yourself!'*

11. When my grandson Billy and I entered our vacation cabin, we kept the lights off until we were inside to keep from attracting pesky insects. Still, a few fireflies followed us in. Noticing them before I did, Billy whispered, *'It's no use Grandpa. Now the mosquitoes are coming after us with flashlights.'*

12 A second grader came home from school and said to her grandmother, *'Grandma, guess what? We learned how to make babies today.'*

   The grandmother, more than a little surprised, tried to keep her cool. *'That's interesting.'* she said, *'How do you make babies?'*

   'It's simple,' replied the girl. *'You just change 'y' to 'i' and add 'es'.'*

13. Children's Logic: *'Give me a sentence about a public servant,'* said a teacher. The small boy wrote: *'The fireman came down the ladder pregnant.'*

   The teacher took the lad aside to correct him. *'Don't you know what pregnant means?'* she asked.

   'Sure,' said the young boy confidently. *'It means carrying a child.'*

14. A grandfather was delivering his grandchildren to their home one day when a fire truck zoomed past. Sitting in the front seat of the fire truck was a Dalmatian dog. The children started discussing the dog's duties. *'They use him to keep crowds back,'* said one child.

   'No,' said another. *'He's just for good luck.'*

A third child brought the argument to a close. *'They use the dogs,'* she said firmly, *'to find the fire hydrants.'*

15. Grandparents are a lady and a man who have no little children of their own. They like other people's children.
16. A grandfather is a man and a grandmother is a lady!
17. Grandparents don't have to do anything except be there when we come to see them. They are so old they shouldn't play hard or run. It is good if they drive us to the shops and give us money.
18. When they take us for walks, they slow down past things like pretty leaves and caterpillars.
19. They show us and talk to us about the colours of the flowers and also why we shouldn't step on 'cracks.'
20. They don't say, *'Hurry up.'*
21. Usually grandmothers are fat but not too fat to tie your shoes.
22. They wear glasses and funny underwear.
23. They can take their teeth and gums out.
24. Grandparents don't have to be smart.
25. They have to answer questions like *'Why isn't God married?'* and *'How come dogs chase cats?'*
26. When they read to us, they don't skip. They don't mind if we ask for the same story over again.
27. Everybody should try to have a grandmother, especially if you don't have television because they are the only grownups who like to spend time with us.
28. They know we should have snack time before bed time and they say prayers with us and kiss us even when we've acted bad.
29. A 6-year-old was asked where his grandma lived. *'Oh,'* he said, *'she lives at the airport and when we want her, we just go get her. Then when we're done having her visit, we take her back to the airport.'*
30. Grandpa is the smartest man on earth! He teaches me good things, but I don't get to see him enough to get as smart as him!
31. It's funny when they bend over; you hear gas leaks and they blame their dog.

Knickers

Little Susie goes home from school and tells her mum that the boys keep asking her to do cartwheels because she's very good at them ?

Mom said: *'You should say NO - they only want to look at your knickers'*

Susie said: *'I know they do. That's why I hide them in my bag!!'*

8th Grade Final Exam: Salina , KS - 1895

Grammar (Time, one hour)

1. Give nine rules for the use of capital letters.
2. Name the parts of speech and define those that have no modifications.
3. Define verse, stanza and paragraph.
4. What are the principal parts of a verb? Give principal parts of 'lie,' 'play,' and 'run.'
5. Define case; illustrate each case.
6. What is punctuation? Give rules for principal marks of punctuation.
7. Write a composition of (about 150 words) and show therein that you understand the practical use of the rules of grammar.

Arithmetic (Time, 1 hour 15 minutes)

1. Name and define the Fundamental Rules of Arithmetic.
2. A wagon box is 2 ft. deep, 10 feet long and 3 ft. wide. How many bushels of wheat will it hold?
3. If a load of wheat weighs 3,942 lbs., what is it worth at 50 cents/bushel, deducting 1,050 lbs. for tare?
4. District No 33 has a valuation of $35,000. What is the necessary levy to carry on a school seven months at $50 per month and have $104 for incidentals?
5. Find the cost of 6,720 lbs. of coal at $6.00 per ton.
6. Find the interest of $512.60 for 8 months and 18 days at 7 percent.
7. What is the cost of 40 boards 12 inches wide and 16 ft. long at $20 per metre?
8. Find bank discount on $300 for 90 days (no grace) at 10 percent.
9. What is the cost of a square farm at $15 per acre, the distance of which is 640 rods?
10. Write a Bank Check, a Promissory Note and a Receipt.

U.S. History (Time, 45 minutes)

1. Give the epochs into which U.S. History is divided.
2. Give an account of the discovery of America by Columbus.
3. Relate the causes and results of the Revolutionary War.
4. Show the territorial growth of the United States.
5. Tell what you can of the history of Kansas.
6. Describe three of the most prominent battles of the Rebellion.

7. Who were the following: Morse, Whitney, Fulton, Bell, Lincoln, Penn and Howe?
8. Name events connected with the following dates: 1607, 1620, 1800, 1849 and 1860?

Orthography (Time, one hour) [Do we even know what this is??]

1. What is meant by the following: alphabet, phonetic orthography, etymology, syllabication.
2. What are elementary sounds? How classified?
3. What are the following and give examples of each: trigraph, subvocals, diphthong, cognate letters, linguals.
4. Give four substitutes for caret 'u.' (HUH?)
5. Give two rules for spelling words with final 'e.' Name two exceptions under each rule.
6. Give two uses of silent letters in spelling. Illustrate each.
7. Define the following prefixes and use in connection with a word: bi, dis, miss, pre, semi, post, non, inter, mono, sup.
8. Mark diacritically and divide into syllables the following and name the sign that indicates the sound: card, ball, mercy, sir, odd, cell, rise, blood, fare, last.
9. Use the following correctly in sentences: cite, site, sight, fane, fain, feign, vane, vain, vein, raze, raise, rays.
10. Write 10 words frequently mispronounced and indicate pronunciation by use of diacritical marks and by syllabication.

Geography (Time, one hour)

1. What is climate? Upon what does climate depend?
2. How do you account for the extremes of climate in Kansas?
3. Of what use are rivers? Of what use is the ocean?
4. Describe the mountains of North America.
5. Name and describe the following: Monrovia , Odessa , Denver , Manitoba, Hecla, Yukon, St. Helena, Juan Fernandez, Aspinwall and Orinoco.
6. Name and locate the principal trade centres of the U.S.
7. Name all the republics of Europe and give the capital of each.
8. Why is the Atlantic Coast colder than the Pacific in the same latitude?
9. Describe the process by which the water of the ocean returns to the sources of rivers.
10. Describe the movements of the earth. Give the inclination of the earth.

Notice that the exam took five hours to complete (with no calculators, computers or internet help). Gives the saying 'he only had an 8th grade education' a whole new meaning, doesn't it?! Also shows you how poor our education system has become and, NO, I don't have the answers!

Biology Class - final exam

Students in an advanced Biology class were taking their mid-term exam. The last question was, *'Name seven advantages of Mother's Milk,'* worth 70 points or none at all.

One student, in particular, was hard put to think of seven advantages. He wrote:

1. It is perfect formula for the child.
2. It provides immunity against several diseases.
3. It is always the right temperature.
4. It is inexpensive.
5. It bonds the child to mother and vice versa.
6. It is always available as needed.

And then the student was stuck. Finally, in desperation, just before the bell rang indicating the end of the test, he wrote:

7. It comes in two attractive containers.

He got an A.

A Little Golf Story

A father put his 3 year old daughter to bed, told her a story and listened to her prayers which ended by saying: *'God bless Mommy, God bless Daddy, God bless Grandma and goodbye Grandpa.'*

The father asked, *'Why did you say goodbye Grandpa?'*

The little girl said, *'I don't know, Daddy, it just seemed like the thing to do.'*

The next day grandpa died. The father thought it was a strange coincidence. A few months later the father put the girl to bed and listened to her prayers which went like this: *'God bless Mommy, God Bless Daddy and goodbye Grandma.'*

The next day the grandmother died.

'Holy Moley,' thought the father, *'this kid is in contact with the other side.'*

Several weeks later when the girl was going to bed the dad heard her say: *'God bless Mommy and goodbye Daddy.'*

He practically went into shock. He couldn't sleep all night and got up at the crack of dawn to go to his office. He was nervous as a cat all day, had lunch and watched the clock. He figured if he could get by until midnight he would be okay.

He felt safe in the office, so instead of going home at the end of the day he stayed there, drinking coffee, looking at his watch and jumping at every sound.

Finally, midnight arrived; he breathed a sigh of relief and went home. When he got home his wife said, *'I've never seen you work so late. What's the matter?'*

He said, *'I don't want to talk about it but I've just spent the worst day of my life.'*

She said, *'You think you had a bad day. You'll never believe what happened to me this morning. My golf pro dropped dead in the middle of my lesson.'*

All I need to know I learned from the Easter Bunny

- Don't put all your eggs in one basket.
- Everyone needs a friend who is all ears.
- There's no such thing as too much candy.
- All work and no play can make you a basket case.
- A cute tail attracts a lot of attention.
- Everyone is entitled to a bad hare day.
- Let happy thoughts multiply like rabbits.
- Some body parts should be floppy.
- Keep your paws off other people's jelly beans.
- Good things come in small, sugar coated packages.
- The grass is always greener in someone else's basket.
- To show your true colours, you have to come out of the shell.
- The best things in life are still sweet and gooey.

Beer by seven year olds

A handful of 7 year old children were asked *'What they thought of beer.'* Some interesting responses, but the last one is especially touching.

- *'I think beer must be good. My dad says the more beer he drinks the prettier my mom gets.'* - Tim, 7 years old.
- *'Beer makes my dad sleepy and we get to watch what we want on television when he is asleep, so beer is nice.'* - Melanie, 7 years old.

- *'My Mom and Dad both like beer. My Mom gets funny when she drinks it and takes her top off at parties, but Dad doesn't think this is very funny.'* - Grady, 7 years old.
- *'My Mom and Dad talk funny when they drink beer and the more they drink the more they give kisses to each other, which is a good thing.'* - Toby, 7 years old.
- *'My Dad gets funny on beer. He is funny. He also wets his pants sometimes, so he shouldn't have too much.'* - Sarah, 7 years old.
- *'My Dad loves beer. The more he drinks, the better he dances. One time he danced right into the pool.'* - Lilly, 7 years old.
- *'I don't like beer very much. Every time Dad drinks it, he burns the sausages on the barbecue and they taste disgusting.'* - Ethan, 7 years old.
- *'I give Dad's beer to the dog and he goes to sleep.'* - Shirley, 7 years old.
- *'My Mom drinks beer and she says silly things and picks on my father. Whenever she drinks beer she yells at Dad and tells him to go bury his bone down the street again, but that doesn't make any sense.'* - Jack, 7 years.

A little boy

A little boy got on the bus; sat next to a man reading a book and noticed he had his collar on backwards. The little boy asked why he wore his collar backwards.

The man, who was a priest, said, *'I am a Father.'*

The little boy replied, *'My Father doesn't wear his collar like that.'*

The priest looked up from his book and answered, *'I am the Father of many.'*

The boy said, *'My Father has four boys, four girls and two grandchildren and he doesn't wear his collar that way!'*

The priest, getting impatient, said. *'I am the Father of hundreds,'* and went back to reading his book.

The little boy sat quietly thinking for a while, then leaned over and said, *'Maybe you should wear a condom and put your pants on backwards instead of your collar.'*

The Teacher

As she stood in front of her 5th grade class on the very first day of school, she told the children an untruth. Like most teachers, she looked at her students and said that she loved them all the same.

However, that was impossible, because there in the front row, slumped in his seat, was a little boy named Teddy Stoddard.

Mrs. Thompson had watched Teddy the year before and noticed that he did not play well with the other children, that his clothes were messy and that he constantly needed a bath. In addition, Teddy could be unpleasant. It got to the point where Mrs. Thompson would actually take delight in marking his papers with a broad red pen, making bold X's and then putting a big 'F' at the top of his papers.

At the school where Mrs. Thompson taught, she was required to review each child's past records and she put Teddy's off until last. However, when she reviewed his file, she was in for a surprise.

Teddy's first grade teacher wrote, *'Teddy is a bright child with a ready laugh. He does his work neatly and has good manners ... he is a joy to be around.'*

His second grade teacher wrote, *'Teddy is an excellent student, well liked by his classmates, but he is troubled because his mother has a terminal illness and life at home must be a struggle.'*

His third grade teacher wrote, *'His mother's death has been hard on him. He tries to do his best, but his father doesn't show much interest and his home life will soon affect him if some steps aren't taken.'*

Teddy's fourth grade teacher wrote, *'Teddy is withdrawn and doesn't show much interest in school. He doesn't have many friends and he sometimes sleeps in class.'*

By now, Mrs. Thompson realised the problem and she was ashamed of herself. She felt even worse when her students brought her Christmas presents, wrapped in beautiful ribbons and bright paper, except for Teddy's. His present was clumsily wrapped in the heavy, brown paper that he got from a grocery bag. Mrs. Thompson took pains to open it in the middle of the other presents. Some of the children started to laugh when she found a rhinestone bracelet with some of the stones missing and a bottle that was one-quarter full of perfume. But she stifled the children's laughter when she exclaimed how pretty the bracelet was, putting it on and dabbing some of the perfume on her wrist.

Teddy Stoddard stayed after school that day just long enough to say, *'Mrs. Thompson, today you smelled just like my Mom used to.'*

After the children left, she cried for at least an hour. On that very day, she quit teaching reading, writing and arithmetic. Instead, she began to teach children. Mrs. Thompson paid particular attention to Teddy. As she worked with him, his mind seemed to come alive. The more she encouraged him, the faster he responded. By the end of the year, Teddy had become one of the smartest children in the class and, despite her lie that she would love all the children the same, Teddy became one of her 'teacher's pets.'

A year later, she found a note under her door, from Teddy, telling her that she was the best teacher he ever had in his whole life. Six years went by before she got another note from Teddy. He then wrote that he had finished high school, third in his class and she was still the best teacher he ever had in life.

Four years after that, she got another letter, saying that while things had been tough at times, he'd stayed in school, had stuck with it and would soon graduate from college with the highest of honours. He assured Mrs. Thompson that she was still the best and favourite teacher he had ever had in his whole life.

Then four more years passed and yet another letter came. This time he explained that after he got his bachelor's degree, he decided to go a little further. The letter explained that she was still the best and favourite teacher he ever had. But now his name was a little longer ... The letter was signed, Theodore F. Stoddard, MD.

The story does not end there. You see, there was yet another letter that spring. Teddy said he had met this girl and was going to be married. He explained that his father had died a couple of years ago and he was wondering if Mrs. Thompson might agree to sit at the wedding in the place that was usually reserved for the mother of the groom. Of course, Mrs. Thompson did. And guess what? She wore that bracelet, the one with several rhinestones missing. Moreover, she made sure she was wearing the perfume that Teddy remembered his mother wearing on their last Christmas together.

They hugged each other and Dr. Stoddard whispered in Mrs. Thompson's ear, *'Thank you Mrs. Thompson for believing in me. Thank you so much for making me feel important and showing me that I could make a difference.'*

Mrs. Thompson, with tears in her eyes, whispered back. She said, *'Teddy, you have it all wrong. You were the one who taught me that I could make a difference. I didn't know how to teach until I met you.'*

[For you that don't know, Teddy Stoddard is the Dr. at Iowa Methodist in Des Moines that has the Stoddard Cancer Wing.]

SENIORS

Written by Regina Brett, 90 years old of the Plain Dealer, Cleveland, Ohio.

'To celebrate growing older, I once wrote the 45 lessons life taught me. It is the most requested column I've ever written. My odometer rolled over to 90 in August, so here is the column once more.'

1. Life isn't fair, but it's still good.
2. When in doubt, just take the next small step.
3. Life is too short to waste time hating anyone.
4. Your job won't take care of you when you are sick. Your friends and parents will. Stay in touch.
5. Pay off your credit cards every month.
6. You don't have to win every argument. Agree to disagree.
7. Cry with someone. It's more healing than crying alone.
8. It's okay to get angry.
9. Save for retirement starting with your first paycheque.
10. When it comes to chocolate, resistance is futile.
11. Make peace with your past so it won't screw up the present.
12. It's okay to let your children see you cry.
13. Don't compare your life to others. You have no idea what their journey is all about.
14. If a relationship has to be a secret, you shouldn't be in it.
15. Everything can change in the blink of an eye. But don't worry; God never blinks.
16. Take a deep breath. It calms the mind.
17. Get rid of anything that isn't useful, beautiful or joyful.
18. Whatever doesn't kill you really does make you stronger.
19. It's never too late to have a happy childhood. But the second one is up to you and no one else.
20. When it comes to going after what you love in life, don't take no for an answer.
21. Burn the candles, use the nice sheets and wear the fancy lingerie. Don't save it for a special occasion. Today is special.
22. Over-prepare, then go with the flow.
23. Be eccentric now. Don't wait for old age to wear purple.
24. The most important sex organ is the brain.
25. No one is in charge of your happiness but you.

26. Frame every so-called disaster with these words *'In five years, will this matter?'*
27. Always choose life.
28. Forgive everyone everything.
29. What other people think of you is none of your business.
30. Time heals almost everything. Give time time.
31. However good or bad a situation is; it will change.
32. Don't take yourself so seriously. No one else does.
33. Believe in miracles.
34. God loves you because of who God is, not because of anything you did or didn't do.
35. Don't audit life. Show up and make the most of it now.
36. Growing old beats the alternative - dying young.
37. Your children get only one childhood.
38. All that truly matters in the end is that you loved.
39. Get outside every day. Miracles are waiting everywhere.
40. If we all threw our problems in a pile and saw everyone else's, we'd grab ours back.
41. Envy is a waste of time. You already have all you need.
42. The best is yet to come.
43. No matter how you feel, get up, dress up and show up.
44. Yield.
45. Life isn't tied with a bow, but it's still a gift.

Free trip

A travel agent looked up from his desk to see an old lady and an old gentleman peering in the shop window at the posters showing the glamorous destinations around the world. The agent had had a good week and the dejected couple looking in the window gave him a rare feeling of generosity.

He called them into his shop: *'I know that on your pension you could never hope to have a holiday, so I am sending you off to a fabulous resort at my expense and I won't take no for an answer.'*

He took them inside and asked his secretary to write two flight tickets and book a room in a five star hotel. They, as can be expected, gladly accepted and were off!

About a month later the little old lady came in to his shop.

'And how did you like your holiday?' he asked eagerly.

'The flight was exciting and the room was lovely,' she said. *'I've come to thank you but, one thing puzzled me. Who was that old guy I had to share the room with?'*

Actually, some of us ask the same question every morning!

Sex and good grammar

For all my grammatically correct friends.

On his 74th birthday, a man got a gift certificate from his wife. The certificate paid for a visit to a medicine man living on a nearby reservation who was rumoured to have a wonderful cure for his erectile dysfunction. After being persuaded, he drove to the reservation, handed his ticket to the medicine man and wondered what he was in for.

The old man handed a potion to him and with a grip on his shoulder, warned, *'This is a powerful medicine. You take only a teaspoonful and then say '1-2-3. When you do, you will become more manly than you have ever been in your life and you can perform as long as you want.'* The man was encouraged.

As he walked away, he turned and asked, *'How do I stop the medicine from working?'*

'Your partner must say '1-2-3-4,' he responded, *'but when she does, the medicine will not work again until the next full moon.'*

He was very eager to see if it worked so he went home, showered, shaved, took a spoonful of the medicine and then invited his wife to join him in the bedroom. When she came in, he took off his clothes and said, *'1-2-3!'* Immediately, he was the manliest of men.

His wife was excited and began throwing off her clothes and then she asked *'What was the 1-2-3 for?'*

And that, boys and girls, is why we should never end our sentences with a preposition, because we could end up with a dangling participle.

Grandparents

- Grandmas are moms with lots of frosting - Author Unknown
- What a bargain grandchildren are! I give them my loose change and they give me a million dollars' worth of pleasure. - Gene Perret
- Grandmothers are just 'antique' little girls. - Author Unknown
- Perfect love sometimes does not come until the first grandchild. - Welsh Proverb
- A grandmother is a babysitter who watches the kids instead of the television. - Author Unknown
- Never have children - only grandchildren!- Gore Vidal

- Becoming a grandmother is wonderful. One moment you're just a mother. The next you are all-wise and prehistoric. - Pam Brown
- Grandchildren don't stay young forever, which is good because Grandfathers have only so many horsey rides in them. - Gene Perret
- When grandparents enter the door, discipline flies out the window. - Ogden Nash
- Grandma always made you feel she had been waiting to see just you all day and now the day as complete. - Marcy DeMaree
- Grandmas never run out of hugs or cookies. - Author unknown
- Grandmas hold our tiny hands for just a little while, but our hearts forever. - Author Unknown
- If I had known how wonderful it would be to have grandchildren, I'd have had them first. - Lois Wyse
- My grandkids believe I'm the oldest thing in the world. And after two or three hours with them, I believe it, too. - Gene Perret
- If becoming a grandmother was only a matter of choice, I should advise every one of you straight away to become one. There is no fun for old people like it! - Hannah Whithall Smith
- It's such a grand thing to be a mother of a mother - that's why the world calls her grandmother. - Author Unknown
- Grandchildren are God's way of compensating us for growing old. - Mary H. Waldrip
- You do not really understand something unless you can explain it to your grandmother. - Proverb
- An hour with your grandchildren can make you feel young again. Anything longer than that and you start to age quickly. - Gene Perret
- The best baby-sitters of course, are the baby's grandparents. You feel completely comfortable entrusting your baby to them for long periods, which is why most grandparents flee to Florida. - Dave Barry
- I wish I had the energy that my grandchildren have - if only for self-defence. - Gene Perret
- Grandmother-grandchild relationships are simple. Grandmas are short on criticism and long on love. - Author Unknown
- Nobody can do for little children what grandparents do. Grandparents sort of sprinkle stardust over the lives of little children. - Alex Haley

- Grandmother - A wonderful mother with lots of practice. - Author Unknown
- A grandparent is old on the outside but young on the inside. - Author Unknown
- One of the most powerful handclasps is that of a new grandbaby around the finger of a grandfather. - Joy Hargrove
- It's amazing how grandparents seem so young once you become one. - Author Unknown
- If your baby is 'beautiful *and perfect, never cries or fusses, sleeps on schedule and burps on demand, an angel all the time,'* you're the grandma. - Teresa Bloomingdale
- Grandparents are similar to a piece of string - handy to have around and easily wrapped around the fingers of their grandchildren. - Author Unknown

'Girl's' Night Out

Last night, my Grannie friends and I went to a Ladies Night Club. One of the girls wanted to impress the rest of us, so she pulled out a $10 bill. When the male dancer came over to us, my friend licked the $10 bill and stuck it to his butt cheek!

Not to be outdone, another friend pulls out a $20 bill. She called the guy back, licks the $20 bill and sticks it to his other butt cheek. In another attempt to impress the rest of us, my third friend pulls out a $50 bill and calls the guy over and licks the $50 bill. I'm worried about the way things are going, but fortunately, she just stuck it on one of his butt cheeks again.

My relief was short-lived. Seeing the way things are going, the guy races over to me. Now everyone's attention is focused on me and the guy is egging me on to try to top the $50. My brain was churning as I reached for my wallet.

What could I do??? The woman in me took over! I got out my ATM card, swiped it down the crack of his butt, grabbed the eighty bucks and left!!

Carnation Milk 70 years ago'

A little old lady from Wisconsin had worked in and around her family dairy farms since she was old enough to walk, with hours of work and little compensation. When canned Carnation Milk became available in grocery stores in the 1940's, she read an advertisement offering $5,000 for the best slogan. The producers wanted a rhyme beginning with *'Carnation Milk is best of all.'*

She thought to herself, I know all about milk and dairy farms. I can do this! She sent in her entry and several weeks later, a black limo pulled up in front of her home. A man got out and said, *'Carnation loved your entry so much! We are here to award you $2,000 even though we will not be able to use it.'*

Her entry read: *'Carnation milk is best of all, no tits to pull, no hay to haul, no buckets to wash, no shit to pitch - just poke a hole in the son-of-a-bitch.'*

The Hypnotist

It was entertainment night at the Old Folks home. Claude the hypnotist exclaimed: *'I'm here to put you into a trance; I intend to hypnotise each and every member of the audience.'*

The excitement was almost electric as Claude withdrew a beautiful antique pocket watch from his coat.

'I want you each to keep your eye on this antique watch. It's a very special watch. It's been in my family for six generations.'

He began to swing the watch gently back and forth while quietly chanting, *'Watch the watch, watch the watch and watch the watch.'*

The crowd became mesmerised as the watch swayed back and forth, light gleaming off its polished surface. Hundreds of pairs of eyes followed the swaying watch, until, suddenly, it slipped from the hypnotist's fingers and fell to the floor, breaking into a hundred pieces.

'SHIT!' said the Hypnotist.

It took three days to clean up the Old Folks home.

Makin' Woopie

Two elderly residents, a man and a woman, are sitting alone in the lobby of their nursing home one evening. The old man looks over and says to the old lady, *'I know just what you want and for $5 I'll have sex with you right over there in that rocking chair.'*

The old lady looks surprised but doesn't say a word.

The old man continues, *'For $10 I'll do it with you on the nice soft sofa by the window, but for $20 I'll take you back to my room, light some candles and give you the most romantic evening you've ever had in your life.'*

The old lady still says nothing but after a couple of moments, starts digging down in her purse. She pulls out a wrinkled $20 and holds it up.

'So you want the nice romantic evening in my room,' says the old man.

'Get serious.' she says, *'Four times in the rocker.'*

Older women are so reasonable

After being married for 44 years, I took a careful look at my wife one day and said, *'Forty-four years ago we had a cheap apartment, a cheap car, slept on a sofa bed and watched a ten-inch black and white TV, but I got to sleep every night with a hot twenty-five-year-old girl. Now I have a $1,500,000.00 home, a $45,000.00 car, a nice big bed and plasma screen TV, but I'm sleeping with a sixty-five-year-old woman. It seems to me that you're not holding up your side of things.'*

My wife is a very reasonable woman ... She told me to go out and find a hot twenty-five-year-old girl and she would make sure that I would once again live in a cheap apartment, drive a cheap car, sleep on a sofa bed and watching a ten-inch black and white TV.

Aren't older women great? They really know how to solve your mid-life crises.

The Ring

An older, white haired man walked into a jewellery store a Friday evening, with a beautiful much younger gal at his side. He told the jeweller he was looking for a special ring for his girlfriend. The jeweller looked through his stock and brought out a $5,000 ring.

The old man said, *'No, I'd like to see something more special.'*

At that statement, the jeweller went to his special stock and brought another ring over. *'Here's a stunning ring at only $40,000'* the jeweller said.

The lady's eyes sparkled and her whole body trembled with excitement. The old man seeing this said, *'We'll take it.'*

The jeweller asked how payment would be made and the old man stated: *'By check. I know you need to make sure my check is good, so I'll write it now and you can call the bank Monday to verify the funds and I'll pick the ring up Monday afternoon.'*

On Monday morning, the jeweller angrily phoned the old man and said *'There's no money in that account.'*

'I know,' said the old man, *'but let me tell you about my great weekend!'*

See ... Not all seniors are senile!

Grandpa's Bet

The ATO (Australian Taxation Office) decides to audit Grandpa and summons him to the ATO office. The ATO auditor was not surprised when Grandpa showed up with his lawyer.

The auditor said, *'Well, sir, you have an extravagant lifestyle and no full-time employment, which you explain by saying that you win money gambling. I'm not sure the ATO finds that believable.'*

'I'm a great gambler and I can prove it,' says Grandpa. *'How about a demonstration?'*

The auditor thinks for a moment and said, *'Okay. Go ahead.'*

Grandpa says, *'I'll bet you a thousand dollars that I can bite my own eye.'*

The auditor thinks a moment and says, *'It's a bet.'*

Grandpa removes his glass eye and bites it. The auditor's jaw drops.

Grandpa says, *'Now, I'll bet you two thousand dollars that I can bite my other eye.'*

Now the auditor can tell Grandpa isn't blind, so he takes the bet. Grandpa removes his dentures and bites his good eye.

The stunned auditor now realises he has wagered and lost three grand, with Grandpa's lawyer as a witness. He starts to get nervous.

'Want to go double or nothing?' Grandpa *asks 'I'll bet you six thousand dollars that I can stand on one side of your desk and pee into that wastebasket on the other side and never get a drop anywhere in between.'*

The auditor, twice burned, is cautious now, but he looks carefully and decides there's no way this old guy could possibly manage that stunt, so he agrees again.

Grandpa stands beside the desk and unzips his pants, but although he strains mightily, he can't make the stream reach the wastebasket on the other side, so he pretty much urinates all over the auditor's desk.

The auditor leaps with joy, realising that he has just turned a major loss into a huge win. But Grandpa's own attorney moans and puts his head in his hands.

'Are you okay?' the auditor asks.

'Not really,' says the attorney.

'This morning, when Grandpa told me he'd been summoned for an audit, he bet me twenty-five thousand dollars that he could come in here and pee all over your desk and that you'd be happy about it!'

Aids warning!

Senior citizens are the nation's leading carriers of aids!

- Hearing aids
- Band aids
- Roll aids
- Walking aids
- Medical aids
- Government aids
- Most of all, Monetary aid to their kids!
- Not forgetting HIV (Hair is Vanishing)

Your Yearly Dementia Test

It's that time of year to take our annual senior citizen test. Exercise of the brain is as important as exercise of the muscles. As we grow older, it's important to keep mentally alert ... If you don't use it, you lose it! Below is a very private way to gauge your loss or non-loss of intelligence.

Take the test presented here to determine if you're losing it or not. The spaces below are so you don't see the answers until you've made your answer. Okay, relax, clear your mind and begin.

1. What do you put in a toaster?
   Answer: 'bread.' If you said 'toast,' give up now and do something else.
   Try not to hurt yourself. If you said, bread, go to:
2. Say ' silk' five times. Now spell 'silk.' What do cows drink?
   Answer: Cows drink water. If you said 'milk,' don't attempt the next question. Your brain is over-stressed and may even overheat. Content yourself with reading a more appropriate literature such as Auto World. However, if you said 'water', proceed to:
3. If a red house is made from red bricks and a blue house is made from blue bricks and a pink house is made from pink bricks and a black house is made from black bricks, what is a green house made from?
   Answer: Greenhouses are made from glass. If you said 'green bricks,' why are you still reading these? If you said 'glass,' go on to:
4. It's thirty years ago and a plane is flying at 20,000 feet over Germany (If you will recall, Germany at the time was politically divided into West Germany and East Germany).

Anyway, during the flight, two engines fail. The pilot, realising that the last remaining engine is also failing, decides on a crash landing procedure. Unfortunately the engine fails before he can do so and the plane fatally crashes smack in the middle of 'no man's land' between East Germany and West Germany. Where would you bury the survivors? East Germany, West Germany or no man's land'?
Answer: You don't bury survivors. If you said ANYTHING else, you're a dunce and you must stop. If you said, 'You don't bury survivors', proceed to the next question.

5. Without using a calculator - You are driving a bus from London to Milford Haven in Wales. In London, 17 people get on the bus. In Reading, six people get off the bus and nine people get on. In Swindon, two people get off and four get on. In Cardiff, 11 people get off and 16 people get on. In Swansea, three people get off and five people get on. In Carmathen, six people get off and three get on. You then arrive at Milford Haven. What was the name of the bus driver?
Answer: Oh, for crying out loud! Don't you remember your own name? It was YOU!!

Health Care

You're a sick senior citizen and the government says there is no nursing home available for you. What do you do?

The new plan would put pensioners in jail and the criminals in a nursing home. It gives anyone 65 years or older (you) a gun and four bullets and you would be allowed to shoot two members of parliament and two illegal immigrants! Of course, this means you will be sent to prison where you will get three meals a day, a roof over your head, central heating, air conditioning, access to showers, hobbies and walks and all the health care you need!

Need a prescription, dental and medical treatment? Need new teeth? - No problem. Need glasses? - Great. Need new hip, knees, kidney, lungs and heart? All covered. You'd have constant video monitoring so if assistance was needed you'd have immediate help.

Bedding would be washed twice a week and all clothing would be washed and ironed as needed. There would be an attendant to check you every twenty minutes and staff to bring your meals and snacks to your cell. And you will be given free condoms - Yipeee.

You would have a private, secure room with an exercise outdoor yard, with gardens for anyone who felt the need to exercise.

And your kids can come and visit you as often as they do now.

You would have access to a library, weight room, spiritual counselling, pool and education. Simple clothing, shoes, slippers, PJ's and legal aid would be free on request.

Each senior would have a PC and TV, radio and daily phone calls and there would be a board of directors to hear complaints and all guards would have a code of conduct that would have to be strictly adhered to.

Criminals would get cold food, be left all alone and unsupervised day and night. Lights off at 8 pm and showers once a week; live in a tiny room and pay $1,000 per week without any hope of ever getting out.

And who would be paying for all of this? The same government that just told you that they cannot afford for you to go into a home. Plus, because you are a prisoner, you don't have to pay income tax any more.

Is this a great country or what?

Here's another alternative

Check into a Holiday Inn! With the average cost for a nursing home care costing $188.00 per day, there is a better way when we get old and too feeble. I've already checked on reservations at the Holiday Inn. For a combined long term stay discount and senior discount, it's $59.23 per night.

Breakfast is included and some have happy hours in the afternoon. That leaves $128.77 a day for lunch and dinner in any restaurant we want or room service, laundry, gratuities and special TV movies. Plus, they provide a spa, swimming pool, a workout room, a lounge and washer-dryer, etc.

Most have free toothpaste and razors and all have free shampoo and soap. $5 worth of tips a day you'll have the entire staff scrambling to help you.

TV broken? Light bulbs need changing? Need a mattress replaced? No problem. They fix everything and apologise for the inconvenience. The Inn has a night security person and daily room service. The maid checks to see if you are okay. If not, they'll call an ambulance ... or the undertaker.

If you fall and break a hip, Medicare will pay for the hip and Holiday Inn will upgrade you to a suite for the rest of your life.

They treat you like a customer, not a patient. There's a city bus stop out front and seniors ride free. The handicap bus will also pick you up (if you fake a decent limp). To meet other nice people, call a church bus on Sundays.

For a change of scenery, take the airport shuttle bus and eat at one of the nice restaurants there. While you're at the airport, fly somewhere. Otherwise, the cash keeps building up.

It takes months to get into decent nursing homes. Holiday Inn will take your reservation today. And you're not stuck in one place forever - you can move from Inn to Inn or even from city to city. Want to see Hawaii? They have Holiday Inns there too.

Tell me this won't happen to me

An elderly Floridian called 911 on her cell phone to report that her car has been broken into. She is hysterical as she explains her situation to the dispatcher*: 'They've stolen the stereo, the steering wheel, the brake pedal and even the accelerator!'* she cried.

The dispatcher said, *'Stay calm. An officer is on the way.'*

A few minutes later, the officer radios in. *'Disregard.'* He says. *'She got in the back-seat by mistake.'*

Family

Three sisters ages 92, 94 and 96 live in a house together. One night the 96 year old draws a bath. She puts her foot in and pauses. She yells to the other sisters, *'Was I getting in or out of the bath?'*

The 94 year old yells back, *'I don't know. I'll come up and see.'* She starts up the stairs and pauses *'Was I going up the stairs or down?'*

The 92 year old is sitting at the kitchen table having tea listening to her sisters. She shakes her head and says, *'I sure hope I never get that forgetful, knock on wood.'*

She then yells, *'I'll come up and help both of you as soon as I see who's at the door.'*

My Years of Job Hunting

1. My first job was working in an Orange Juice factory, but I got canned. Couldn't concentrate.
2. Then I worked in the woods as a Lumberjack, but just couldn't hack it, so they gave me the axe.
3. After that, I tried being a Tailor, but wasn't suited for it - mainly because it was a sew-sew job.
4. Next, I tried working in a Muffler Factory, but that was too exhausting.

5. Then, tried being a Chef - figured it would add a little spice to my life, but just didn't have the thyme.
6. Next, I attempted being a Deli Worker, but any way I sliced it ... I couldn't cut the mustard.
7. My best job was a Musician, but eventually found I wasn't noteworthy.
8. I studied a long time to become a Doctor, but didn't have any patience.
9. Next, was a job in a Shoe Factory. Tried hard but just didn't fit in.
10. Then I became a Professional Fisherman, but discovered that I couldn't live on my net income.
11. Managed to get a good job working for a Pool Maintenance Company, but the work was just too draining.
12. So then I got a job in a Gymnasium/Workout Centre, but they said I wasn't fit for the job.
13. After many years of trying to find steady work, I finally got a job as a Historian - until I realised there was no future in it.
14. My last job was working in Starbucks, but had to quit because it was the same old grind.
15. So this year, I tried Retirement and ... guess what ... I found that I'm perfect for the job. There's no better feeling than going to bed at night and not having to set an alarm for tomorrow Super sex

A little old lady was running up and down the halls in a nursing home. As she ran, she would flip up the hem of her nightgown and say *'Super sex.'*

She walked up to an elderly man in a wheelchair flipping her gown at him, she said, *'Super sex.'*

He sat silently for a moment or two and finally answered, *'I'll just take the soup.'*

Down at the retirement center

80-year old Bessie bursts into the rec room at the retirement home. She holds her clenched fist in the air and announces, *'Anyone who can guess what's in my hand can have sex with me tonight!!'*

An elderly gentleman in the rear shouts out, *'An elephant?'*

Bessie thinks a minute and says, *'Close enough.'*

Three old ladies were sitting side by side in their retirement home reminiscing. The first lady recalled shopping at the green grocers and demonstrated with her hands, the length and thickness of a cucumber she could buy for a penny.

The second old lady nodded, adding that onions used to be much bigger and cheaper also and demonstrated the size of two big onions she could buy for a penny a piece.

The third old lady remarked, *'I can't hear a word you're saying, but I remember the guy you're talking about.'*

The Importance of walking

- Walking can add minutes to your life. This enables you at 85 years old to spend an additional 5 months in a nursing home at $4,000 per month.
- I like long walks, especially when they are taken by people who annoy me.
- The only reason I would take up walking is so that I could hear heavy breathing again.
- I joined a health club last year, spent about 250 bucks. Haven't lost a pound. Apparently you have to go there!
- Every time I hear the dirty word 'exercise,' I wash my mouth out with chocolate.
- I do have flabby thighs, but fortunately my stomach covers them.
- The advantage of exercising every day is so when you die, they'll say, *'Well, he looks good doesn't he.'*
- If you are going to try cross-country skiing, start with a small country.
- I know I got a lot of exercise the last few years ... just getting over the hill.
- We all get heavier as we get older, because there's a lot more information in our heads. That's my story and I'm sticking to it. And:
- Every time I start thinking too much about how I look, I just find a pub with a Happy Hour and by the time I leave, I look just fine.
- I have to walk early in the morning, before my brain figures out what I'm doing.

Old friends

Two elderly ladies had been friends for many decades. Over the years, they had shared all kinds of activities and adventures. Lately, their activities had been limited to meeting a few times a week to play cards.

One day, they were playing cards when one looked at the other and said, *'Now don't get mad at me. I know we've been friends for a long time but I just can't think of your name! I've thought and thought, but I can't remember it. Please tell me what your name is.'*

Her friend glared at her. For at least three minutes she just stared and glared at her. Finally she said, *'How soon do you need to know?'*

Senior driving

As a senior citizen was driving down the freeway, his car phone rang. Answering, he heard his wife's voice urgently warning him, *'Herman, I just heard on the news that there's a car going the wrong way on Interstate 77. Please be careful!'*

'Hell,' said Herman, *'It's not just one car. It's hundreds of them!'*

Two elderly women were out driving in a large car; both could barely see over the dashboard. As they were cruising along, they came to an intersection. The stoplight was red, but they just went on through. The woman in the passenger seat thought to herself *'I must be losing it. I could have sworn we just went through a red light.'*

After a few more minutes, they came to another intersection and the light was red again. Again, they went right through. The woman in the passenger seat was almost sure that the light had been red but was really concerned that she was losing it. She was getting nervous at the next intersection and sure enough, the light was red and they went on through. So, she turned to the other woman and said, *'Mildred, did you know that we just ran through three red lights in a row? You could have killed us both!'*

Mildred turned to her and said, *'Oh! Am I driving?'*

Fender skirts

I came across this phrase yesterday *'fender skirts.'* A term I haven't heard in a long time and thinking about *'fender skirts'* started me thinking about other words that quietly disappear from our language with hardly a notice like *'curb feelers'* and *'steering knobs.'* (AKA) *'suicide knob or Necker's Knobs.'*

Since I'd been thinking of cars, my mind naturally went that direction first. Any kids will probably have to find some elderly person over 60 to explain some of these terms to you.

Remember 'Continental kits?' They were rear bumper extenders and spare tire covers that were supposed to make any car as cool as a Lincoln Continental.

When did we quit calling them *'emergency brakes?'* At some point *'parking brake'* became the proper term. But I miss the hint of drama that went with *'emergency brake.'*

I'm sad, too, that almost all the old folks are gone who would call the accelerator the *'foot pedal.'* Many today do not even know what a *'clutch'* is or that the *'dimmer switch'* used to be on the floor. Didn't you ever wait at the street for your daddy to come home, so you could ride the *'running board'* up to the house?

Here's a phrase I heard all the time in my youth but never any more - *'store-bought.'* Of course, just about everything is store-bought these days. But once it was bragging material to have a store-bought dress or a store-bought bag of candy.

'Coast to coast' is a phrase that once held all sorts of excitement and now means almost nothing. Now we take the term *'world-wide'* for granted. This floors me.

On a smaller scale, *'wall-to-wall'* was once a magical term in our homes. In the '50s, everyone covered his or her hardwood floors with, wow, *wall-to-wall carpeting!* Today, everyone replaces their wall-to-wall carpeting with hardwood or timber floors. Go figure.

When's the last time you heard the quaint phrase *'in a family way?'* It's hard to imagine that the word *'pregnant'* was once considered a little too graphic, a little too clinical for use in polite company, so we had all that talk about *'stork visits'* and *'being in a family way'* or simply *'expecting.'*

Apparently *'brassiere'* is a word no longer in usage. I said it the other day and my daughter cracked up. I guess it's just *'bra'* now. *'Unmentionables'* probably wouldn't be understood at all.

I always loved going to the *'picture show,'* but I considered *'movie'* an affectation.

Most of these words go back to the '50s, but here's a pure-'60s word I came across the other day - *'rat fink.'* Ooh, what a nasty put-down!

Here's a word I miss - *'percolator.'* That was just a fun word to say. And what was it replaced with? *'Coffee maker.'* How dull. Mr. Coffee, I blame you for this.

I miss those made-up marketing words that were meant to sound so modern and now sound so retro. Words like *'Dyna Flow'* and *'Electrolux.'* Introducing the 1963 Admiral TV, now with *'Spectra Vision!'*

Food for thought - Was there a telethon that wiped out *'lumbago?'* Nobody complains of that anymore. Maybe that's what castor oil cured, because I never hear mothers threatening kids with *'castor oil'* any more.

Some words aren't gone, but are definitely on the endangered list. The one that grieves me most, *'supper.'* Now everybody says *'dinner.'* Save a great word. Invite someone to supper and discuss fender skirts.

Smart ass

Two businessmen in were sitting down for a break in their soon-to-be-opened new store. As yet, the store wasn't ready, with only a few shelves set up.

One said to the other, *'I bet any minute now some senior is going to walk by, put his face to the window and ask what we're selling.'*

No sooner were the words out of his mouth when, sure enough, a curious senior walked to the window, had a peek and in a soft voice asked, *'What are you selling' here?'*

One of the men replied sarcastically, *'We're selling ass holes.'*

Without skipping a beat, the old timer said, *'Must be doing well ... Only two left.'*

Seniors - don't mess with them!

My Forgetter

My forgetter's getting better, but my rememberer is broke.
To you that may seem funny, but to me, that is no joke.
For when I'm 'here' I'm wondering if I really should be 'there.'
And, when I try to think it through, I haven't got a prayer!
Oft times I walk into a room, say, *'What am I here for?'*
I wrack my brain, but all in vain a zero, is my score.
At times I put things away where they are safe, but, Gee the person it is safest from is generally me!
When shopping, I may see someone, say *'Hi'* and have a chat, then, when the person walks away,
I ask myself, *'Who the Hell was that?'*
Yes, my forgetter's getting better while my rememberer is broke and it's driving me plumb crazy and that isn't any joke!

A Well-Planned Retirement (From the Bristol Evening Post)

Outside England's Bristol Zoo there is a parking lot for 150 cars and 8 coaches. For 23 years, its parking fees were managed by a very pleasant attendant. The fees were £1 for cars £5 for coaches.

On Monday, June 1st, after 23 solid years of never missing a day of work, he just didn't show up; so the Zoo Management called the Bristol City Council and asked them to send them a replacement parking attendant.

The Council did some research and replied that the parking lot was the Zoo's own responsibility.

The Zoo said *'The attendant was employed by the City Council ... wasn't he?'*

The Council said *'What attendant? We've never had an attendant for the zoo on the City payroll.'*

Gone missing from his home is a man who has been taking daily the car park fees amounting to about £400 per day for the last twenty-three years ...! Total sum just short £2.9 million.

Meanwhile, sitting in his villa somewhere on the coast of Spain (or some such scenario) is a man who'd apparently had a ticket machine installed completely on his own; and then had simply begun to show up every day, commencing to collect and keep the parking fees. And no one even knows his name.

Now that's a long-term pension plan that worked!

Wal Mart Applicant

Below is an actual job application that this 75 year old senior citizen submitted to Wal Mart in California. They hired him because he was so funny.

- Name: Kenneth Way (Grumpy Old Bastard.)
- Sex: Not lately, but I am looking for the right woman (or at least one who will cooperate.)
- Desired Position: Company President or Vice President. But seriously, whatever's available. If I was in a position to be picky, I wouldn't be applying here in the first place
- Desired Salary: $185,000 a year plus stock options and a Michael Ovitz style severance package. If that's not possible, make an offer and we can haggle.
- Education: Yes.
- Last Position Held: Target for middle management hostility.
- Previous salary: A lot less than I'm worth.

- Most notable achievement: My incredible collection of stolen pens and post-it notes.
- Reason for leaving: It sucked.
- Hours available to work: Any.
- Preferred Hours: 1:30-3:30 pm Monday, Tuesday and Thursday.
- Do you have any special skills? Yes, but they're better suited to a more intimate environment.
- May we contact your current employer? If I had one, would I be here?
- Do you have any physical conditions that would prohibit you from lifting up to 50 lbs? Of what?
- Do you have a car? I think the more appropriate question here would be 'Do you have a car that runs?'
- Do you smoke? On the job - no! On my breaks - yes!
- Nearest Relative: 7 miles
- Have you received any special awards or recognition? I may already be a winner of the Publishers Clearing House Sweepstakes, so they tell me.
- What would you like to be doing in five years? Living in the Bahamas with a fabulously wealthy dumb sexy blonde supermodel who thinks I'm the greatest thing since sliced bread. Actually, I'd like to be doing that now.
- Do you certify that the above is true and complete to the best of your knowledge? Oh yes, absolutely.

Old People Rock!

Remember your specs!!!

Yesterday my daughter asked why I didn't do something useful with my time. She suggested I go down to the senior centre and hang out with the guys.

I did this and when I got home last night I told her that I had joined a parachute club.

She said *'Are you nuts? You're almost 70 years old and you're going to start jumping out of airplanes?'*

I proudly showed her that I even got a membership card.

She said to me, *'You idiot, where are your glasses! This is a membership to a Prostitute Club, not a Parachute Club!'*

I'm in trouble again and don't know what to do! I signed up for five jumps a week! Life as a senior citizen is not getting any easier.

Old is just old - Old is not dumb

A strong young man at a construction site was bragging that he could out-do anyone in a feat of strength. He made a special case of making fun of one of the older workmen.

After several minutes, the older worker had enough.

'Why don't you put your money where your mouth is,' he said.

'I'll bet a week's wages that I can haul something in a wheelbarrow over to that building that you won't be able to wheel back.'

'You're on, old man,' the braggart replied. *'Let's see you do it.'*

The old man reached out and grabbed the wheelbarrow by the handles. Then, nodding to the young man, he said, *'All right, Dummy, get in.'*

As the saying goes, Old age and treachery will beat youth and skill every time.

'Old' is when:

- Your sweetie says, *'Let's go upstairs and make love,'* and you answer, *'Pick one; I can't do both!'*
- Your friends compliment you on your new alligator shoes and you're barefoot.
- Going bra-less pulls all the wrinkles out of your face.
- You don't care where your spouse goes, just as long as you don't have to go along.
- You are cautioned to slow down by the doctor instead of by the police.
- *'Getting a little action'* means you don't need to take a laxative today.
- *'Getting lucky'* means you find your car in the parking lot.
- An *'all nighter'* means not getting up to use the bathroom.
- You're not sure if these are facts or jokes.

Drafting Guys over 60

New Direction for any war: Send Service Vets over 60!

I am over 60 and the Armed Forces think I'm too old to track down terrorists. You can't be older than 42 to join the military. They've got the whole thing ass-backwards. Instead of sending 18-year olds off to fight, they ought to take us old guys. You shouldn't be able to join a military unit until you're at least 35.

For starters:

Researchers say 18-year-olds think about sex every 10 seconds. Old guys only think about sex a couple of times a day, leaving us more than 28,000 additional seconds per day to concentrate on the enemy.

Young guys haven't lived long enough to be cranky and a cranky soldier is a dangerous soldier. *'My back hurts! I can't sleep, I'm tired and hungry'* We are impatient and maybe letting us kill some asshole that desperately deserves it will make us feel better and shut us up for a while.

An 18-year-old doesn't even like to get up before 10 am. Old guys always get up early to pee so what the hell. Besides, like I said, *'I'm tired and can't sleep and since I'm already up, I may as well be up killing some fanatical s-of-a-b....'*

If captured we couldn't spill the beans because we'd forget where we put them. In fact, name, rank and serial number would be a real brainteaser.

Boot camp would be easier for old guys. We're used to getting screamed and yelled at and we're used to soft food. We've also developed an appreciation for guns. We've been using them for years as an excuse to get out there and do some hunting.

They could lighten up on the obstacle course however. I've been in combat and didn't see a single 20-foot wall with rope hanging over the side, nor did I ever do any push-ups after completing basic training.

Actually, the running part is kind of a waste of energy, too. I've never seen anyone outrun a bullet.

An 18-year-old has the whole world ahead of him. He's still learning to shave, to start up a conversation with a pretty girl. He still hasn't figured out that a baseball cap has a brim to shade his eyes, not the back of his head.

These are all great reasons to keep our kids at home to learn a little more about life before sending them off into harm's way.

Let us old guys track down those dirty rotten coward terrorists. The last thing an enemy would want to see is a couple of million pissed off old farts with attitudes and automatic weapons who know that their best years are already behind them.

And how about recruiting Women with PMS??? You think Men have attitudes!!! Ohhhhhhhhhhhh!!!

If nothing else, put us on border patrol ... we would have it secured the first night!

Ramblings of a Retired Mind

I was thinking about how a status symbol of today is those cell phones that everyone has clipped onto their belt or purse. I can't afford one. So, I'm wearing my garage door opener.

I also made a cover for my hearing aid and now I have what I think they call blue teeth.

You know, I spent a fortune on deodorant before I realised that people didn't like me anyway.

I was thinking that women should put pictures of missing husbands on beer cans!

I was thinking about old age and decided that old age is *'when you still have something on the ball, but you are just too tired to bounce it.'*

I thought about making a fitness movie for folks my age and call it *'Pumping Rust'*.

I've gotten that dreaded furniture disease. That's when your chest is falling into your drawers!

When people see a cat's litter box, they always say, *'Oh, have you got a cat?'* Just once I want to say, *'No, it's for company!'*

Employment application blanks always ask who is to be notified in case of an emergency. I think you should write, *'A Good Doctor!'*

I was thinking about how people seem to read the Bible a whole lot more as they get older. Then, it dawned on me. They were cramming for their finals. As for me, I'm just hoping God grades on the curve.

Lovemaking tips for seniors

1. Wear your glasses to make sure your partner is actually in the bed.
2. Set timer for 3 minutes, in case you doze off in the middle.
3. Set the mood with lighting. (Turn them ALL OFF!)
4. Make sure you put the emergency number on your speed dial before you begin.
5. Write partner's name on your hand in case you can't remember.
6. Use extra polygrip so your teeth don't end up under the bed.
7. Have Tylenol ready in case you actually complete the act.
8. Make all the noise you want ... the neighbours are deaf, too.
9. If it works, call everyone you know with the good news!!
10. Don't even think about trying it twice.

An Elderly Irish Virgin

In a tiny village on the Irish coast lived an old lady, a virgin and very proud of it. Sensing that her final days were rapidly approaching and desiring to make sure everything was in proper order when she dies, she went to the town's undertaker (who also happened to be the local postal clerk) to make proper 'final' arrangements. As a last wish, she informed the Undertaker that she wanted the following inscription engraved on her tombstone: ***'Born a virgin, lived as a virgin, died a virgin.'***

Not long after, the old maid died peacefully. A few days after the funeral, as the undertaker/postal clerk went to prepare the tombstone that the lady had requested. It became quite apparent that the tombstone she had selected was much too small for the wording that she had chosen.

He thought long and hard about how he could fulfil the old maid's final request considering the very limited space available on the small piece of stone. For days, he agonised over the dilemma, but finally his experience as a postal worker allowed him to come up with what he thought was the appropriate solution to the problem.

The virgin's tombstone was finally completed and duly engraved and it read as follows: ***'Returned - Unopened'***

Being Healed

Grandma and grandpa were watching a religious healing program on TV. The evangelist called to all who wanted to be healed, to put one hand on the TV and the other on the body part they wanted healed. Grandma hobbled to the TV and put one hand on the TV and the other on her arthritic hip. Grandpa made his way to the set and put one hand on the TV and the other on his crotch.

Grandma looked at him with disgust: *'you just don't understand, you old coot. The purpose of this program is to heal the sick, not raise the dead.'*

As I Mature:

- I've learned that you cannot make someone love you. All you can do is stalk them and hope they panic and give in.
- It's important to have a twinkle in your wrinkles.
- Age is mind over matter. If you don't mind, it doesn't matter.
- I've learned that no matter how much I care, some people are just assholes.

- I've learned that it takes years to build up trust and only takes suspicion, not proof, to destroy it.
- I've learned that you can get by on charm for about fifteen minutes. After that, you'd better have a big willy or huge boobs.
- I've learned that you shouldn't compare yourself to others - they are more screwed up than you think.
- I've learned that we are responsible for what we do, unless we are celebrities.
- I've learned that regardless of how hot and steamy a relationship is at first, the passion fades and there had better be a lot of money to take its place!
- I've learned that 99% of the time when something isn't working in your home, one of your kids did it.
- I've learned that the people you care most about in life are taken from you too soon and all the less important ones just never go away.

Advice to an Old Guy

An old guy (not in the best of shape) was working out in the gym when he spotted a sweet young thing. He asked the trainer that was nearby, *'What machine in here should I use to impress that sweet thing over there?'*

The trainer looked him up and down and said, *'I'd try the ATM in the lobby'*

One night, an 87-year-old woman came home from Bingo to find her 92-year-old husband in bed with another woman. She became violent and ended up pushing him off the balcony of their 20th floor apartment, killing him instantly.

Brought before the court, on the charge of murder, she was asked if she had anything to say in her own defence.

'Your Honour,' she began coolly, *'I figured that at 92, if he could screw, he could fly.'*

An old lady was standing at the railing of the cruise ship holding her hat on tightly so that it would not blow off in the wind.

A gentleman approached her and said: *'Pardon me, madam. I do not intend to be forward, but did you know that your dress is blowing up in this high wind?'*

'Yes, I know,' said the lady, *'I need both hands to hold onto this hat.'*

'But, madam, you must know that your privates are exposed!' said the gentleman in earnest.

The woman looked down, then back up at the man and replied, *'Sir anything you see down there is 85 years old. I just bought this hat yesterday!*

A Doctor was addressing a large audience in Tampa. *'The material we put into our stomachs is enough to have killed most of us sitting here, years ago. Red meat is awful. Soft drinks corrode your stomach lining. Chinese food is loaded with MSG. High fat diets can be disastrous and none of us realises the long-term harm caused by the germs in our drinking water.*

However, there is one thing that is the most dangerous of all and we all have eaten or will eat it. Can anyone here tell me what food it is that causes the most grief and suffering for years after eating it?'

After several seconds of quiet, a 75-year-old man in the front row raised his hand and softly said, *'Wedding Cake.'*

Bob, a 70-year-old, extremely wealthy widower, shows up at the Country Club with a breathtakingly beautiful and very sexy 25-year-old blonde-haired woman who knocks everyone's socks off with her youthful sex appeal and charm and who hangs over Bob's arm and listens intently to his every word. His buddies at the club are all aghast.

At the very first chance, they corner him and ask, *'Bob, how'd you get the trophy girlfriend?'* Bob replies, *'Girlfriend? She's my wife!'*

They are knocked over, but continue to ask. *'So, how'd you persuade her to marry you?'*

'I lied about my age', Bob replies.

'What? Did you tell her you were only 50?'

Bob smiles and says, *'No, I told her I was 90.'*

Groups of Americans were travelling by tour bus through Holland. As they stopped at a cheese farm, a young guide led them through the process of cheese making, explaining that goat's milk was used. She showed the group a lovely hillside where many goats were grazing.

'These' she explained, *'Are the older goats put out to pasture when they no longer produce.'*

She then asked, *'What do you do in America with your old goats?'*

A spry old gentleman answered, *'They send us on bus tours!'*

Because they had no reservations at a busy restaurant, my elderly neighbour and his wife were told there would be a 45-minute wait for a table. *'Young man, we're both 90 years old,'* the husband said, *'We may not have 45 minutes.'* They were seated immediately.

Question: Where can single men over the age of 60 find younger women who are interested in them?
Answer: Try a bookstore, under fiction.

Question: What can a man do while his wife is going through menopause?
Answer: Keep busy. If handy with tools, you can finish the basement. When done, you have a place to live.

Question: Someone has told me that menopause is mentioned in the bible. Is that true? Where is it?
Answer: Yes: Matthew 14.92: 'And Mary rode Joseph's ass all the way to Egypt.'

Question: How can I increase the heart rate of my over 60-year-old mate?
Answer: Tell him you're pregnant.

Question: How can I avoid that terrible curse of unsightly wrinkles?
Answer: Take off your glasses.

Question: Seriously! What can I do for those crow's feet and all those wrinkles on my fade?
Answer: Go braless. It will usually pull them out.

Question: Why should 60-plus people use valet parking?
Answer: Valets don't forget where they park your car.

Question: Is it common for 60-plus year olds to have problems with short term memory storage?
Answer: Storing memory is not the problem - retrieving it is the problem.

Question: As people age, do they sleep more soundly?
Answer: Yes, but usually in the afternoon.

Question: Where should 60-plus year olds look for eyeglasses?
Answer: On their foreheads.

Question: What is the most common remark made by 60-plus year olds when they enter antique stores?

Answer: *'Gosh I remember all these!'*

Q. Half of all Americans live within 50 miles of what?
A. Their birthplace.

Q. Most boat owners name their boats. What is the most popular boat name requested?
A. Obsession.

Q. If you were to spell out numbers, how far would you have to go until you would find the letter 'A'?
A. One thousand.

Q. What do bulletproof vests, fire escapes, windshield wipers and laser printers have in common?
A. All were invented by women.

Q. What is the only food that doesn't spoil?
A. Honey.

Q. Which day are there more collect calls than any other day of the year?
A. Father's Day.

Been in jail

Russ and Sam, two friends, met in the park every day to feed the pigeons, watch the squirrels and discuss world problems. One day Russ didn't show up. Sam didn't think much about it and figured maybe he had a cold or something. But after Russ hadn't shown up for a week or so, Sam really got worried. However, since the only time they ever got together was at the park, Sam didn't know where Russ lived, so he was unable to find out what had happened to him.

A month had passed and Sam figured he had seen the last of Russ, until one day, Sam approached the park and - lo and behold! - there sat Russ! Sam was very excited and happy to see him and told him so. Then he said, *'For crying out loud Russ, what in the world happened to you?'*

Russ replied, *'I have been in jail.'*

'Jail!' cried Sam. *'What in the world for?'*

'Well,' Russ said, *'You know Sue, that cute little blonde waitress at the coffee shop where I sometimes go?'*

'Yeah,' said Sam, *'I remember her. What about her?'*

'Well, one day she filed rape charges against me; and, at 89 years old, I was so proud that when I got into court, I pled 'guilty.'

'The damned judge gave me 30 days for perjury.'

Test Tickets

A Kiwi was in Australia to watch an upcoming Rugby Test match, for which he had tickets. He wasn't feeling well, so he decided to see a doctor. *'Hey doc, I dun't feel so good, ey'* said Wiremu.

The doctor gave him a thorough examination and informed Wiremu that he had long existing and advanced prostate problems and that the only cure was testicular removal.

'No way doc' replied Wiremu *'I'm gitting a sicond opinion!'*

The second Aussie doctor gave Wiremu the same diagnosis and also advised him that testicular removal was the only cure. Not surprisingly he refused the treatment.

Wiremu was devastated, but with the rugby match just around the corner he found an expat Kiwi doctor working in Australia and decided to get one last opinion from someone he could trust. The Kiwi doctor examined him and said: *'Wiremu Cuzzy Bro, you huv prostate suckness ey'*

'What's the cure thin doc?' asked Wiremu hoping for a different answer.

'Wull, Wiremu,' said the Kiwi doctor *'Wi're gonna huv to cut off your balls.'*

'Phew, thunk God for thut!' said Wiremu, *'Those Aussie bastards wanted to take my test tickets off me!'*

[I apologise to all the Kiwi's out there - but it is a cute joke!]

Deserted Island

Abe and Esther are flying to Australia for a two-week vacation to celebrate their 40th anniversary. Suddenly, over the public address system, the Captain announces, *'Ladies and Gentlemen, I am afraid I have some very bad news. Our engines have ceased functioning and we will attempt an emergency landing. Luckily, I see an uncharted island below us and we should be able to land on the beach. However, the odds are that we may never be rescued and will have to live on the island for the rest of our lives!'*

Thanks to the skill of the flight crew, the plane lands safely on the island. An hour later Abe turns to his wife and asks, *'Esther, did we pay our $5,000 PBS pledge cheque yet?'*

'No, sweetheart,' she responds.

Abe, still shaken from the crash landing, then asks, *'Esther, did we pay our American Express card yet?'*

'Oh, no! I'm sorry. I forgot to send the cheque,' she says.

'One last thing, Esther. Did you remember to send cheques for the Visa and MasterCard this month?' he asks.

'Oh, forgive me, Abe,' begged Esther. *'I didn't send that one, either.'*

Abe grabs her and gives her the biggest kiss in 40 years. Esther pulls away and asks him, *'What was that for?'*

Abe answers, *'They'll find us!'*

Obituary

Today we mourn the passing of a beloved old friend, Common Sense who has been with us for many years. No one knows for sure how old he was since his birth records were long ago lost in bureaucratic red tape. He will be remembered as having cultivated such valuable lessons as: Knowing when to come in out of the rain and why the early bird gets the worm; Life isn't always fair; and maybe it was my fault.

Common Sense lived by simple, sound financial policies: (Don't spend more than you can earn) and reliable strategies: (Adults, not children, are in charge).

His health began to deteriorate rapidly when well-intentioned but overbearing regulations were set in place. Reports of a 6-year old boy charged with sexual harassment for kissing a classmate; teens suspended from school for using mouthwash after lunch; and a teacher fired for reprimanding an unruly student, only worsened his condition.

Common Sense lost ground when parents attacked teachers for doing the job that they themselves had failed to do in disciplining their unruly children. It declined even further when schools were required to get parental consent to administer sun lotion or an Aspirin to a student; but could not inform parents when a student became pregnant and wanted to have an abortion.

Common Sense lost all the will to live as the churches became businesses and criminals received better treatment than their victims. Common Sense took a beating when you couldn't defend yourself from a burglar in your own home and the burglar could sue for assault.

Common Sense finally gave up the will to live after a woman failed to realise that a steaming cup of coffee was hot. She spilled it on her lap and was awarded a huge settlement.

Common Sense was preceded in death by his parents; Truth and Trust; by his wife Discretion; by his daughter Responsibility and his son Reason. He is survived by his four stepbrothers:

I know my rights!
I want it NOW!
Someone else is to blame; and
I am a victim.

Not many attended his funeral because so few realised he was gone. If you still remember him, pass this on. If not, join the majority and do nothing.

Recently, I was diagnosed with A.A.A.D.D

[Age Activated Attention Deficit Disorder]

Thank goodness there's a name for this disorder. Somehow I feel better even though I have it!! This is how it manifests:

I decide to water my garden. As I turn on the hose in the driveway, I look over at my car and decide it needs washing. As I start toward the garage, I notice mail on the porch table that I brought up from the mail box earlier. I decide to go through the mail before I wash the car. I lay my car keys on the table, put the junk mail in the garbage can under the table and notice that the can is full. So, I decide to put the bills back on the table and take out the garbage first.

But then I think, since I'm going to be near the mailbox when I take out the garbage anyway, I may as well pay the bills first. I take my cheque book off the table and see that there is only one cheque left. My extra cheques are in my desk in the study, so I go inside the house to my desk where I find the can of Pepsi I'd been drinking. I'm going to look for my cheques, but first I need to push the Pepsi aside so that I don't accidentally knock it over. The Pepsi is getting warm and I decide to put it in the refrigerator to keep it cold.

As I head toward the kitchen with the Pepsi, a vase of flowers on the counter catches my eye - they need water. I put the Pepsi on the counter and discover my reading glasses that I've been searching for all morning. I decide I better put them back on my desk, but first I'm going to water the flowers.

I set the glasses back down on the counter, fill a container with water and suddenly spot the TV remote. Someone left it on the kitchen table. I realise that tonight when we go to watch TV, I'll be looking for the remote, but I won't remember that it's on the kitchen table, so I decide to put it back in the den where it belongs, but first I'll water the flowers. I pour some water in the flowers, but quite a bit of it spills on the floor.

So, I set the remote back on the table, get some towels and wipe up the spill. Then, I head down the hall trying to remember what I was planning to do. At the end of the day:

- The car isn't washed
- The bills aren't paid
- There is a warm can of Pepsi sitting on the counter
- The flowers don't have enough water
- There is still only one check in my cheque book
- I can't find the remote (God forbid!)
- I can't find my glasses and
- I don't remember what I did with the car keys.

Then, when I try to figure out why nothing got done today, I'm really baffled because I know I was busy all day and I'm really tired. I realise this is a serious problem and I'll try to get some help for it, but first I'll check my e-mail ...

Do me a favour. Forward this message to everyone you know, because I don't remember who I've sent it to. Don't laugh - if this isn't you yet, your day is coming!

Senior Ladies!!

Remember, a layer of dust protects the wood beneath it. A house becomes a home when you can write *'I love you'* on the furniture.

I used to spend at least eight hours every weekend making sure things were just perfect *'in case someone came over.'* Finally I realised one day that no-one came over; they were all out living life and having fun!

NOW, when people visit, I don't have to explain the *'condition'* of my home. They are more interested in hearing about the things I've been doing while I was away living life and having fun. If you haven't figured this out yet, please heed this advice.

Life is short. Enjoy it!

Dust if you must, but wouldn't it be better to paint a picture or write a letter, bake cookies or a cake and lick the spoon or plant a seed. Ponder the difference between want and need?

Dust if you must, but there's not much time, with wine to drink, rivers to swim and mountains to climb, music to hear and books to read, friends to cherish and life to lead.

Dust if you must, but the world is out there with the sun in your eyes, the wind in your hair, a flutter of snow, a shower of rain. This day will not come around, again.

Dust if you must, but bear in mind, old age will come and it's not kind. And when you go - and go you must - you, yourself will make more dust!

Five Old Ladies

Sitting on the side of the highway waiting to catch speeding drivers, a Police Officer sees a car puttering along at 22 kph. Says he to himself: *'This driver is just as dangerous as a speeder!'* So he turns on his lights and pulls the driver over. Approaching the car, he notices that there are five old ladies - two in the front seat and three in the back - wide eyed and white as ghosts.

The driver, obviously confused, says to him *'Officer, I don't understand, I was doing exactly the speed limit! What seems to be the problem?'*

'Ma'am,' the officer replies, *'You weren't speeding, but you should know that driving slower than the speed limit can also be a danger to other drivers.'*

'Slower than the speed limit? No sir, I was doing the speed limit exactly twenty-two kilometres an hour!' the old woman says a bit proudly.

The Police officer, trying to contain a chuckle explains to her that 22 is the highway number, not the speed limit.

A bit embarrassed, the woman grins and thanks the officer for pointing out her error.

'But before I let you go, Ma'am, I have to ask. Is everyone in this car okay? These women seem awfully shaken and they haven't made a peep this whole time,' the officer asks.

'Oh, they'll be all right in a minute officer. We just got off Highway 189.'

Dead son

When the police arrived, they found a very upset senior mother who explained that she had just found her son Marcus dead in his chair as he watched TV. She had been out buying vegetables to put in with the roast that was cooking in the oven.

The police inspected the scene and determined that her son had been murdered - that he'd been hit with a smooth but hard weapon.

The mother rallied and automatically prepared her veggies and added them to the roast.

It took a long time for the forensic team to finish their investigation and the aroma of the cooking dinner was decidedly enticing, so when the mother invited the remaining two officers to enjoy the food with her, they decided to please her and tucked into the delicious meal.

After they left, the old woman chuckled to herself as she washed the dishes. Her son Marcus had been abusing her for years and she'd finally had enough. She had taken a frozen leg of lamb out of the freezer and while he watched TV she bashed him on the head with it, then calmly put the roast in the oven and went shopping for the veggies. Imagine - she served the murder weapon to the police for dinner!

Where I've been:

I have been in many places, but I've never been in **Cahoots**. Apparently, you can't go alone. You have to be in **Cahoots** with someone.

I have also never been in **Cognito**. I hear no one recognises you there.

I have, however, been in **Sane**. They don't have an airport; you have to be driven there. I have made several trips there, thanks to my friends, family and work.

I would like to go to **Conclusions**, but you have to jump and I'm not too much on physical activity any more since my knee replacements.

I have also been in **Doubt**. That is a sad place to go and I try not to visit there too often.

I have been in **Flexible**, but only when it was very important to stand firm.

Sometimes I'm in **Capable and** I go there more often as I'm getting older.

One of my favourite places to be is in **Suspense**! It really gets the adrenalin flowing and pumps up the old heart! At my age I need all the stimuli I can get.

The Neighbour

Tom had been in Police work for twenty-five years. Finally sick of the stress, he quit his job and bought fifty acres of land in Western Australia as far from humanity as possible. He sees the postman once a week and gets groceries once a month. Otherwise, it's total peace and quiet. After six months or so of almost total isolation, someone knocks on his door. He opens it and a huge, bearded man is standing there.

'Name's Cliff, your neighbour from forty miles up the road. Having a Christmas party Friday night. Thought you might like to come at about 5:00'

'Great,' says Tom, *'After six months out here I'm ready to meet some local folks. Thank you.'*

As Cliff is leaving, he stops. *'Gotta warn you. Be some drinking'.'*

'Not a problem' says Tom. *'After 25 years in the business, I can drink with the best of 'em'.*

Again, the big man starts to leave and stops. *'More 'n' likely gonna be some fighting' too.'*

'Well, I get along with people, I'll be all right! I'll be there. Thanks again.'

'More'n likely be some wild sex, too,'

'Now that's really not a problem' says Tom, warming to the idea. *'I've been all alone for six months! I'll definitely be there. By the way, what should I wear?'*

'Don't much matter. Just gonna be the two of us.'

Crabby old man

When an old man died in the geriatric ward of a small hospital near Tampa, Florida, it was believed that he had nothing left of any value. Later, when the nurses were going through his meagre possessions, they found this poem. Its quality and content so impressed the staff that copies were made and distributed to every nurse in the hospital. And this little old man, with nothing left to give to the world is now the author of this 'anonymous' poem winging across the Internet.

What do you see nurses? What do you see?
What are you thinking, when you're looking at me?
A crabby old man, not very wise,
Uncertain of habit, with faraway eyes?
Who dribbles his food and makes no reply.
When you say in a loud voice, *'I do wish you'd try!'*
Who seems not to notice .the things that you do.
And forever is losing a sock or a shoe?
Who, resisting or not, lets you do as you will,
With bathing and feeding, the long day to fill?
Is that what you're thinking? Is that what you see?

Then open your eyes, nurse, you're not looking at me.
I'll tell you who I am as I sit here so still,
As I do what you're bidding, as I eat at your will.
I'm a small child of ten, with a father and mother,
Brothers and sisters who love one another.
A young boy of sixteen with wings on his feet
Dreaming that soon now. a lover he'll meet.
A groom soon at twenty, my heart gives a leap.
Remembering, the vows that I promised to keep.
At twenty-five, now, I have young of my own.
Who need me to guide and a secure, happy home.
A man of thirty, my young now grown fast,
Bound to each other with ties that should last.
At forty, my young sons have grown and are gone,
But my woman's beside me, to see I don't mourn.
At fifty, once more, babies play 'round my knee,
Again, we know children, my loved one and me.
Dark days are upon me, my wife is now dead.
I look at the future, I shudder with dread.
For my young are all rearing young of their own.
And I think of the years and the love that I've known.
I'm now an old man and nature is cruel.
'Tis jest to make old age look like a fool.
The body, it crumbles, grace and vigour, depart.
There is now a stone, where I once had a heart.
But inside this old carcass, a young guy still dwells,
And now and again, my battered heart swells
I remember the joys, I remember the pain.
And I'm loving and living, life over again.
I think of the years, all too few, gone too fast.
And accept the stark fact that nothing can last.
So open your eyes, people, open and see
Not a crabby old man.
Look closer - see ... ME!!

Remember this poem when you next meet an older person who you might brush aside without looking at the young soul within. We will all, one day, be there, too!

Looking for Grandma

The computer swallowed Grandma,
Yes, honestly it's true!

She pressed 'control' and 'enter'
And disappeared from view.

It devoured her completely,
The thought just makes me squirm.
She must have caught a virus
Or been eaten by a worm.

I've searched through the recycle bin,
And files of every kind;
I've even used the Internet,
But nothing did I find.

In desperation, I asked Mr. Google
My searches to refine.
The reply from him was negative,
Not a thing was found 'online.'

So, if inside your 'Inbox,'
My grandma you should see,
Please 'Copy, Scan and Paste' her.
And send her back to me.

This is a tribute to all the Grandmas and Grandpas, Nannas and Popps, who have been fearless and learned to use the Computer … They are the greatest!!

BLONDE

A Wise Old Biker

A crusty old biker out on a long summer ride in the country pulls up to a tavern in the middle of nowhere; parks his bike and walks inside. As he passes through the swinging doors, he sees a sign hanging over the bar:

- Cold beer: $2.00
- Hamburger: $2.25
- Cheeseburger: $2.50
- Chicken sandwich: $3.50
- Hand job: $50.00

Checking his wallet to be sure he has the necessary payment, the old biker walks up to the bar and beckons to the exceptionally attractive blonde female bartender who is serving drinks to a couple of sun-wrinkled farmers. She glides down behind the bar to the old biker.

'Yes?' she inquires with a wide, knowing smile, *'May I help you?'*

The old biker leans over the bar, *'I was wondering young lady,'* he whispers, *'Are you the one who gives the hand-jobs?'*

She looks into his eyes with that wide smile and purrs *'Why yes, yes, I sure am.'*

The old biker leans closer and into her left ear whispers softly, *'Well, wash your hands real good, cause I want a cheeseburger.'*

Blonde Girl

A girl came skipping home from school one day.

'Mommy, Mommy,' she yelled, *'we were counting today and all the other kids could only count to four, but I counted to 10. See? 1, 2, 3, 4, 5, 6, 7, 8, 9. 10!'*

'Very good,' said her mother.

'Is it because I'm blonde, Mommy?'

'Yes, It's because you're blonde.'

The next day the girl came skipping home from school. *'Mommy, Mommy,'* she yelled, *'We were saying the alphabet today and all the other kids could only say it to D, but I said it to G. See? A, B, C, D, E, F, G!'*

'Very good,' said her mother.

'Is it because I'm blonde, Mommy?'

'Yes, it's because you're blonde.'

The next day the girl came skipping home from school. *'Mommy, Mommy,'* she yelled *'We were in gym class today and when we showered, all the other girls have flat chests, but I have these!'* And she lifted her tank top to reveal a pair of 36c's.

'Very good,' said her embarrassed mother.

'Is it because I'm blonde, Mommy?'

'No, honey. It's because you're 24!'

Crocodile Shoes

A blonde was on vacation and driving through Darwin. She desperately wanted to take home a pair of genuine crocodile shoes but was very reluctant to pay the high prices the local vendors were asking. After becoming very frustrated with the 'no haggle on prices' attitude of one of the shopkeepers, the blonde shouted, *'Well then, maybe I'll just go out and catch my own crocodile, so I can get a pair of shoes for free.'*

The shopkeeper said with a sly, knowing smile, *'Little lady, just go and give it a try!'*

The blonde headed out toward the river, determined to catch a crocodile! Later in the day, as the shopkeeper is driving home, he pulls over to the side of the bank where he spots the same young woman standing waist deep in the murky water, shotgun in hand. Just then, he spots a huge three metre croc swimming rapidly toward her. With lightning speed, she takes aim, kills the creature and hauls it onto the slimy banks of the river. Lying nearby were seven more of the dead creatures, all lying on their backs. The shopkeeper stood on the bank, watching in silent amazement. The blonde struggled and flipped the croc onto its back.

Rolling her eyes heavenward and screaming in great frustration, she shouts out, *'Sh*t, Sh*t, Sh*t, This one's barefoot too!'*

Idiotic 'millionaire' contestant makes worst use of lifelines ever

In New York, Idaho resident Kathy Evans brought humiliation to her friends and family when she set a new standard for stupidity with her appearance on the popular TV show, *'Who wants to be a millionaire.'*

It seems that Evans, a 32-year-old wife and mother of two, got stuck on the first question and proceeded to make what fans of the show are dubbing *'the absolute worst use of lifelines ever.'* After being introduced to the show's host Meredith Vieira, Evans assured her that she was ready to play, whereupon she was posed with an extremely easy $100 question. The question was: *'Which of the following is the largest?'*

a) A Peanut
b) An Elephant
c) The Moon
d) Hey, who you calling large?

Immediately Mrs. Evans was struck with an all consuming panic as she realised that this was a question to which she did not readily know the answer. *'Hmm, oh boy, that's a toughie,'* said Evans, as Vieira did her level best to hide her disbelief and disgust. *'I mean, I'm sure I've heard of some of these things before, but I have no idea how large they would be.'*

Evans made the decision to use the first of her three lifelines, the 50/50. Answers a) and d) were removed, leaving her to decide which was bigger, an elephant or the moon. However, faced with an incredibly easy question, Evans still remained unsure.

'Oh! It removed the two I was leaning towards!' exclaimed Evans. *'Darn. I think I better phone a friend.'*

Using the second of her two lifelines on the first question, Mrs. Evans asked to be connected with her friend Betsy, who is an office assistant.

'Hi Betsy! How are you? This is Kathy! I'm on TV!' said Evans, wasting the first seven seconds of her call. *'Ok, I got an important question. Which of the following is the largest? b) an elephant or c) the moon. 15 seconds hun.'*

Betsy quickly replied that the answer was c) the moon. Evans proceeded to argue with her friend for the remaining ten seconds.

'Come on Betsy, are you sure?' asked Evans.

'How sure are you? Duh, that can't be it.'

To everyone's astonishment, the moronic Evans declined to take her friend's advice and pick *'The Moon.'*

'I just don't know if I can trust Betsy. She's not all that bright. So I think I'd like to ask the audience,' said Evans.

Asked to vote on the correct answer, the audience returned 98% in favour of answer c), 'The Moon.' Having used up all her lifelines, Evans then made the dumbest choice of her life.

'Wow, seems like everybody is against what I'm thinking,' said the too-stupid-to-live Evans. *'But you know, sometimes you just got to go with your gut. So, let's see. For which is larger, an elephant or the moon, I'm going to have to go with b) an elephant. Final answer.'*

Evans sat before the dumbfounded audience, the only one waiting with bated breath and was told that she was wrong and that the answer was in fact, c) *'The Moon.'*

[We never did find out whether she was a blonde!]

Death Row

There was a German, an American and a blonde Australian on death row. The Warden gave them a choice of three ways to die:

1) be shot;
2) be hung; or
3) be injected with the AIDS virus.

So the German said, *'Shoot me right in the head.'* Boom! He was dead instantly.

Then the American said, *'Just hang me.'* Snap! He was dead instantly.

Then the Australian said, *'Give me some of that AIDS stuff!'*

They gave him his injection and he fell down laughing. The guards looked at each other and wondered what was wrong with this guy.

Then the Australian said, *'Give me another one of those shots.'* So the guards did. Now he was laughing so hard he almost was peeing in his pants.

So finally the Warden said, *'What the hell is wrong with you?'*

The Australian replied *'You guys are so stupid. I'm wearing a condom!'*

Two Hunters

Two hunters were out in the woods when one of them collapses. He doesn't seem to be breathing and his eyes are glazed. The other guy (a blonde) takes out his phone and calls the emergency services.

He gasps: *'My friend is dead. What can I do?'*

The operator replies, *'Calm down. I can help. First, let's make sure he's dead.'*

There is a silence and then a gunshot is heard.

Back on the phone, the guy says, *'Okay. Now what?'*

Horse Ride

A blonde decides to try horseback riding, even though she has had no lessons or prior experience. She mounts the horse, unassisted and the horse immediately springs into action. As it gallops along at its steady and rhythmic pace, the blonde begins to slip from the saddle.

In terror, she grabs for the horse's mane, but cannot seem to get a firm grip. She tries to throw her arms around the horse's neck, but despite her best efforts, slides down the horse's flanks. The horse continues to gallop along, seemingly oblivious to its slipping rider. Finally, giving up her frail grip, the blonde attempts to leap away from the horse and throw herself to safety. Unfortunately, her foot has become entangled in the stirrup.

She is now at the mercy of the horse's pounding hooves as her head is struck against the ground time and time again.

As her head is battered against the ground, she is mere moments away from unconsciousness when to her great fortune, Frank, the Woolworth's trolley boy, sees her dilemma and unplugs the horse.

The Blonde Mortician

A man who'd just died is delivered to a local mortuary wearing an expensive, expertly tailored black suit. The female blonde mortician asks the deceased's wife how she would like the body dressed. She points out that the man does look good in the black suit he is already wearing. The widow, however, says that she always thought her husband looked his best in blue and that she wants him in a blue suit. She gives the Blonde mortician a blank check and says, *'I don't care what it costs, but please have my husband in a blue suit for the viewing.'*

The woman returns the next day for the wake. To her delight, she finds her husband dressed in a gorgeous blue suit with a subtle chalk stripe; the suit fits him perfectly. She says to the mortician, *'Whatever this cost, I'm very satisfied. You did an excellent job and I'm very grateful. How much did you spend?*

To her astonishment, the blonde mortician presents her with the blank check.

'There's no charge,' she says.

'No, really, I must compensate you for the cost of that exquisite blue suit!' she says.

'Honestly, ma'am,' the blonde says, *'it cost nothing. You see, a deceased gentleman of about your husband's size was brought in shortly after you left yesterday and he was wearing an attractive blue suit. I asked his wife if she minded him going to his grave wearing a black suit instead and she said it made no difference as long as he looked nice. So I just switched the heads.'*

[Bet you didn't see that coming!!!]

Ace Hardware

'Hi Mom!'

'Hi Sally, where are you? I thought you were with your father at the Ace Hardware.'

'Yeah we were, but I got arrested and they've let me make one phone call.'

'What happened?'

'Oh, I punched this African-American woman in the head.'

'What on earth happened? Why did you do that?'

'Well it wasn't my fault. Dad told me to find a Black & Decker.'

Leaving the office early

Three girls all worked in the same office with the same female boss. Each day, they noticed the boss left work early. One day the girls decided that when the boss left, they would leave right behind her. After all, she never called or came back to work, so how would she know they went home early?

The brunette was thrilled to be home early. She did a little gardening, spent playtime with her son and went to bed early.

The redhead was elated to be able to get in quick workout at the spa before meeting dinner date.

The blonde was happy to get home early and surprise her husband, but when she got to her bedroom, she heard a muffled noise from inside. Slowly and quietly, she cracked open the door and was mortified to see her husband in bed with her lady boss!! Gently, she closed the door and crept out of her house.

The next day, at their coffee break, the brunette and redhead planned to leave early again and they asked the blonde if she was going to go with them.

'No way,' the blonde exclaimed. *'I almost got caught yesterday!'*

Mailman's last day

It was the mail man's last day on the job after 35 years of carrying the mail through all kinds of weather to the same neighbourhood. When he arrived at the first house on his route he was greeted by the whole family there, who congratulated him and sent him on his way with a big gift envelope.

At the second house they presented him with a box of fine cigars. The folks at the third house handed him a selection of terrific fishing lures.

At the fourth house he was met at the door by a strikingly beautiful blonde in a revealing negligee. She took him by the hand, gently led him through the door (which she closed behind him) and led him up the stairs to the bedroom where she blew his mind with the most passionate love he had ever experienced.

When he had enough they went downstairs, where she fixed him a giant breakfast: eggs, potatoes, ham, sausage, blueberry waffles and fresh-squeezed orange juice. When he was truly satisfied she poured him a cup of steaming coffee. As she was pouring, he noticed a dollar bill sticking out from under the cup's bottom edge.

'All this was just too wonderful for words,' he said, *'but what's the dollar for?'*

'Well,' she said, *'last night, I told my husband that today would be your last day and that we should do something special for you. I asked him what to give you.'*

He said, *'Screw him - give him a dollar.'*

The blonde then blushed and said, *'The breakfast was my idea.'*

Ahh to be

During a recent password audit, it was found that a blond female employee was using the following password:

MickeyMinniePlutoHueyLouieDeweyDonaldGoofySacramento

When asked why such a long password, she said she was told that it had to be at least eight characters long and include at least one capital.

Cooter and Gome (Two male blondes)

Stanley died in a fire and his body was burned pretty badly. The morgue needed someone to identify the body, so they sent his two best friends, Cooter and Gomer. The three men had always done everything together.

Cooter arrived first and when the mortician pulled back the sheet, Cooter said, *'Yup, his face is burned up pretty bad. You better roll him over.'*

The mortician rolled him over and Cooter said, *'Nope, ain't Stanley.'*

The mortician thought this was rather strange. So he brought Gomer in to confirm the identity of the body.

Gomer looked at the body and said, *'Yup, he's pretty well burnt up. Roll him over.'*

The mortician rolled him over and Gomer said, *'No, it ain't Stanley.'*

The mortician asked, *'How can you tell?'*

Gomer said, *'Well, Stanley had two assholes.'*

'What? He had two assholes?' asked the mortician.

'Yup, we never seen 'em, but everybody used to say: 'There's Stanley with them two assholes.'

Crabs

A lawyer boarded an airplane in New Orleans with a box of frozen crabs and asked a blonde stewardess to take care of them for him. She took the box and promised to put it in the crew's refrigerator onboard.

He advised her that he was holding her personally responsible for them staying frozen, mentioning in a very haughty manner that he was a lawyer and proceeded to rant at her about what would happen if she let them thaw out.

Needless to say, she was annoyed by his behaviour.

Shortly before landing in New York, she used the intercom to announce to the entire cabin, *'Would the gentleman who gave me the crabs in New Orleans, please raise your hand?'*

Not one person's hand went up, so she took them home and ate them.

Two lessons here:

1. Lawyers aren't as smart as they think they are.
2. Blonds aren't as dumb as most folks think they are.

Trucker's Breakfast

A trucker came into a truck stop cafe and placed his order. He said, *'I want three flat tires, a pair of headlights and a pair of running boards.'*

The brand new blonde waitress, not wanting to appear stupid, went into the kitchen and said to the cook, *'This guy out there just ordered three flat tires, a pair of headlights and a pair of running boards. What does he think this place is? An auto parts store?'*

'No,' the cook said. *'Three flat tires ... means three pancakes; a pair of headlights is two eggs sunny side up; and a pair of running boards ... are two slices of crisp bacon!'*

'Oh, ... Okay!' said the blonde. She thought about it for a moment and then spooned up a bowl of beans and gave it to the customer.

The trucker asked, *'What are the beans for Blondie?'*

She replied, *'I thought while you were waiting for the flat tires, headlights and running boards, you might as well gas up!'*

Golf Balls

A man entered the bus with both front pockets full of golf balls and sat beside a beautiful (you guessed it) blonde. The puzzled blonde kept looking at him and his bulging pockets.

Finally, he said, *'It's golf balls.'*

Nevertheless, the blonde continued to look at him. Finally not being able to contain her curiosity any longer, she asked; *'Does it hurt as much as tennis elbow?'*

TGIF

A Blonde goes over to her friend's house wearing a TGIF tee-shirt.

'Why are you wearing a Thank God It's Friday tee-shirt on Monday?'

'Oh crap!' the blonde says ... *'I didn't realise it was a religious T-shirt. I thought it meant Tits Go In Front.'*

Naked Blonde

A naked and drunken woman boards a taxi in London one night. The driver keeps staring and does not start the taxi.

The woman sneers: *'Haven't you ever seen a naked woman before?'*

Driver: *'I'm not staring at you lady ... I'm just wondering where you're storing the money to pay me.'*

Judge Judy

Judge Judy asks the prostitute, *'So when did you realise you were raped?'*

The prostitute replies while wiping away her tears, *'When the cheque bounced.'*

Buying Christmas Cards

A blonde goes to the post office to buy stamps for Christmas cards. She says to the clerk, *'May I have 50 Christmas stamps please?'*

The clerk replies, *'Which denomination?'*

The blonde says, *'Good God help us. Has it come to this? Okay - give me 22 Catholic, 12 Presbyterian, 10 Lutheran and 6 Baptist.'*

Housework

One day my housework-challenged husband decided to wash his sweatshirt. Seconds after he stepped into the laundry room, he shouted to me, *'What setting do I use on the washing machine?'*

'It depends,' I replied. *'What does it say on your shirt?'*

He yelled back, *'OHIO STATE!'*

And they say blondes are dumb ...

MISCELLANEOUS

Under the kilt

A Scotsman is sitting in a bar in Cuba and is minding his business when a man with a large black beard walks in. The man goes to the bar and orders a shot of whisky. The bartender serves him; the man drinks the whisky then starts walking out the door.

The bartender says, *'Hey aren't you going to pay for that?'*

The man says, *'Excuse me, Castro's Army.'*

The bartender says, *'All right then.'* and the man leaves.

A few minutes later another man with a large black beard walks in. The man goes to the bar and orders a shot of whisky. The bartender serves him; the man drinks the whisky then starts walking out the door.

The bartender says, *'Hey aren't you going to pay for that?'*

The man says, *'Excuse me, Castro's Army.'*

The bartender says *'All right then.'* and the man leaves.

The Scotsman gets an idea and walks up to the bar and orders a shot of whisky. He drinks the whisky then starts walking out the door.

The bartender says, *'Hey aren't you going to pay for that?'*

The Scotsman says, *'Excuse me, Castro's Army.'*

The bartender says, *'Hey where is your big black beard?'*

The Scotsman thinks quickly. He lifts his Kilt and says, *'Secret Service!'*

One day a Scotsman, who had been stranded on a deserted island for over 10 years, saw a speck on the horizon. He thought to himself, *'It's certainly not a ship.'* And, as the speck got closer and closer, he began to rule out the possibilities of a small boat or even a raft.

Suddenly there emerged from the surf a wet-suited black clad figure. Putting aside the scuba gear and the top of the wet suit, there stood a drop-dead gorgeous blonde! The glamorous blonde strode up to the stunned Scotsman and said to him, *'Tell me. How long has it been since you've had a cigarette?'*

'Ten years,' replied the amazed Scotsman. With that, she reached over and unzipped a waterproofed pocket on the left sleeve of her wet suit and pulled out a fresh pack of cigarettes. He takes one, lights it and takes a long drag. *'Aye,'* said the man, *'that is so good I'd almost forgotten how great a smoke can be!'*

'And how long has it been since you've had a drop of good Scotch whiskey?' asked the blonde.

Trembling, the castaway replied, *'Ten years.'*

Hearing that, the blonde reaches over to her right sleeve unzips a pocket and removes a flask and hands it to him. He opened the flask and took a long drink. *''Tis nectar of the gods!'* stated the Scotsman. '*Tis truly fantastic!!!'*

At this point the gorgeous blonde started to slowly unzip the long front of her wet suit, right down the middle. She looked at the trembling man and asked, *'and how long has it been since you played around?'*

With tears in his eyes, the Scotsman fell to his knees and sobbed; *'Sweet Jesus! Don't tell me you've got golf clubs in there too!'*

Scottish compassion

A man was sitting on a blanket at the beach. He had no arms and no legs.

Three women, from England, Wales and Scotland, were walking past and felt sorry for the poor man.

The English woman said, *'Have you ever had a hug?'*

The man said, *'No,'* so she gave him a hug and walked on.

The Welsh woman said, *'Have you ever had a kiss?'* The man said, *'No,'* so she gave him a kiss and walked on.

The Scottish woman came to him and said, *'ave ya ever been fooked laddie?'*

The man broke into a big smile and said, *'No.'*

She said, *'Aye - Ya will be when the tide comes in.'*

The Outhouse/Biffie/Dunny

They were funny looking buildings, that were once a way of life. If you couldn't sprint the distance, then you really were in strife. They were nailed, they were wired, but were mostly falling down. There was one in every yard, in every house, in every town.

They were given many names, some were even funny, but to most of us, we knew them as the outhouse, biffie or the dunny. I've seen some of them all gussied up, with painted doors and all, but it really made no difference, they were just a port of call.

Now my old man would take a bet, he'd lay an even pound, that you wouldn't make the dunny with them turkeys hangin' round. They had so many uses, these buildings out the back. You could even hide from mother, so you wouldn't get the strap.

That's why we had good cricketers, never mind the bumps. We used the pathway for the wicket and the dunny door for stumps. Now my old man would sit for hours, the smell would rot your socks, He read the daily back to front in that good old thunderbox. And if by chance that nature called sometime through the night, you always sent the dog in first, for there was no flamin' light. And the dunny seemed to be the place where crawlies liked to hide, but never ever showed themselves until you sat inside.

There was no such thing as Sorbent, no tissues there at all, just squares of well read newspaper, a hangin' on the wall. If you had some friendly neighbours, as neighbours sometimes are, you could sit and chat to them, if you left the door ajar.

When suddenly you got the urge and down the track you fled. Then of course the magpies were there to peck you on your head. Then the time there was a wet, the rain it never stopped. If you had an urgent call, you ran between the drops.

The dunny man came once a week, to these buildings out the back and he would leave an extra can, if you left for him a zac. For those of you who've no idea what I mean by a zac, then you're too young to have ever had, a dunny out the back.

For it seems today they call them the bathroom or the loo. If you've never had one out the back, then I feel sorry for you. For it used to be a way of life, to race along the track, to answer natures call, at these buildings out the back.

The Kohl's shopping trip

Clutching their Kohl's shopping bags, Ellen and Kay woefully gazed down at a dead cat in the mall parking lot. Obviously a recent hit - no flies, no smell.

'What business could that poor kitty have had here?' murmured Ellen.

'Come on, Ellen, let's just go.'

But Ellen had already grabbed her shopping bag and was explaining, *'I'll just put my things in your bag and then I'll use this tissue.'*

She dumped her purchases into Kay's bag and then used the tissue paper to cradle and lower the former feline into her own Kohl's bag and cover it.

They continued the short trek to the car in silence, stashing their goods in the trunk.

But it occurred to both of them that if they left Ellen's burial bag in the trunk, warmed by the Texas sunshine while they ate,

Kay's Lumina would soon lose that new-car smell. They decided to leave the bag on top of the trunk and they headed over to K & W Cafeteria.

After they went through the serving line, they sat down at a window table. They had a view of Kay's Chevy with the Kohl's bag still on the trunk but not for long! As they ate, they noticed a woman in a red gingham shirt stroll by their car. She looked quickly this way and that and then took the Kohl's bag without breaking stride. She quickly walked out of their line of vision Kay and Ellen shot each other a wide-eyed look of amazement.

It all happened so fast that neither of them could think how to respond.

'Can you imagine?' finally sputtered Ellen. *'The nerve of that woman!'*

Kay sympathised with Ellen, but inwardly a laugh was building as she thought about the grand surprise awaiting the female thief. Just when she thought she'd have to giggle into her napkin, she noticed Ellen's eyes freeze in the direction of the serving line. Following her gaze, Kay recognised the woman in the red gingham shirt with *The Kohl's bag* hanging from her arm.

She was brazenly pushing her tray toward the cashier. Helplessly they watched the scene unfold: After leaving the register, the woman settled at a table across from theirs, put the bag on an empty chair and began to eat.

After a few bites of baked whitefish and green beans, she casually lifted the bag into her lap to survey her treasure. Looking from side to side, but not far enough to notice her rapt audience three tables over, she pulled out the tissue paper and peered into the bag. Her eyes widened and she began to make a sort of gasping noise. The noise grew.

The bag slid from her lap as she sank to the floor, wheezing and clutching her upper chest. The beverage cart attendant quickly recognised a customer in trouble and sent the busboy to call 911, while she administered the Heimlich manoeuvre.

A crowd quickly gathered that did not include Ellen and Kay, who remained riveted to their chairs for seven whole minutes until the ambulance arrived. In a matter of minutes, the woman with the red gingham shirt emerged from the crowd, still gasping and securely strapped on a gurney.

Two well-trained EMS volunteers steered her to the waiting ambulance, while a third scooped up her belongings. The last they saw of the distressed cat-burglar was as she disappeared behind the ambulance doors, the Kohl's Bag perched on her stomach!!

God does take care of those who do bad things! [And once in a while ... He allows us to witness it!]

Stud Fees

A Missouri farmer in his pickup, drove to a neighbour's and knocked at the door. A boy, about 9, opened the door.

'Is your Dad home?'

'No sir, he isn't; he went to town.'

'Well, is your Mother here?'

'No sir, she went to town with Dad.'

'How about your brother Howard? Is he here?'

'No sir, He went with Mom and Dad.'

The rancher stood there for a few minutes, shifting from one foot to the other and mumbling to himself.

'Is there anything I can do for you? I know where all the tools are, if you want to borrow one or I can give dad a message.'

'Well,' said the rancher uncomfortably, *'I really wanted to talk to your Dad. It's about your brother Howard getting my daughter, Suzie, pregnant."*

The boy thought for a moment. *'You would have to talk to Dad about that. I know he charges $500 for the bull and $50 for the hog, but I don't know how much he charges for Howard.'*

Modern Nursery Rhymes

- Mary had a little pig. She kept it fat and plastered; and when the price of pork went up, she shot the little bastard.
- Mary had a little lamb. Her father shot it dead. Now it goes to school with her, between two hunks of bread.
- Jack and Jill went up the hill to have a little fun. Stupid Jill forgot the pill and now they have a son.
- Simple Simon met a pie man going to the fair. Said Simple Simon to the pie man, *'What have you got there?'* Said the pie man unto Simon, *'Pies, you dumb ass!!'*
- Humpty Dumpty sat on a wall. Humpty Dumpty had a great fall. All the kings' horses and all the kings' men had scrambled eggs, for breakfast again.
- Hay diddle, diddle, the cat took a piddle, all over the bedside clock. The little dog laughed to see such fun then died of electric shock.

- Georgie Porgy pudding and pie; kissed the girls and made them cry. And when the boys came out to play, he kissed them too 'cause he was gay.
- There was a little girl who had a little curl right in the middle of her forehead. When she was good, she was very, very good. But when she was bad, she got a fur coat, jewels, a waterfront condo and a sports car.

The Charlie Schultz Philosophy

The following is the philosophy of Chares Schultz, the creator of the 'Peanuts' comic strip. You don't have to actually answer the questions - just ponder them:

1. Name the five wealthiest people in the world.
2. Name the last five Heisman trophy winners.
3. Name the last five winners of the Miss Universe pageant.
4. Name ten people who have won the Nobel or Pulitzer Prize.
5. Name the last half dozen Academy Award winners for best actor and actress.
6. Name the last decade's worth of Tennis champions.

How did you do? The point is, none of us remembers the headliners of yesterday. These are no second-rate achievers - they are the best in their fields. But the applause dies, awards tarnish, achievements are forgotten, accolades and certificates are buried with their owners. Here's another quiz. See how you do on this one:

1. List a few teachers who aided your journey through school.
2. Name three friends who have helped you through a difficult time.
3. Name five people who have taught you something worthwhile.
4. Think of a few people who have made you feel appreciated and special.
5. Think of five people you enjoy spending time with.

Easier? The lesson:

The people who make a difference in your life are not the ones with the most credentials, the most money ... or the most awards. They're simply the ones who care the most.

Don't worry about the world coming to an end today. It's already tomorrow - in Australia!

'Be yourself. Everyone else is taken!'

Babies' names

Patrick's pregnant sister was in a terrible car accident and went into a deep coma. After being in the coma for nearly six months, she wakes up and sees that she is no longer pregnant.

Frantically, she asks the doctor about her baby.

The doctor replies, *'Ma'am, you had twins ... a boy and a girl. The babies are fine, however, they were poorly at birth and had to be christened immediately so your brother Patrick came in and named them.'*

The woman groans to herself, *'Oh suffering Jesus, no, not me brother, he's a clueless idiot.'*

Expecting the worst, she asks the doctor,*' Well, what's my daughter's name?'*

'Denise' says the doctor.

The new mother is somewhat relieved, *'Wow, that's a beautiful name. I guess I was wrong about my brother,'* she thought *'I really like Denise '*

Then she asks, *'What's the boy's name?'*

The doctor replies *'Denephew.'*

The two brooms

Two brooms were hanging in the closet and after a while they got to know each other so well, they decided to get married. One broom was, of course, the bride broom, the other the groom broom. The bride broom looked very beautiful in her white dress. The groom broom was handsome and suave in his tuxedo. The wedding was lovely.

After the wedding, at the wedding dinner, the bride-broom leaned over and said to the groom-broom, *'I think I am going to have a little broom!'*

'Impossible!' said the groom broom.

Are you ready for this? Brace yourself; this is going to hurt!!

'We haven't even swept together!'

One of the brooms at the reception added, *'I think she must have been sweeping around!'*

[I heard you groaning!]

The Wheelie Bin

A refuse collector is driving along a street picking up the wheelie bins and emptying them into his compactor. He goes to one house where the bin hasn't been left out and in the spirit of kindness and after having a quick look about for the bin, he gets out of his truck goes to the front door and knocks. There's no answer.

Being a kindly and conscientious bloke, he knocks again - much harder. Eventually a Japanese man comes to the door.

'Harro!' says the Japanese man.

'Gidday, mate! Where's ya bin?' asks the collector.

'I bin on toiret,' explains the Japanese bloke, a bit perplexed.

Realising the little foreign fellow had misunderstood him, the bin man smiles and tries again. *'No! No! Mate, where's your wheelie bin?'*

'I dust been to toiret, I toll you!' says the Japanese man, still perplexed.

'Listen,' says the collector. *'You're misunderstanding me.'*

'Where's your 'wheelie' bin?'

'Okay, okay.' replies the Japanese man with a sheepish grin and whispers in the collector's ear, *'I wheelie bin having sex wirra wife's sista!'*

Newfie poetry contest

The National Poetry Contest had come down to two semi-finalists: A Yale graduate and a Newfoundlander. They were given a single word and then allowed two minutes to come up with a poem that contained that word. The word they were given was *'Timbuktu.'*

First to recite his poem was the Yale Graduate. He stepped up to the microphone and said:

'Slowly across the desert sand trekked a lonely caravan, men on camels, two by two destination - Timbuktu!!'

The crowd went crazy! No way could the Newfie top that they thought.

The Newfoundlander calmly made his way to the microphone and recited,

'Me and Tim a huntin' we went, met three whores in a pop-up tent. They was three and we was two so I bucked one and Timbuktu!!'

The Newfie won hands down!!

Newfoundland charm

Two informally dressed ladies happened to start-up a conversation during an endless wait in Toronto's Terminal 3 airport. The first lady was an arrogant Upper Canadian married to a wealthy business man. The second was a well-mannered elderly woman from Bell Island, Newfoundland.

When the conversation cantered on whether they had any children, the Upper Canadian woman started by saying, *'When my first child was born, my husband built a beautiful mansion for me.'*

The lady from Bell Island commented, *'Well, isn't that precious?'*

The first woman continued, *'When my second child was born, my husband bought me a beautiful Mercedes-Benz.'*

Again, the lady from Bell Island commented, *'Well, isn't that precious?'*

The first woman continued boasting, *'Then, when my third child was born, my husband bought me this exquisite diamond bracelet.'*

Yet again, the Bell Island lady commented, *'Well, isn't that precious?'*

The first woman then asked her companion, *'What did your husband buy for you when you had your first child?'*

'My husband sent me to charm school,' declared the Bell Island lady.

'Charm school?' the first woman cried, *'Oh, my Lord! What on earth for?'*

The elderly Bell Island lady responded, *'Well as an example. Instead of saying, Who gives a Damn, I learned to say, Well, isn't that precious ...'*

You can't outsmart a Newfie

Each Friday night after work, sun, snow or rain, Jack, being a Newfie, would fire up his outdoor grill and cook a moose steak. But, all of Jack's neighbours were Catholic. And especially since it was Lent, they were forbidden from eating meat on Friday.

The delicious aroma from the grilled moose steaks was causing such a problem for the Catholic faithful that they finally talked to their priest. The priest came to visit Jack and suggested that he become a Catholic. After several classes and much study, Jack attended Mass and as the priest sprinkled holy water over him, he said: *'You were born a Protestant and raised a Protestant, but now you are a Catholic.'*

Jack's neighbours were greatly relieved, until Friday night arrived and the wonderful aroma of grilled moose filled the neighbourhood. The priest was called immediately by the neighbours and, as he rushed into Jack's yard, clutching a rosary and prepared to scold him, he stopped and watched in amazement.

There stood Jack, clutching a small bottle of holy water which he carefully sprinkled over the grilling meat and chanted: *'You wuz born a Moose, you wuz raised a Moose, but now you is a Codfish.'*

Newfie's Vacation

Paddy and Murphy, two friends from Leading Tickles, Newfoundland, were talking one afternoon when Paddy tells Murphy, *'Ya know, I reckon I'm 'bout ready for a vacation. Only this year I'm gonna do it a little different. The last few years, I took your advice about where to go. Three years ago you said to go to Hawaii. I went to Hawaii and Molly got pregnant.'*

'Then two years ago, you told me to go to the Bahamas and Molly got pregnant again.'

'Last year you suggested Tahiti and darn me, if Molly didn't get pregnant again.'

Murphy asks Paddy, *'So, what you gonna do this year that's different?'*

Paddy says, *'This year I'm taking Molly with me.'*

To Maintain a Healthy Level of Insanity

1. At lunch time, sit in your parked car with sunglasses on and point a hair dryer at passing cars ... See if they slow down.
2. Page yourself over the intercom. Don't disguise your voice.
3. Every time someone asks you to do something, ask them if they want fries with that.
4. Put decaf in the coffee maker for three weeks. Once everyone has gotten over their caffeine addictions, switch to Espresso.
5. In the memo field of all your cheques, write 'for marijuana.'
6. Skip down the hall, rather than walk and see how many looks you get.
7. Order a diet water whenever you go out to eat, with a serious face.
8. Specify that your drive through order is 'to go.'
9. Sing along at the opera.
10. Five days in advance, tell your friends you can't attend their party because you have a headache.
11. When the money comes out of the ATM, scream 'I won, I won.'
12. When Leaving the Zoo, start running towards the parking lot yelling 'Run for your lives! They're loose!'
13. Tell your children over dinner, 'Due to the economy, we are going to have to let one of you go.'

And the final way to keep a healthy level of insanity:

14. Pick up a box of condoms at the pharmacy; go to the counter and ask where the fitting room is.

This was written by a Black gentleman from Texas

- When I was born, I was Black,
- When I grew up, I was Black,
- When I went in the sun, I stayed Black
- When I got cold, I was Black,
- When I was scared, I was Black,
- When I was sick, I was Black,
- And when I die, I'll still be Black.

NOW, you 'white' folks ...

- When you're born, you're Pink,
- When you grow-up, you're White,
- When you go in the sun, you get Red,
- When you're cold, you turn Blue,
- When you're scared, you're Yellow,
- When you get sick, you're Green,
- When you bruise, you turn Purple,
- And when you die, you look Gray.
- So why y'all callin' us Blacks - Coloured Folks?

Bill Cosby

'They're standing on the corner and they can't speak English. I can't even talk the way these people talk:

- Why you ain't,
- Where you is,
- What he drive,
- Where he stay,
- Where he work,
- *Who you be ...*

And I blamed the kid until I heard the mother talk. And then I heard the father talk.

Everybody knows it's important to speak English except these knuckleheads. You can't be a doctor with that kind of crap coming out of your mouth. In fact you will never get any kind of job making a decent living.

People marched and were hit in the face with rocks to get an Education and now we've got these knuckleheads walking around. The lower economic people are not holding up their end in this deal. These people are not parenting. They are buying things for kids. $500 sneakers for what? And they won't spend $200 for Hooked on Phonics.

I am talking about these people who cry when their son is standing there in an orange suit.

Where were you when he was 2?

Where were you when he was 12?

Where were you when he was 18 and how come you didn't know that he had a pistol?

And where is the father? Or who is his father?

People putting their clothes on backward: Isn't that a sign of something gone wrong? People with their hats on backward, pants down around the crack, isn't that a sign of something? Or are you waiting for Jesus to pull his pants up?

Isn't it a sign of something when she has her dress all the way up and got all type of needles [piercing] going through her body? What part of Africa did this come from?

We are not Africans. Those people are not Africans; they don't know a thing about Africa.

I say this all the time. It would be like white people saying they are European-American. That is totally stupid. I was born here and so were my parents and grandparents and, very likely my great grandparents. I don't have any connection to Africa, no more than white Americans have to Germany, Scotland, England, Ireland or the Netherlands. The same applies to 99 percent of all the black Americans as regards to Africa. So stop, already!

With names like Shaniqua, Taliqua and Mohammed and all of that crap ... and all of them are in jail. Brown or black versus the Board of Education is no longer the white person's problem. We have got to take the neighbourhood back.

People used to be ashamed. Today a woman has eight children with eight different 'husbands' - or men or whatever you call them now.

We have millionaire football players who cannot read. We have million-dollar basketball players who can't write two paragraphs. We, as black folks have to do a better job. Someone working at Wal-Mart with seven kids, you are hurting us.

We have to start holding each other to a higher standard. We cannot blame the white people any longer.'

Dr. William Henry 'Bill' Cosby, Jr., Ed.D.

Well said Bill. It's NOT about colour, it's about behaviour!'

Sunny Okanagan - will you come visit?

May 30th:
Just moved to the sunny Okanagan! Now this is the place to live! Beautiful sunny days and warm balmy evenings. What a place! It is beautiful. I've finally found my home. I love it here.

June 14th:
Really heating up, got to 38 Celsius today. Not a problem. Live in an air-conditioned home, drive an air-conditioned car. What a pleasure to see the sun every day like this. I'm turning into a sun worshipper.

June 30th:
Had the backyard landscaped with western plants today, lots of cactus and rocks. What a breeze to maintain. No more mowing lawn for me. Another scorcher today, but I love it here.

July 10th:
The temperature hasn't been below 38 Celsius all week. How do people get used to this kind of heat? At least it's kind of windy though. But getting used to the heat is taking longer than I expected.

July 15th:
Fell asleep by the community pool. Got 3rd degree burns over 60% of my body, missed 3 days of work. What a dumb thing to do. I learned my lesson though, got to respect the ol' sun in a climate like this.

July 20th:
I missed Lomita (my cat) sneaking into the car when I left this morning. By the time I got to the hot car at noon, Lomita had died and swollen up to the size of a shopping bag and stunk up the upholstery. The car now smells like Kibbles and shits. I learned my lesson though. No more pets in this heat.

July 25th:
The wind sucks. It feels like a giant freaking blow dryer!! And it's hot as hell. The home air-conditioner is on the fritz and the A/C repairman charged $200 just to drive by and tell me he needed to order parts.

July 30th:
Been sleeping outside on the patio for three nights now, $300,000 house and I can't even go inside. Why did I ever come here?

Aug. 4th:
It's 46 degrees Celsius! Finally got the air-conditioner fixed today. It cost $500 and gets the temperature down to 30 Celsius. I hate this stupid city.

Aug. 8th:
If another wise-ass cracks, *'Hot enough for you today?'* I'm going to strangle him. Damn heat. By the time I get to work the radiator is boiling over, my clothes are soaking wet and I smell like baked cat!!

Aug. 9th:
Tried to run some errands after work, wore shorts and when I sat on the seats in the car, I thought my ass was on fire. I lost two layers of flesh and all the hair on the back of my legs and ass. Now my car smells like burnt hair, fried ass and baked cat.

Aug. 10th:
The weather report might as well be a damn recording. Hot and sunny! Hot and sunny! Hot and sunny! It's been too hot to do shit for two damn months and the weatherman says it might really warm up next week. Doesn't it ever rain in this damn desert? Water rationing will be next, so my $1,700 worth of cactus will just dry up and blow over. Even the cactus can't live in this damn heat.

Aug. 14th:
Welcome to HELL!!! Temperature got to 46 Celsius today. Forgot to crack the window and blew the damn windshield out of the car. The installer came to fix it and said, *'Hot enough for you today?'* My sister had to spend $1,500 to bail me out of jail. Freaking OKANAGAN! What kind of a sick demented idiot would want to live here??

Will write later to let you know how the trial went.

Restaurant Waiter

For all of you who frequent restaurants and understand the need for the service to be faster, this short story is a timeless lesson on how consultants can make a difference to an organisation.

Last week, we took some friends out to a new restaurant and noticed that the waiter who took our order carried a spoon in his shirt pocket. It seemed a little strange. When another waiter brought our water and utensils I noticed he also had a spoon in his shirt pocket. Then I looked around and saw that all the staff had spoons in their pockets.

When the waiter came back to serve our soup I asked, *'Why the spoon?'*

'Well', he explained, *'the restaurant's owners hired Andersen Consulting to revamp all our processes. After several months of analysis, they concluded that the spoon was the most frequently dropped utensil. It represents a drop frequency of approximately 3 spoons per table per hour. If our personnel are better prepared, we can reduce the number of trips back to the kitchen and save 15 man-hours per shift.'*

As luck would have it, I dropped my spoon and he was able to replace it with his spare. *'I'll get another spoon next time I go to the kitchen, instead of making an extra trip to get it right now.'*

I was impressed. I also noticed that there was a string hanging out of the waiter's fly. Looking around, I noticed that all the waiters had the same string hanging from their flies. So before he walked off, I asked the *waiter 'Excuse me, but can you tell me why you have that string right there?'*

'Oh, certainly!' Then he lowered his voice. *'Not everyone is so observant. That consulting firm I mentioned also found out that we can save time in the restroom. By tying this string to the tip of you know what, we can pull it out without touching it and eliminate the need to wash our hands, shortening the time spent in the restroom by 76.39 percent.'*

I asked *'After you get it out, how do you put it back?'*

'Well,' he whispered, *'I don't know about the others, but I use the spoon.'*

Just a tap on the shoulder

A passenger in a taxi leaned over to ask the driver a question and tapped him on the shoulder. The driver screamed, lost control of the cab, nearly hit a bus, drove up over the curb and stopped just inches from a large plate glass window.

For a few moments everything was silent in the cab and then the still shaking driver said, *'I'm sorry, but you scared the daylights out of me.'*

The frightened passenger apologised to the driver and said he didn't realise a mere tap on the shoulder could frighten him so much. The driver replied, *'No, no, I'm sorry, it's entirely my fault. Today is my first day driving a cab ... I've been driving a hearse for the last 25 years.'*

Signs

- Sign over a Gynaecologist's Office: *' Dr. Jones, at your cervix.'*
- In a Podiatrist's office: *'Time wounds all heels.'*

- On a Septic Tank Truck: '*Yesterday's Meals on Wheels.'*
- On a Plumber's truck: *'We repair what your husband fixed.'*
- On another Plumber's truck: *'Don't sleep with a drip. Call your plumber.'*
- On a Church's Bill board: *'7 days without God makes one weak.'*
- At a Tire Store: *'Invite us to your next blowout.'*
- On an Electrician's truck: *'Let us remove your shorts.'*
- In a Non-smoking Area: *'If we see smoke, we will assume you are on fire and take appropriate action.'* [This is my favourite!]
- On a Maternity Room door: *'Push. Push. Push.'*
- On a Taxidermist's window: *'We really know our stuff.'*
- At an Optometrist's Office: *'If you don't see what you're looking for, you've come to the right place.'*
- On a Fence: *'Salesmen welcome! Dog food is expensive!'*
- At a Car Dealership: *'The best way to get back on your feet - miss a car payment.'*
- Outside a Car Exhaust Store: *'No appointment necessary. We hear you coming.'*
- In a Vets waiting room: *'Be back in 5 minutes. Sit! Stay!'*
- In a Restaurant window: *'Don't stand there and be hungry; come on in and get fed up.'*
- In the front yard of a Funeral Home: *'Drive carefully. We'll wait.'*
- And don't forget the sign at a Radiator shop: *'Best place in town to take a leak.'*
- Sign on the back of yet another Septic Tank Truck**: '***We are in the number 2 business'*
- Sign on the back of yet another Septic Tank Truck*: 'Caution - This Truck is full of Political Promises'*
- Another sign (aimed at teenagers) read: Teenagers; tired of being hassled by your stupid parents? Act NOW! Move out, get a job and pay your own bills. Do it now while you still know everything.
- Whatever hits the fan will not be distributed evenly.
- I have kleptomania, but when it gets bad, I just take something for it.
- Suicidal twin kills sister by mistake.
- In just two days from now, tomorrow will be yesterday.
- I may be schizophrenic, but at least I have each other.
- I am nobody; nobody is perfect - therefore I am perfect!

- Money isn't everything, but it sure keeps the kids in touch.
- Don't sweat the petty things. Don't pet the sweaty things.
- Corduroy pillows are making headlines.
- I found Jesus - he was hiding in my trunk when I returned from Mexico.
- Sign on shop front: Family Jewels
- Private sign - do not read.
- Danger Stripper in use. Keep Out. (stripping the floor)
- Caution: Please be aware that the balcony is NOT on ground level.
- We will no longer accept money out of undergarments.
- Please note: As of 27th October, all staff will be required to arrive at work with teeth. If you don't have, please provide proof that you are getting some.
- Sign on street during rush hour: You'll never get to work on time. Ha Ha!!
- Attn: Do not leave items of value in vehicle. You are in Stockton, not Fairyland.
- Please do not walk on grass (near a tiny patch of scruffy grass). Guess nobody listened!
- Slow down - the cop hides behind this sign.
- (On light switch) Save Energy! How would you like it if someone turned you on and then left?
- Cows: Please close gate.
- Anyone caught exiting thru this door will be asked to leave.
- Warning: Fasten bra straps and remove dentures - very bumpy Road: Kosi Bay Bush Camp
- Please refrain from standing on the toilet bowl as an accident is bound to happen!

Investment tips

For all of you with any money left, be aware of the next expected mergers so that you can get in on the ground floor and make some BIG bucks. Watch for these consolidations:

- FedEx is expected to join its major competitor, UPS and become: FedUp
- Hale Business Systems, Mary Kay Cosmetics, Fuller Brush and W. R.Grace Co. will merge and become: Hale, Mary, Fuller, Grace.

- Polygram Records, Warner Bros. and Zesta Crackers join forces and become: Poly, Warner Cracker
- 3M will merge with Goodyear and become: MMMGood.
- Zippo Manufacturing, Audi Motors, Dofasco and Dakota Mining will merge and become: ZipAudiDoDa.
- Fairchild Electronics and Honeywell Computers will become: Fairwell Honeychild.
- Grey Poupon and Docker Pants are expected to become: Poupon Pants [I like this one!]
- Knotts Berry Farm and the National Organisation of Women will become: Knott NOW!
- Victoria's Secret and Smith & Wesson will merge under the new name: Titty Titty Bang Bang [I like this one even better!]

Blood Transfusions

American Medical Association researchers have made a remarkable discovery. It seems that some patients needing blood transfusions may benefit from receiving chicken blood rather than human blood. It tends to make the men cocky and the women lay better.

Thought you should know this, just in case.

Golf Tees

'How's she cuttin' bye' (boy) says the attendant. Mike nods a quick *'Hello'* and bends forward to pick up the nozzle.

As he does so, two tees fall out of his shirt pocket onto the ground.

'What are dose?' asks the attendant.

'They're called tees' replies Mike.

'Well, what on God's earth are dey for?' inquires the attendant.

'They're for resting my balls on when I'm driving', says Mike.

'Jaysus,' says the Newfoundlander, *'Ford tinks of everyting!'*

Idiot sightings

Idiot sighting 1

My daughter and I went through the McDonalds take-away window and I gave the girl a £5 note. Our total was £4.20, so I also handed her a twenty pence piece.

She said, *'You gave me too much money.'*

I said, *'Yes I know, but this way you can just give me £1 back.'*

She sighed and went to get the manager who asked me to repeat my request. I did so and he handed me back the 20 pence and said *'We're sorry but they could not do that kind of thing.'*

The girl then proceeded to give me back 80 pence in change.

Do not confuse the girls at MacD's.

Idiot sighting 2

We had to have the garage door repaired. The Garador repairman told us that one of our problems was that we did not have a 'large' enough motor on the opener.

I thought for a minute and said that we had the largest one Garador made at that time, a 1/2 horsepower. He shook his head and said, *'Lady, you need a ¼ horsepower.'*

I responded that 1/2 was larger than 1/4 and he said, *'NOOO, it's not. Four is larger than two.'*

We haven't used Garador repair since. Happened in Bromley, Kent UK

Idiot sighting 3

I live in a semi rural area. We recently had a new neighbour call the Highways Department to request the removal of the DEER CROSSING sign on our road. The reason: *'Too many deer are being hit by cars out here! I don't think this is a good place for them to be crossing any more.'*

Story from Crayford, Kent, UK

Idiot sighting 4

My daughter went to a local Kentucky Fried and ordered a Mexican taco. She asked the person behind the counter for' 'minimum lettuce.' He said he was sorry, but they only had iceberg lettuce.

From Gillingham Kent, UK

Idiot sighting 5

I was at the airport, checking in at the gate when an Irish airport employee asked, *'Has anyone put anything in your baggage without your knowledge?'*

To which I replied, *'If it was without my knowledge, how would I know?'*

He smiled knowingly and nodded, *'That's why we ask.'*

Happened Luton Airport UK

Idiot sighting 6

The stoplight on the corner buzzes when it's safe to cross the street. I was crossing with an intellectually challenged co-worker of mine. She asked if I knew what the buzzer was for. I explained that it signals blind people when the light is red.

Appalled, she responded, *'What on earth are blind people doing driving?!'*

She is a Local County Council employee in Dartford Kent, UK

Idiot sighting 7

When my husband and I arrived at Our Local Ford dealer to pick up our car, we were told the keys had been locked in it. We went to the service department and found a mechanic working feverishly to unlock the driver's side door. As I watched from the passenger side, I instinctively tried the door handle and discovered that it was unlocked. *'Hey,' I announced to the Mechanic 'It's open!'*

His reply, *'I know. I already did that side.'*

This was at the Ford dealership in St Albans, Hertfordshire UK.

Idiot sighting 8

I was at the checkout of a K-Mart. The cashier rang up $46.64 charges. I gave her a fifty dollar bill. She gave me back $46.64. I gave the money back to her and told her that she had made a mistake in MY favour.

She became indignant and informed me she was educated and knew what she was doing and returned the money again. I gave her the money back same scenario! I departed the store with the $46.64.

Idiot sighting 9

I walked into a Starbucks with a buy-one-get- one-free coupon for a Grande Latte. I handed it to the girl and she looked over at a little chalkboard that said 'buy one-get one free.'

'They're already buy-one- get-one-free,' she said, *'So I guess they're both free'*. She handed me my free Lattes and I walked out the door.

Idiot sighting 10

One day I was walking down the beach with some friends when one of them shouted, *'Look at that dead bird!'*

Someone looked up at the sky and said, *'Where?'*

Idiot sighting 11

While looking at a house, my brother asked the real estate agent which direction was north because, he explained, he didn't want the sun waking him up every morning. She asked, *'Does the sun rise in the North?'*

When my brother explained that the sun rises in the East and has for some time, she shook her head and said, *'Oh I don't keep up with all that stuff.'*

Idiot sighting 12

I used to work in technical support for a 24/7 call centre. One day I got a call from an individual who asked what hours the call centre was open. I told him, *'The number you dialled is open 24 hours a day, 7 days a week.'*

He responded, *'Is that Eastern or Pacific time?'*

Wanting to end the call quickly, I said, *'Uh, Pacific.'*

Idiot sighting 13

My sister has a lifesaving tool in her car designed to cut through a seat belt if she gets trapped. She keeps it in the trunk (boot) of her car.

Idiot sighting 14

My friends and I went out to buy beer and noticed that the cases were discounted 10%. Since it was a big party, we bought 2 cases. The cashier multiplied 2 times 10% and gave us a 20% discount.

Idiot sighting 15

I couldn't find my luggage at the airport baggage area, so I went to the lost luggage office and told the woman there that my bags never showed up. She smiled and told me not to worry because she was a trained professional and I was in good hands.

'Now,' she asked me, *'Has your plane arrived yet?'*

Idiot sighting 16

While working at a pizza place I observed a man ordering a small pizza to go. He appeared to be alone and the cook asked him if he would like it cut into 4 pieces or 6. He thought about it for some time before responding. *'Just cut it into 4 pieces; I don't think I'm hungry enough to eat 6 pieces.'*

Idiot sighting 17

I work with an individual who plugged her power strip back into itself and for the sake of her life, couldn't understand why her system would not turn on. A deputy with the Dallas County Sheriff's office, no less.

Idiot Sighting 18

How would you pronounce this child's name 'Le-a'

Leah? No.

Lee - ah? Nope.

Lay - ah? No.

Lei? Guess again.

This child attends a school in Kansas City, Mo. Her mother is irate because everyone is getting her name wrong. When the Mother was asked about the pronunciation of the name, she said, *'the dash don't be silent. It's pronounced 'Ledasha,'*

So, if you see something come across your desk like this (-) please remember to pronounce the dash. If dey axe you why - tell dem de dash don't be silent.

Idiot Sighting 19

At a good-bye luncheon for an old and dear co-worker who was leaving the company due to 'downsizing,' our manager commented cheerfully, *'This is fun. We should do this more often.'* Not another word was spoken. We all just looked at each other with that deer-in-the-headlights stare. This was a lunch at Texas Instruments.

Idiot Sighting 20

I am a medical student currently doing a rotation in toxicology at the poison control centre. A woman called in very upset because she caught her little daughter eating ants. I quickly reassured her that the ants are not harmful and there would be no need to bring her daughter into the hospital. She calmed down and at the end of the conversation happened to mention that she gave her daughter some ant poison to eat in order to kill the ants.

I told her that she better bring her daughter into the emergency room right away.

Idiot Sighting 21

Early last year, some Boeing employees on the airfield decided to steal a life raft from one of the 747s. They were successful in getting it out of the plane and home. Shortly after they took it for a float on the river, they noticed a Westpac Rescue Helicopter coming towards them. It turned out that the chopper was homing in on the emergency locator beacon that activated when the raft was inflated. They are no longer employed at Boeing.

Idiot Sighting 22

Seems this guy wanted some beer pretty badly. He decided that he'd just throw a brick through a liquor store window, grab some booze and run. So he lifted the brick and heaved it over his head at the window. The brick bounced back knocking him unconscious. It seems the liquor store window was made of Flexi-Glass ... The whole event was caught on videotape. Perth WA.

Stay alert! They walk amongst us ... and the scary part is that is they have the right to vote and reproduce!

Be sure to cancel your credit card before you die

A lady died this past January and Citibank billed her for February and March for their annual service charges on her credit card and added late fees and interest on the monthly charge. The balance had been $0.00 when she died, but now somewhere around $60.00. A family member placed a call to Citibank. Here is the exchange:

Family Member: *'I am calling to tell you she died back in January.'*

Citibank: *'The account was never closed and the late fees and charges still apply.'*

Family Member: *'Maybe, you should turn it over to collections.'*

Citibank: *'Since it is two months past due, it already has been.'*

Family Member: *'So, what will they do when they find out she is dead?'*

Citibank: *'Either report her account to frauds division or report her to the credit bureau, maybe both!'*

Family Member: *'Do you think God will be mad at her?'*

Citibank: *'Excuse me?'*

Family Member: *'Did you just get what I was telling you - the part about her being dead?'*

Citibank: *'Sir, you'll have to speak to my supervisor.'*

Supervisor gets on the phone:

Family Member: 'I'm *calling to tell you, she died back in January with a $0 balance.'*

Citibank: *'The account was never closed and late fees and charges still apply.'*

Family Member: *'You mean you want to collect from her estate?'*

Citibank: (Stammer) *'Are you her lawyer?'*

Family Member: *'No, I'm her great nephew.'* (Lawyer info was given)

Citibank: *'Could you fax us a certificate of death?'*

Family Member: *'Sure.'* (Fax number was given)

After they get the fax:

Citibank: *'Our system just isn't set up for death. I don't know what more I can do to help.'*

Family Member: *'Well, if you figure it out, great! If not, you could just keep billing her. She won't care.'*

Citibank: *'Well, the late fees and charges do still apply.'* (What is wrong with these people?!?)

Family Member: *'Would you like her new billing address?'*

Citibank: *'That might help.'*

Family Member: *' Odessa Memorial Cemetery, Highway 129, Plot Number 69.'*

Citibank: *'Sir, that's a cemetery!'*

Family Member: *'And what do you do with dead people on your planet???'*

Trivia

- A pig's orgasm lasts 30 minutes. [In my next life, I want to be a pig.]
- Some lions mate over 50 times a day. [I still want to be a pig in my next life ... quality over quantity.]
- [Something I always wanted to know.] Humans and dolphins are the only species that have sex for pleasure. [Is that why Flipper was always smiling? And what about the pig?]
- In Hong Kong, a betrayed wife is legally allowed to kill her adulterous husband, but may only do so with her bare hands. The husband's illicit lover, on the other hand, may be killed in any manner desired. [Ah! Justice!]
- [30 minutes. Lucky pig! Can you imagine?]
- Topless saleswomen are legal in Liverpool, England but only in tropical fish stores. [But of course!]
- In Cali, Colombia, a woman may only have sex with her husband and the first time this happens, her mother must be in the room to witness the act. [Makes one shudder at the thought.]

- In Santa Cruz, Bolivia, it is illegal for a man to have sex with a woman and her daughter at the same time. [I presume this was a big enough problem that they had to pass this law?]
- In Lebanon, men are legally allowed to have sex with animals, but the animals must be female. Having sexual relations with a male animal is punishable by death. [Like THAT makes sense.]
- In Bahrain, a male doctor may legally examine a woman's genitals, but is prohibited from looking directly at them during the examination. He may only see their reflection in a mirror. [Do they look different reversed?]
- Muslims are banned from looking at the genitals of a corpse. This also applies to undertakers. The sex organs of the deceased must be covered with a brick or piece of wood at all times. [A brick??]
- The penalty for masturbation in Indonesia is decapitation. [Much worse than 'going blind!']
- There are men in Guam whose full-time job is to travel the countryside and deflower young virgins, who pay them for the privilege of having sex for the first time. Reason: under Guam law, it is expressly forbidden for virgins to marry. [Let's just think for a minute; is there any job anywhere else in the world that even comes close to this?]
- In Maryland, it is illegal to sell condoms from vending machines with one exception: Prophylactics may be dispensed from a vending machine only 'in places where alcoholic beverages are sold for consumption on the premises.' [Is this a great country or what? Well ... not as great as Guam!]
- Turtles can breathe through their butts. [And I thought I had bad breath in the morning!]
- It is impossible to lick your elbow.
- The percentage of Africa that is wilderness: 28%
- The cost of raising a medium-size dog to the age of eleven: $16,400
- The average number of people airborne over the U.S. in any given hour: 61,000.
- The first novel ever written on a typewriter, Tom Sawyer.
- The San Francisco Cable cars are the only mobile National Monuments.
- Each king in a deck of playing cards represents a great king from history:
    - Spades - King David

    - Hearts - Charlemagne
    - Clubs -Alexander, the Great
    - Diamonds - Julius Caesar
- Cure for a headache - take a lime, cut in half and rub on forehead. The throbbing will go away. Alternative: Take a lime, mix with tequila, chill and drink. All your pains will go away.
- In Shakespeare's time, mattresses were secured on bed frames by ropes. When you pulled on the ropes, the mattress tightened, making the bed firmer to sleep on. Hence the phrase ... *'Goodnight , sleep tight'*
- It was the accepted practice in Babylon 4,000 years ago that for a month after the wedding the bride's father would supply his son-in-law with all the mead he could drink. Mead is a honey beer and because their calendar was lunar based, this period was called the honey month, which we know today as the honeymoon.
- In English pubs, ale is ordered by pints and quarts ... So in old England, when customers got unruly, the bartender would yell at them *'Mind your pints and quarts and settle down.'* It's where we get the phrase *'mind your P's and Q's'*
- Many years ago in England, pub frequenters had a whistle baked into the rim or handle of their ceramic cups. When they needed a refill, they used the whistle to get some service. *'Wet your whistle'* is the phrase inspired by this practice.

Lexophiles - lovers of words - will enjoy these.

1. A bicycle can't stand alone; it is two tired.
2. A will is a dead giveaway.
3. Time flies like an arrow; fruit flies like a banana.
4. A backward poet writes inverse.
5. In a democracy it's your vote that counts; in feudalism, it's your Count that votes.
6. A chicken crossing the road: poultry in motion.
7. If you don't pay your exorcist you may be repossessed.
8. With her marriage she got a new name and a dress.
9. Show me a piano falling down a mine shaft and I'll show you A-flat miner.
10. When a clock is hungry it goes back four seconds.
11. The guy who fell onto an upholstery machine was fully recovered.

12. A grenade fell onto a kitchen floor in France resulting in Linoleum Blownapart.
13. You are stuck with your debt if you can't budge it.
14. Local Area Network in Australia: The LAN down under.
15. He broke into song because he couldn't find the key.
16. A calendar's days are numbered.
17. A lot of money is tainted: 'Taint yours and 'taint mine.
18. A boiled egg is hard to beat.
19. He had a photographic memory that was never developed.
20. A plateau is a high form of flattery.
21. The short fortune teller who escaped from prison: a small medium at large.
22. Those who get too big for their britches will be exposed in the end.
23. When you've seen one shopping center you've seen the mall.
24. If you jump off a Paris bridge, you are in Seine.
25. When she saw her first strands of gray hair, she thought she'd dye.
26. Bakers trade bread recipes on a knead to know basis.
27. Santa's helpers are subordinate clauses.
28. Acupuncture: a jab well done.
29. Marathon runners with bad shoes suffer the agony of de feet.

Ambidextrous Golfer

A group of guys lived and died for their Saturday morning round of golf. One transferred to another city. It wasn't the same without him. A new woman joined their Club. She overheard the guys talking about their golf round. She said, *'You know, I used to play on my golf team in college and I was pretty good. Would you mind if I joined you next week?'*

The three guys looked at each other. Not one of them wanted to say *'yes',* but she had them on the spot. Finally, one man said it would be okay, but they would be starting early - at 6:30 am.

He figured the early tee-time would discourage her. The woman said this may be a problem and asked if she could be up to 15 minutes late. They rolled their eyes, but said okay. She smiled and said, *'Good, I'll be here at 6:30 or 6:45.'*

She showed up at 6:30 sharp and beat all three of them with an eye-opening 2-under par round. She was fun and a pleasant person and the guys were impressed. Back at the clubhouse, they congratulated her and invited her back the next week. She smiled and said, *'I'll be there at 6:30 or 6:45.'*

The next week she again showed up at 6:30 sharp. Only this time, she played left-handed. The three guys were incredulous as she still beat them with an even par round, despite playing with her off-hand. They were totally amazed.

They couldn't figure her out. She was again very pleasant and didn't seem to be purposely showing them up. They invited her back again, but each man harboured a burning desire to beat her.

The third week, the guys had their game faces on. But this time, she was 15 minutes late, which made the guys irritable. This week the lady played right-handed and narrowly beat all three of them.

The men mused that her late arrival was due to petty gamesmanship on her part. However, she was so gracious and so complimentary of their strong play, they couldn't hold a grudge.

Back in the clubhouse, all three guys were shaking their heads. This woman was a riddle no one could figure out. They had a couple of beers and finally, one of the men asked her point blank, *'How do you decide if you're going to golf right-handed or left-handed?'*

The lady blushed and grinned. *'That's easy,'* she said. *'When my Dad taught me to play golf, I learned I was ambidextrous. I like to switch back and forth. When I got married after college, I discovered my husband always sleeps in the nude. From then on, I developed a silly habit. Right before I left in the morning for golf practice, I would pull the covers off him. If his you-know-what was pointing to the right, I golfed right-handed; if it was pointed to the left, I golfed left-handed.'*

The guys on the team thought this was hysterical. Astonished at this bizarre information, one of the guys shot back, *'But what if it's pointing straight up?'*

She said, *'Then, I'm fifteen minutes late.'*

Ya gotta love a drunk

A man and his wife are awakened at 3 o'clock in the morning by a loud pounding on the door. The man gets up and goes to the door where a drunken stranger, standing in the pouring rain, is asking for a push.

'Not a chance,' says the husband. *'It is 3 o'clock in the morning.'*

He slams the door and returns to bed.

'Who was that?' asked his wife.

'Just some drunk guy asking for a push!'

'Did you help him?' she asks.

'No. I did not. It is 3 o'clock in the morning and it is pouring rain outside!'

His wife said, *'Don't you remember about three months ago when we broke down and those two guys helped us? You should be ashamed of yourself!'*

The man gets dressed and goes out into the pouring rain. He calls out into the dark, *'Hello. Are you still there?'*

'Yes,' comes back the answer.

'Do you still need a push?' calls out the husband.

'Yes! Please!' comes the reply from the darkness.

'Where are you?' asks the husband.

'Over here on the swing!' replies the drunk.

The Pit Crew

The Ferrari F1 team fired their pit crew yesterday. The announcement followed Ferrari's decision last month to take advantage of the New Zealand government's *'work for the dole scheme'* and to hire unemployed Maori youths.

The decision to hire them was brought on by a recent television documentary on how Maori youths were able to remove a set of car wheels in less than 6 seconds without proper equipment, whereas Ferrari's pit crew can only do it in 8 seconds with the aid of millions of dollars of high tech gear.

This was thought to be an excellent yet bold move by Ferrari management. As most races are won and lost in the pits, Ferrari would have a decided advantage over every other F1 team. However Ferrari got more than they bargained for.

On Sunday during the first pit stop the Maori crew changed all four tyres in under six seconds, but within twelve seconds they had re-sprayed, re-badged and sold the car over to the McLaren team for ten dozen beer and an HQ Holden and had even had time for a quick look at David Coulthard's girlfriend in the shower.

The Value of a Drink

'Sometimes when I reflect back on all the wine I drink I feel shame.' Then I look into the glass and think about the workers in the vineyards and all of their hopes and dreams. If I didn't drink this wine, they might be out of work and their dreams would be shattered. Then I say to myself, *'It is better that I drink this wine and let their dreams come true than be selfish and worry about my liver.'* - Jack Handy

Warning: The consumption of alcohol may leave you wondering what the hell happened to your bra and panties.

'I feel sorry for people who don't drink. When they wake up in the morning, that's as good as they're going to feel all day.' - Frank Sinatra

Warning: The consumption of alcohol may create the illusion that you are tougher, smarter, faster and better looking than most people.

'When I read about the evils of drinking, I gave up reading.' - Henny Youngman

Warning: The consumption of alcohol may lead you to think people are laughing WITH you.

'24 hours in a day, 24 beers in a case. Coincidence? I think not.' - Stephen Wright

Warning: The consumption of alcohol may cause you to think you can sing.

If we fall asleep, we commit no sin. When we commit no sin, we go to heaven. So, let's all get drunk and go to heaven!' - Brian O'Rourke

Warning: The consumption of alcohol may cause pregnancy.

'Beer is proof that God loves us and wants us to be happy.' - Benjamin Franklin

Warning: The consumption of alcohol is a major factor in dancing like a retard.

'Without question, the greatest invention in the history of mankind is beer. Oh, I grant you that the wheel was also a fine invention, but the wheel does not go nearly as well with pizza.' - Dave Barry

Warning: The consumption of alcohol may cause you to tell your friends over and over again that you love them.

'To some it's a six-pack, to me it's a Support Group. Salvation in a can!' - Dave Howell

Warning: The consumption of alcohol may make you think you can logically converse with members of the opposite sex without spitting.

And saving the best for last, as explained by Cliff Clavin of Cheers. One afternoon at Cheers, Cliff Clavin was explaining the Buffalo Theory to his buddy Norm. Here's how it went:

'Well ya see, Norm, it's like this ... A herd of buffalo can only move as fast as the slowest buffalo. And when the herd is hunted, it is the slowest and weakest ones at the back that are killed first. This natural selection is good for the herd as a whole, because the general speed and health of the whole group keeps improving by the regular killing of the weakest members. In much the same way, the

human brain can only operate as fast as the slowest brain cells. Excessive intake of alcohol, as we know, kills brain cells. But naturally, it attacks the slowest and weakest brain cells first. In this way, regular consumption of beer eliminates the weaker brain cells, making the brain a faster and more efficient machine. That's why you always feel smarter after a few beers.'

Warning: The consumption of alcohol may make you think you are whispering when you are not.

Geography lesson

The teacher of the Earth Science class was lecturing on map reading. He spent the class explaining about latitude, longitude, degrees and minutes. Towards the end of class, the teacher asked his students, *'Suppose I asked you to meet me for lunch at 23 degrees, 4 minutes north latitude and 45 degrees, 15 minutes east longitude...'* A student's voice broke the confused silence and volunteered, *'I guess you'd be eating alone, sir.'*

Cheap Suits

Bubba and Billy Joe are walking down the street in Dallas and they see a sign on a store which reads, 'Suits $5.00 each! Shirts $2.00 each, trousers $2.50 each.'

Bubba says to his pal, *'Billy Joe, Look here! We could buy a whole gob of these, take 'em back to Sand Mountain, sell 'em to our friends and make a fortune. Just let me do the talkin' 'cause if they hear your accent, they might think we're ignorant and not wanna sell that stuff to us. Now, I'll talk in a slow Georgia drawl so's they don't know we is from Texas.'*

They go in and Bubba says with his best fake Georgia drawl, *'I'll take 50 of them suits at $5.00 each, 100 of them there shirts at $2.00 each, 50 pairs of them there trousers at $2.50 each. I'll back up my pickup and ...'*

The owner of the shop interrupts, *'Ya'll from East Texas, ain't ya?'*

'Well ... yeah,' says a surprised Bubba. *'How come you knowed that?'*

'Because this is a dry cleaners.'

Tickle Me Elmo toys

There is a factory in Northern Minnesota that makes the Tickle Me Elmo toys. The toy laughs when you tickle it under the arms. Well,

Lena is hired at The Tickle Me Elmo factory and she reports for her first day promptly at 8:00 am.

The next day at 8:45 am there is a knock at the Personnel Manager's door. The Foreman throws open the door and begins to rant about the new employee. He complains that she is incredibly slow and the whole line is backing up, putting the entire production line behind schedule.

The Personnel Manager decides he should see this for himself, so the two men march down to the factory floor.

When they get there the line is so backed up that there are Tickle Me Elmos all over the factory floor and they're really beginning to pile up. At the end of the line stands Lena surrounded by mountains of Tickle Me Elmos. She has a roll of plush red fabric and a huge bag of small marbles.

The two men watch in amazement as she cuts a little piece of fabric, wraps it around two marbles and begins to carefully sew the little package between Elmo's legs. The Personnel Manager bursts into laughter.

After several minutes of hysterics he pulls himself together and approaches Lena. *'I'm sorry,'* he says to her, barely able to keep a straight face, *'but I think you misunderstood the instructions I gave you yesterday ... 'Your job is to give Elmo two test tickles.'*

What would you do?

Scenario: You are driving in a car at a constant speed. On your left side is a valley and on your right side is a fire engine travelling at the same speed as you. In front of you is a galloping pig that is the same size as your car and you cannot overtake it. Behind you is a helicopter flying at ground level. Both the giant pig and the helicopter are also travelling at the same speed as you. What must you do to safely get out of this highly dangerous situation?

Answer: Get off the children's Merry Go Round; you're drunk.

Dear Tide:

I am writing to say what an excellent product you have! I've used it all of my married life, as my Mom always told me it was the best. Now that I am in my fifties I find it even better! In fact, about a month ago, I spilled some red wine on my new white blouse. My inconsiderate and uncaring husband started to belittle me about how clumsy I was and generally started becoming a pain in the neck.

One thing led to another and somehow I ended up with his blood on my new white blouse! I grabbed my bottle of Tide with bleach alternative and to my surprise and satisfaction; all of the stains came out! In fact, the stains came out so well the detectives who came by yesterday told me that the DNA tests on my blouse were negative and then my attorney called and said that I was no longer considered a suspect in the disappearance of my husband.

What a relief! Going through menopause is bad enough without being a murder suspect! I thank you, once again, for having a great product. Well, gotta go, have to write to the Hefty bag people.

Only in Saskatchewan, Canada

Did you hear about the two duck hunters from Prince Albert, Saskatchewan? Absolutely true story heard on a Saskatoon radio station reporting on the incident.

A guy buys a new Lincoln Navigator in Saskatoon for $42,500.00 (with monthly payments of $560.00). He and a friend go duck hunting at Tobin Lake in mid-October; and of course the lake is frozen. These two guys go on a lake with their guns, a dog and of course the New Navigator. They decide they want to make a natural looking water area for the ducks, something for the decoys to float on. Now making a hole in the ice large enough to invite a passing duck is going to take a little more power than the average drill auger can produce.

So, out of the back of the new Navigator comes a stick of dynamite with a short 40-second-fuse. Now our two Rocket Scientists, afraid they might slip on the ice while trying to run away after lighting the fuse (and becoming toast, along with the Navigator) decide on the following course of action: they light the 40-second fuse; then with a mighty thrust, they throw the stick of dynamite as far away as possible.

Remember a couple of paragraphs back when I mentioned the Navigator, the guns and the dog? Let's talk about the dog: A highly trained Black Lab used for retrieving, especially things thrown by the owner. You guessed it: the dog takes off across the ice at a high rate of speed and grabs the stick of dynamite, with the burning 40-second fuse, just as it hits the ice. The two men swallow, blink, start waving their arms and, with veins in their necks swelling to resemble stalks of rhubarb, scream and holler at the dog to stop.

The dog, now apparently cheered on by his master, keeps coming. One hunter panics, grabs the shotgun and shoots the dog! The shotgun is loaded with #8 bird shot, hardly big enough to stop a Black Lab. The dog stops for a moment, slightly confused then continues on.

Another shot and this time the dog, still standing, becomes really confused and of course terrified, thinks these two geniuses have gone insane. The dog takes off to find cover, under the brand new Navigator. The men continue to scream as they run. The red hot exhaust pipe on the truck touches the dog's rear end; he yelps, drops the dynamite under the truck and takes off after his master.
Then""""BOOOOOOOOOOOOM""""!!!!

The truck is blown to bits and sinks to the bottom of the lake, leaving the two idiots standing there with an, *'I can't believe this just happened'* looks on their faces.

The SGI insurance company says that sinking a vehicle in a lake by illegal use of explosives is not covered by the policy. He still had yet to make the first of those $560.00 monthly payments. The dog is okay. And they make fun of people in Newfoundland?

The Negative Hairdresser

A woman was at her hairdresser's getting her hair styled for a trip to Rome with her husband. She mentioned the trip to the hairdresser, who responded: *'Rome? Why would anyone want to go there? It's crowded and dirty. You're crazy to go to Rome. So, how are you getting there?'*

'We're taking Continental,' was the reply. *'We got a great rate!'*
'Continental?' exclaimed the hairdresser, *'That's a terrible airline. Their planes are old, their flight attendants are ugly and they're always late.'*

'So, where are you staying in Rome?'

'We'll be at this exclusive little place over on Rome's Tiber River called Teste.'

'Don't go any further. I know that place. Everybody thinks it's gonna be something special and exclusive, but it's really a dump, the worst hotel in the city! The rooms are small, the service is surly and they're overpriced.'

'So, whatcha' doing when you get there?'

'We're going to go to see the Vatican and we hope to see the Pope.'

'That's rich,' laughed the hairdresser. *'You and a million other people trying to see him. He'll look the size of an ant. Boy, good luck on this lousy trip of yours. You're going to need it.'*

A month later, the woman again came in for a hairdo. The hairdresser asked her about her trip to Rome.

'It was wonderful,' explained the woman, *'Not only were we on time in one of Continental's brand new planes, but it was*

overbooked and they bumped us up to first class. The food and wine were wonderful and I had a handsome 28-year-old steward who waited on me hand and foot. And the hotel was great! They'd just finished a $5 million remodelling job and now it's a jewel, the finest hotel in the city. They, too, were overbooked, so they apologised and gave us their owner's suite at no extra charge!'

'Well,' muttered the hairdresser, *'that's all well and good, but I know you didn't get to see the Pope.'*

'Actually, we were quite lucky, because as we toured the Vatican, a Swiss Guard tapped me on the shoulder and explained that the Pope likes to meet some of the visitors and if I'd be so kind as to step into his private room and wait, the Pope would personally greet me. Sure enough, five minutes later, the Pope walked through the door and shook my hand! I knelt down and he spoke a few words to me.'

'Oh, really! What'd he say?'

He said: *'Where'd you get the horrible hair do?*

Another mind bender

Only great minds can read this. This is weird, but interesting!

fi yuo cna raed tihs, yuo hvae a sgtrane mnid too .

Cna yuo raed tihs? Olny 55 plepoe out of 100 can.

I cdnuolt blveiee taht I cluod aulaclty uesdnatnrd waht I was rdanieg. The phaonmneal pweor of the hmuan mnid, aoccdrnig to a rscheearch at Cmabrigde Uinervtisy, it dseno't mtaetr in waht oerdr the ltteres in a wrod are, the olny iproamtnt tihng is taht the frsit and lsat ltteer be in the rghit pclae. The rset can be a taotl mses and you can sitll raed it whotuit a pboerlm. Tihs is bcuseae the huamn mnid deos not raed ervey lteter by istlef, but the wrod as a wlohe. Azanmig huh? yaeh and I awlyas tghuhot slpeling was ipmorantt! if you can raed tihs forwrad it

From the British newspapers

Commenting on a complaint from a Mr Arthur Purdey about a large gas bill, a spokesman for North West Gas said, *'We agree it was rather high for the time of year. It's possible Mr. Purdey has been charged for the gas used up during the explosion that destroyed his house.'* (The Daily Telegraph)

Irish police are being handicapped in a search for a stolen van, because they cannot issue a description. It's a Special Branch vehicle and they don't want the public to know what it looks like. (The Guardian)

A young girl who was blown out to sea on a set of inflatable teeth was rescued by a man on an inflatable lobster. A coastguard spokesman commented, *'This sort of thing is all too common.'* (The Times)

At the height of the gale, the harbourmaster radioed a coastguard on the spot and asked him to estimate the wind speed. He replied he was sorry, but he didn't have a gauge. However, if it was any help, the wind had just blown his Land Rover off the cliff. (Aberdeen Evening Express)

Mrs Irene Graham of Thorpe Avenue, Boscombe, delighted the audience with her reminiscence of the German prisoner of war who was sent each week to do her garden. He was repatriated at the end of 1945, she recalled *'He'd always seemed a nice friendly chap, but when the crocuses came up in the middle of our lawn in February 1946, they spelt out 'Heil Hitler.'* (Bournemouth Evening Echo)

Some actual announcements that London Tube train drivers have made to their passengers:

'Ladies and Gentlemen, I do apologise for the delay to your service. I know you're all dying to get home, unless, of course, you happen to be married to my ex-wife, in which case you'll want to cross over to the Westbound and go in the opposite direction'.

'Your delay this evening is caused by the line controller suffering from E & B syndrome, not knowing his elbow from his backside. I'll let you know any further information as soon as I'm given any.

'We are now travelling through Baker Street, as you can see Baker Street is closed. It would have been nice if they had actually told me, so I could tell you earlier, but no, they don't think about things like that.'

'Beggars are operating on this train, please do NOT encourage these professional beggars, if you have any spare change, please give it to a registered charity, failing that, give it to me.'

During an extremely hot rush hour on the Central Line the driver announced in a West Indian drawl: *'Step right this way for the sauna, ladies and gentleman ... unfortunately towels are not provided.'*

'To the gentleman wearing the long grey coat trying to get on the second carriage - what part of 'stand clear of the doors' don't you understand?'

'May I remind all passengers that there is strictly no smoking allowed on any part of the Underground. However, if you are

smoking a joint, it's only fair that you pass it round the rest of the carriage.'

The year's best (actual!) headlines!

- Red Tape Holds Up New Bridges. [You mean there's something stronger than duct tape?!]
- Something Went Wrong in Jet Crash, Expert Says. [No, really?]
- Police Begin Campaign to Run Down Jaywalkers. [Now that's taking things a bit far!]
- Miners Refuse to Work after Death. [Those good-for-nothing lazy so-and-sos!]
- Juvenile Court to Try Shooting Defendant. [See if that works any better than a fair trial!]
- War Dims Hope for Peace. [I can see where it might have that effect!]
- If Strike Isn't Settled Quickly, It May Last Awhile. [Really?!]
- Cold Wave Linked to Temperatures. [Who would have thought!]
- Enfield Couple Slain; Police Suspect Homicide. [They may be on to something!]
- Man Struck By Lightning: Faces Battery Charge. [He probably IS the battery charge!]
- New Study of Obesity Looks for Larger Test Group. [Weren't they fat enough?!]
- Astronaut Takes Blame for Gas in Spacecraft. [That's what he gets for eating those beans!]
- Kids Make Nutritious Snacks. [Do they taste like chicken?]
- Local High School Dropouts Cut in Half. [Chain-saw Massacre all over again!]
- Hospitals are Sued by 7 Foot Doctors. [Boy, are they tall!]

And the winner is ...

- Typhoon Rips Through Cemetery; Hundreds Dead. [Did I read that right?]

Real Newspaper Ads

- Free Yorkshire Terrier. 8 years old. Hateful little dog. Bites.
- Free Puppies. 1/2 Cocker Spaniel, 1/2 sneaky neighbour's dog.
- Free Puppies. Mother, German Shepherd. Father, Super Dog ... able to leap tall fences in a single bound.

- Found – Dirty white dog. Looks like a rat ... been out a while. Better be a reward.
- Joining Nudist Colony! Must sell washer and dryer $300.
- Wedding dress for sale. Worn once by mistake. Call Stephanie.

And the best one:

- For sale by owner: Complete set of Encyclopaedia Britannica, 45 volumes. Excellent condition. $1,000 or best offer. No longer needed, got married last month. Wife knows everything.

Drafted

Fifty-one years ago, Herman James, a North Carolina mountain man, was drafted by the Army. On his first day in basic training, the Army issued him a comb. That afternoon the Army barber sheared off all his hair. On his second day, the Army issued Herman a toothbrush. That afternoon the Army dentist yanked seven of his teeth. On the third day, the Army issued him a jock strap. The Army has been looking for Herman for 51 years.

Polish Immigrant

A Polish immigrant went to the DMV to apply for a driver's license. First, of course, he had to take an eye sight test. The optician showed him a card with the letters 'C Z W I X N O S T A C Z.'

'Can you read this?' the optician asked.

'Read it?' the Polish guy replied, *'I know the guy.'*

Questions that haunt me

1. Can you cry under water?
2. How important does a person have to be before they are considered assassinated instead of just murdered?
3. Why do you have to 'put your two cents in' but it's only a 'penny for your thoughts?' Where's that extra penny going to?
4. Once you're in heaven, do you get stuck wearing the clothes you were buried in for eternity?
5. Why does a round pizza come in a square box?
6. What disease did cured ham actually have?
7. How is it that we put man on the moon before we figured out it would be a good idea to put wheels on luggage?
8. Why is it that people say they 'slept like a baby' when babies wake up like every two hours?
9. If a deaf person has to go to court, is it still called a hearing?
10. Why are you IN a movie, but you're ON TV?

11. Why do people pay to go up tall buildings and then put money in binoculars to look at things on the ground?
12. Why do doctors leave the room while you change? They're going to see you naked anyway.
13. Why is 'bra' singular and 'panties' plural?
14. Did you ever notice that when you blow in a dog's face, he gets mad at you, but when you take him for a car ride, he sticks his head out the window?
15. Why do toasters always have a setting that burns the toast to a horrible crisp, which no decent human being would eat?
16. If Jimmy cracks corn and no one cares, why is there a stupid song about him?
17. Can a hearse carrying a corpse drive in the carpool lane?
18. If the professor on Gilligan's Island can make a radio out of a coconut, why can't he fix a hole in a boat?
19. Do the Alphabet song and Twinkle, Twinkle Little Star have the same tune?

    Why did you just try singing the two songs above?
20. Why do they call it an asteroid when it's outside the hemisphere, but call it a haemorrhoid when it's in your butt?
21. Why does Goofy stand erect while Pluto remains on all fours? They're both dogs!
22. If Wylie E. Coyote had enough money to buy all that ACME crap to catch the roadrunner for dinner, why didn't he just buy dinner?
23. If corn oil is made from corn and vegetable oil is made from vegetables, what is baby oil made from?
24. If electricity comes from electrons, does morality come from morons?
25. If you have sex with a prostitute against her will, is it considered rape or shoplifting?

Something educational for a change!!

Albert Einstein was born on March 14, 1879. Few people remember that the Nobel Prize winner married his cousin, Elsa Lowenthal, after his first marriage dissolved in 1919. He stated that he was attracted to Elsa because she was well endowed and postulated that if you are attracted to women with large breasts; the attraction is stronger if there is a DNA connection.

This came to be known as Einstein's Theory of Relative Titty.

Oh be quiet ... I don't write this stuff - I just forward it!

Thoughts for the weekend

- Wouldn't it be nice if whenever we messed up our life we could simply press 'Ctr Alt Delete' and start all over?
- Just remember, if the world didn't suck, we'd all fall off.
- Brain cells come and brain cells go, but fat cells live forever.
- A friend is someone who reaches for your hand, but touches your heart.

One of my fondest memories

As I recall the days of yore
Was the little house, behind the house,
With the crescent o'er the door.

'Twas a place to sit and ponder
With your head all bowed down low;
Knowing that you wouldn't be there,
If you didn't have to go.

Ours was a multi-holer, three,
With a size for every one.
You left there feeling better,
After your job was done.

You had to make those frequent trips
In snow, rain, sleet or fog -
To that little house where you usually
Fund the Eaton's catalogue.

Oft times in dead of winter,
The seat was spread with snow.
'Twas then with much reluctance,
To that little house you'd go.

With a swish you'd clear that wooden seat,
Bend low, with dreadful fear
You'd shut your eyes and grit your teeth
As you settled on your rear.

I recall the day Ol' Granddad,
Who stayed with us one summer,
Made a trip out to that little house
Which proved to be a bummer.

'Twas the same day that my Dad had
Finished painting the kitchen green.

He'd just cleaned up the mess he'd made
With rags and gasoline.

He tossed the rags down in the hole
Went on his usual way
Not knowing that by doing so
He'd eventually rue the day.

Now Granddad had an urgent call,
I never will forget!
This trip he made to the little house
Stays in my memory yet.
He sat down on the wooden seat,
With both feet on the floor.
He filled his pipe and tapped it down
And struck a match on the outhouse door.

He lit the pipe and sure enough,
It soon began to glow.
He slowly raised his rear a bit
And tossed the flaming match below.

The blast that followed, I am told
Was heard for miles around;
And there was poor ol' Granddad
Sprawled out there on the ground.

The smouldering pipe still in his mouth,
His eyes were shut real tight;
The celebrated three-holer
Was blown clear out of sight.

We asked him what had happened,
What he said I'll ne'er forget.
He said he thought it must have been
The pinto beans he et!

Next day we had a new one
Dad put it up with ease.
But this one had a door sign
That reads: *'No Smoking, Please.'*

Black Fella system

An Aboriginal elder sat in his humpy eyeing two government officials sent to interview him. One official said to him, *'You have observed the white man for 90 years. You've seen his wars and his technological advances. You've seen his progress and the damage he has done.'* The elder nodded in agreement.

The official continued, *'Considering all these events, in your opinion, where did the white man go wrong?'*

The Elder stared at the two government officials for over a minute and then he calmly replied: *'When white man found the land, Aboriginals were running it. No taxes, no debt, plenty kangaroo, plenty fish, women did all the work, medicine man free, Aboriginal man spent all day hunting and fishing, all night having sex.'* Then the elder leaned back and smiled before he added, *'Only white man bloody stupid enough to think he could improve system like that.'*

Weather Forecast

It was April and the Aboriginals in a remote part of Northern Australia asked their new elder if the coming winter was going to be cold or mild.

Since he was an elder in a modern community he had never been taught the old secrets. When he looked at the sky he couldn't tell what the winter was going to be like.

Nevertheless, to be on the safe side, he told his tribe that the winter was indeed going to be cold and that the members of the tribe should collect firewood to be prepared.

But being a practical leader, after several days he had an idea. He walked out to the telephone booth on the highway, called the Bureau of Meteorology and asked, *'Is the coming winter in this area going to be cold?'*

The meteorologist responded, *'It looks like this winter is going to be quite cold.'*

So the elder went back to his people and told them to collect even more wood in order to be prepared.

A week later, he called the Bureau of Meteorology again. *'Does it still look like it is going to be a very cold winter?'*

The meteorologist again replied, *'Yes, it's going to be a very cold winter.'*

The elder again went back to his community and ordered them to collect every scrap of firewood they could find.

Two weeks later the elder called the Bureau again. *'Are you absolutely sure that the winter is going to be very cold?'* he asked.

'Absolutely,' the man replied. *'It's looking more and more like it is going to be one of the coldest winters ever.'*

'How can you be so sure?' the elder asked.

The weatherman replied, *'There are reports that the Aboriginals are collecting firewood like crazy and that's always a sure sign.'*

Great truths that adults have learned

1. Raising teenagers is like nailing jelly to a tree.
2. Wrinkles don't hurt.
3. Families are like fudge … mostly sweet, with a few nuts.
4. Today's mighty oak is just yesterday's nut that held its ground.
5. Laughing is good exercise. It's like jogging on the inside.
6. Middle age is when you choose your cereal for the fibre - not the toy.

Ponderisms

- I used to eat a lot of natural foods until I learned that most people die of natural causes.
- Garden Rule: When weeding, the best way to make sure you are removing a weed and not a valuable plant is to pull on it. If it comes out of the ground easily, it is a valuable plant.
- The easiest way to find something lost around the house is to buy a replacement.
- Never take life seriously. Nobody gets out alive anyway.
- Have you noticed since everyone has a camcorder these days no one talks about seeing UFOs like they used to?
- How is it that one careless match can start a forest fire, but it takes a whole box to start a campfire?
- Who was the first person to look at a cow and say, *'I think I'll squeeze these dangly things here and drink whatever comes out?'*
- Do illiterate people get the full effect of Alphabet Soup?
- Why doesn't glue stick to the inside of the bottle?

Great truths about growing old

1. Growing old is mandatory; growing up is optional.
2. Forget the health food. I need all the preservatives I can get.
3. When you fall down, you wonder what else you can do while you're down there.
4. You're getting old when you get the same sensation from a rocking chair that you once got from a roller coaster.
5. It's frustrating when you know all the answers but nobody bothers to ask you the questions
6. Time may be a great healer, but it's a lousy beautician.

7. Wisdom comes with age, but sometimes age comes alone.

New Meanings

These are so apt they should be in a dictionary.

- Adult: A person who has stopped growing at both ends and is now growing in the middle.
- Beauty Parlour: A place where women curl up and dye.
- Cannibal: Someone who is fed up with people.
- Chickens: The only animals you eat before they are born and after they are dead.
- Committee: A body that keeps minutes and wastes hours.
- Dust: Mud with the juice squeezed out.
- Egotist: Someone who is usually me-deep in conversation.
- Handkerchief: Cold Storage.
- Inflation: Cutting money in half without damaging the paper.
- Mosquito: An insect that makes you like flies better.
- Raisin: Grape with sunburn.
- Secret: Something you tell to one person at a time.
- Skeleton: **A** bunch of bones with the person scraped off.
- Toothache: The pain that drives you to extraction.
- Tomorrow: One of the greatest labour saving devices of today.
- Yawn: An honest opinion openly expressed.

And my Favourite!!

- Wrinkles: Something other people have, similar to my character lines.

Success

- At age 4 success is ... not piddling in your pants.
- At age 12 success is ... having friends.
- At age 17 success is ... having a drivers licence.
- At age 35 success is ... having money.
- At age 50 success is ... having money.
- At age 70 success is ... having a drivers licence.
- At age 75 success is ... having friends.
- At age 80 success is ... not piddling in your pants.

The Four Stages of Life

1. You believe in Santa Claus.
2. You don't believe in Santa Claus.
3. You are Santa Claus.

4. You look like Santa Claus.

Hollywood Squares:

These great questions and answers are from the days when 'Hollywood Squares' game show responses were spontaneous, not scripted, as they are now. Peter Marshall was the host asking the questions, of course.

Q. Paul, what is a good reason for pounding meat?
A. Paul Lynde (About fifteen minutes later): Loneliness!
And the audience laughed for another 10 to 15 minutes.

Q. Do female frogs croak?
A. Paul Lynde: If you hold their little heads under water long enough.

Q. If you're going to make a parachute jump, at least how high should you be?
A. Charley Weaver: Three days of steady drinking should do it.

Q. True or False, a pea can last as long as 5,000 years.
A. George Gobel: Boy, it sure seems that way sometimes.

Q. You've been having trouble going to sleep. Are you probably a man or a woman?
A. Don Knotts: That's what's been keeping me awake.

Q. According to Cosmopolitan, if you meet a stranger at a party and you think that he is attractive, is it okay to come out and ask him if he's married.
A. Rose Marie: No wait until morning.

Q. Which of your five senses tends to diminish as you get older?
A. Charley Weaver: My sense of decency.

Q. In Hawaii, does it take more than three words to say *'I Love You?'*
A. Vincent Price: No, you can say it with a pineapple and a twenty.

Q. What are *'Do It,' 'I Can Help,'* and *'I Can't Get Enough?''*
A. George Gobel: I don't know, but it's coming from the next apartment.

Q. As you grow older, do you tend to gesture more or less with your hands while talking?
A. Rose Marie: You ask me one more growing old question Peter and I'll give you a gesture you'll never forget.

Q. Paul, why do Hell's Angels wear leather?
A. Paul Lynde: Because chiffon wrinkles too easily.

Q. Charley, you've just decided to grow strawberries. Are you going to get any during the first year?
A. Charley Weaver: Of course not, I'm too busy growing strawberries.

Q. In bowling, what's a perfect score?
A. Rose Marie: Ralph, the pin boy.

Q. It is considered in bad taste to discuss two subjects at nudist camps. One is politics, what is the other?
A. Paul Lynde: Tape measures.

Q. During a tornado, are you safer in the bedroom or in the closet?
A. Rose Marie: Unfortunately Peter, I'm always safe in the bedroom.

Q. Can boys join the Camp Fire Girls?
A. Marty Allen: Only after lights out.

Q. When you pat a dog on its head he will wag his tail. What will a goose do?
A. Paul Lynde: Make him bark?

Q. If you were pregnant for two years, what would you give birth to?
A. Paul Lynde: Whatever it is, it would never be afraid of the dark.

Q. According to Ann Landers, is there anything wrong with getting into the habit of kissing a lot of people?
A. Charley Weaver: It got me out of the army.

Q. It is the most abused and neglected part of your body, what is it?
A. Paul Lynde: Mine may be abused, but it certainly isn't neglected.

Q. Back in the old days, when Great Grandpa put horseradish on his head, what was he trying to do?

A. George Gobel: Get it in his mouth. [I really laughed at this one ...]

Q. Who stays pregnant for a longer period of time, your wife or your elephant?
A. Paul Lynde: Who told you about my elephant?

Q. When a couple have a baby, who is responsible for its sex?
A. Charley Weaver: I'll lend him the car, the rest is up to him.

Q. Jackie Gleason recently revealed that he firmly believes in them and has actually seen them on at least two occasions. What are they?
A. Charley Weaver: His feet.

Q. According to Ann Landers, what are two things you should never do in bed?
A. Paul Lynde: Point and laugh.

The Old Marine

A crusty old Marine Sergeant Major found himself at a gala event hosted by a local liberal arts college. There was no shortage of extremely young, idealistic ladies in attendance, one of whom approached the Sergeant Major for conversation.

'Excuse me, Sergeant Major, but you seem to be a very serious man. Is something bothering you?'

'Negative, ma'am. Just serious by nature.'

The young lady looked at his awards and decorations and said, *'It looks like you have seen a lot of action.'*

'Yes, ma'am, a lot of action.'

The young lady, tiring of trying to start up a conversation, said, *'You know, you should lighten up a little. Relax and enjoy yourself.'*

The Sergeant Major just stared at her in his serious manner. Finally the young lady said, *'You know, I hope you don't take this the wrong way, but when is the last time you had sex?'*

'1957, ma'am.'

'Well, there you are. You really need to chill out and quit taking everything so seriously! I mean, no sex since 1957!' She took his hand and led him to a private room where she proceeded to 'relax' him several times.

Afterwards, panting for breath, she leaned against his bare chest and said, *'Wow, you sure didn't forget much since 1957!'*

The Sergeant Major, glancing at his watch, said in his matter-of-fact voice, *'I hope not, it's only 2130 now.'*

[Don't ya love military time?]

Famous Quotes:

- Bisexuality immediately doubles your chances for a date on Saturday night. - Rodney Dangerfield
- There are a number of mechanical devices which increase sexual arousal in women. Chief among these is the Mercedes-Benz 380SL. - Lynn Lavner
- Sex at age 90 is like trying to shoot pool with a rope. - Camille Paglia
- Sex is one of the nine reasons for incarnation. The other eight are unimportant. - George Burns
- Women might be able to fake orgasms, but men can fake a whole relationship. - Sharon Stone
- Hockey is a sport for white men. Basketball is a sport for black men. Golf is a sport for white men dressed like black pimps. - Tiger Woods
- My mother never saw the irony in calling me a son-of-a-bitch. - Jack Nicholson
- Clinton lied. A man might forget where he parks or where he lives, but he never forgets oral sex, no matter how bad it is. - Barbara Bush Former US First Lady. [And you didn't think Barbara had a sense of humour?]
- Women need a reason to have sex. Men just need a place. - Billy Crystal
- According to a new survey, women say they feel more comfortable undressing in front of men than they do undressing in front of other women. They say that women are too judgmental, where, of course, men are just grateful. - Robert De Niro
- There's a new medical crisis. Doctors are reporting that many men are having allergic reaction to latex condoms. They say they cause severe swelling. So what's the problem? - Dustin Hoffman
- Sex is one of the most wholesome, beautiful and natural experiences money can buy. - Steve Martin
- There's very little advice in men's magazines, because men think, I know what I'm doing - Just show me somebody naked. - Jerry Seinfeld

- See, the problem is that God gives men a brain and a penis and only enough blood to run one at a time. - Robin Williams
- It's been so long since I've had sex, I've forgotten who ties up whom. - Joan Rivers
- You don't appreciate a lot of stuff in school until you get older. Little things like being spanked every day by a middle-aged woman. Stuff you pay good money for in later life. - Elmo Phillips
- Bigamy is having one spouse too many. Monogamy is the same. - Oscar Wilde;
- It isn't premarital sex if you have no intention of getting married. George Burns
- Santa Claus has the right idea. Visit people only once a year. - Victor Borge
- Sometimes, when I look at my children, I say to myself, Lillian, you should have remained a virgin. - Lillian Carter [mother of Jimmy Carter.]
- I had a rose named after me and I was very flattered. But I was not pleased to read the description in the catalogue: - No good in a bed, but fine against a wall. - Eleanor Roosevelt
- Last week, I stated this woman was the ugliest woman I had ever seen. I have since been visited by her sister and now wish to withdraw that statement. - Mark Twain
- Be careful about reading health books. You may die of a misprint. - Mark Twain
- By all means, marry. If you get a good wife, you'll become happy; if you get a bad one, you'll become a philosopher. - Socrates
- I was married by a judge. I should have asked for a jury. - Groucho Marx
- My wife has a slight impediment in her speech. Every now and then she stops to breathe. - Jimmy Durante
- I have never hated a man enough to give his diamonds back. - Zsa Zsa Gabor
- Only Irish coffee provides in a single glass all four essential food groups: alcohol, caffeine, sugar and fat. - Alex Levine
- My luck is so bad that if I bought a cemetery, people would stop dying. - Rodney Dangerfield
- Money can't buy you happiness ... but it does bring you a more pleasant form of misery. - Spike Milligan

- Until I was thirteen, I thought my name was SHUT UP. - Joe Namath
- I don't feel old. I don't feel anything until noon. Then it's time for my nap. - Bob Hope
- I never drink water because of the disgusting things that fish do in it. - W. C. Fields
- We could certainly slow the aging process down if it had to work its way through Congress. - Will Rogers
- Don't worry about avoiding temptation. As you grow older, it will avoid you. - Winston Churchill
- Maybe it's true that life begins at fifty, but everything else starts to wear out, fall out or spread out. - Phyllis Diller
- By the time a man is wise enough to watch his step, he's too old to go anywhere. - Billy Crystal
- The secret of a good sermon is to have a good beginning and a good ending; and to have the two as close together as possible - George Burns
- I love people who make me laugh. I honestly think it's the thing I like most – to laugh. It cures a multitude of ills. It's probably the most important thing in a person – Audrey Hepburn
- And finally...The cardiologist's diet: - If it tastes good spit it out.

Why, Why, Why

- Why do we press harder on a remote control when we know the batteries are dying or dead?
- Why do banks charge a fee for 'insufficient funds' when they know there is not enough money?
- Why does someone believe you when you say there are four billion stars, but insist on checking when you say the paint is wet?
- Why doesn't Tarzan have a beard?
- Why does Superman stop bullets with his chest, but ducks when you throw a revolver at him?
- Why do Kamikaze pilots wear helmets?
- Whose idea was it to put an 'S' in the word 'lisp'?
- If people evolved from apes, why are there still apes?
- Why do they use sterilised needles for lethal injection?
- Why is it that no matter what colour bubble bath you use the bubbles are always white?

- Is there ever a day that mattresses are not on sale?
- Why do people constantly return to the refrigerator with hopes that something new to eat will have materialised?
- Why do people keep running over a string a dozen times with their vacuum cleaner, then reach down, pick it up, examine it, then put it down to give the vacuum one more chance?
- Why is it that no plastic bag will open from the end on your first try?
- How do those dead bugs get into those enclosed light fixtures?
- When we are in the supermarket and someone rams our ankle with a shopping cart then apologises for doing so, why do we say, *'It's all right?'* Well, it isn't all right, so why don't we say, *'That really hurt, why don't you watch where you're going?'*
- Why is it that whenever you attempt to catch something that's falling off the table you always manage to knock something else over?
- In winter why do we try to keep the house as warm as it was in summer when we complained about the heat?
- How come you never hear father-in-law jokes?

And my favourite ...

- The statistics on sanity is that one out of every four persons is suffering from some sort of mental illness. Think of your three best friends - if they're okay - then it's you!

Why Condoms come in boxes of 3, 6, & 12

A man walks into a drug store with his 12-year old son. They happen to walk by the condom display and the boy asks, *'What are these, Dad?'*

To which the man matter-of-factly replies, *'Those are called condoms, son. Men use them to have safe sex.'*

'Oh I see,' replied the boy. *'Yes, I've heard of that in health class at school.'*

He looks over the display and picks up a Package of 3 and asks, *'Why are there 3 in this package?'*

The dad replies, *'Those are for high schoolboys, one for Friday, one for Saturday and one For Sunday.'*

'Cool.' says the boy. He notices a 6 pack and asks, *'Then who are these for?'*

'Those are for college men,' the dad answers, *'Two for Friday, two for Saturday and two for Sunday.'*

'Wow!' exclaimed the boy, *'Then who uses these?'* he asks, picking up a 12 Pack.

With a sigh and a tear in his eye, the dad replied, *'Those are for Married men. One for January, one for February, one for March.*

Ten Thoughts to Ponder

Number 10: Life is sexually transmitted.
Number 9: Good health is merely the slowest possible rate at which one can die.
Number 8: Men have two emotions: Hungry and Horny. If you see him without an erection, make him a sandwich.
Number 7: Give a person a fish and you feed them for a day, teach a person to use the Internet and they won't bother you for weeks.
Number 6: Some people are like a Slinky ... not really good for anything, but you still can't help but smile when you shove them down the stairs.
Number 5: Health nuts are going to feel stupid someday, lying in hospitals, dying of nothing.
Number 4: All of us could take a lesson from the weather. It pays no attention to criticism.
Number 3: Why does a slight tax increase cost you $200.00 and a substantial tax cut saves you $30.00?
Number 2: In the 60's, people took acid to make the world weird. Now the world is weird and people take Prozac to make it normal.
And The Number 1 Thought: Life is like a jar of Jalapeno peppers; what you do today, might burn your ass tomorrow.

Health Rules

I want to thank all of you for your educational e-mails over the past year. I am totally screwed up now and have little chance of recovery. For instance:

- I no longer open a bathroom door without using a paper towel or have the waitress put lemon slices in my ice water without worrying about the bacteria on the lemon peel.
- I can't use the remote in a hotel room because I don't know what the last person was doing while flipping through the adult movie channels.
- I can't sit down on the hotel bedspread because I can only imagine what has happened on it since it was last washed.

- I can't touch any woman's purse for fear she has placed it on the floor of a public bathroom.
- I have trouble shaking hands with someone who has been driving because the number one pastime while driving is picking one's nose.
- Eating a little snack sends me on a guilt trip because I can only imagine how many gallons of trans fats I have consumed over the years.
- I must send my special thanks to whoever sent me the one about the rat poop in the glue on envelopes because I now have to use a wet sponge with every envelope that needs sealing.
- Also, now I have to scrub the top of every can I open for the same reason.
- I no longer have any savings because I gave it to a sick girl (Penny Brown) who is about to die for the 1,387,258th time.
- I no longer have any money but that will change once I receive the $15,000 that Bill Gates / Microsoft and AOL are sending me for participating in their special mail program.
- I no longer worry about my soul because I have 363,214 Angels looking out for me and a special Novena/TV evangelist has granted my every wish.
- I can't have a drink in a bar because I'll wake up in a bathtub full of ice with my kidneys gone.
- I can't eat at KFC because their chickens are actually horrible mutant freaks with no eyes feet or feathers.
- I can't use cancer causing deodorants even though I smell like a water buffalo on a hot day.
- Thanks to you, I have learned that my prayers only get answered if I forward an e-mail to seven of my friends and make a wish within five minutes.
- Because of your concern, I no longer drink Coca Cola because it can remove toilet stains and tar stains on my car.
- I no longer buy gas without taking someone along to watch the car so a serial killer doesn't crawl in my back seat when I'm filling up.
- I no longer use ClingWrap in the microwave because it causes seven different types of cancer.
- I no longer buy cookies from Neiman-Marcus since I now have their recipe.

- And thanks for letting me know I can't boil a cup of water in the microwave any more because it will blow up in my face disfiguring me for life.
- I no longer go to the movies because I could be pricked with a needle infected with AIDS when I sit down.
- I no longer go to shopping malls because someone will drug me with a perfume sample and rob me.
- I no longer receive packages from UPS or Fed Ex since they are actually Al Qaeda agents in disguise. And I no longer answer the phone because someone will ask me to dial a number for which I will get a phone bill with calls to Jamaica, Uganda, Singapore and Uzbekistan.
- Thanks to you I can't use anyone's toilet but mine because a big black snake could be lurking under the seat and cause me instant death when it bites my butt.
- I can't ever pick up a $2.00 coin dropped in the parking lot because it probably was placed there by a sex fiend waiting to grab me as I bend over.
- I no longer drive my car because buying gas from some companies supports Al Qaeda and buying gas from all the others supports South American dictators.
- I can't do any gardening because I'm afraid I will get bitten by the Violin Spider and my hand will fall off.

Oh, by the way ...

- A German scientist from Argentina, after a lengthy study, has discovered that people with insufficient brain activity read their e-mail with their hand on the mouse.
  Don't bother taking it off now, it's too late.

PS: I now keep my toothbrush in the living room, because I was told by e-mail that water splashes over six feet out of the toilet.

To all who get offended. Enjoy Anyway!

- My neighbour knocked on my door at 2:30 am this morning; can you believe it was 2:30 am?! Luckily for him I was still up playing my Bagpipes.
- I sat on the train this morning opposite a stunning Thai girl. I kept thinking to myself, please don't get an erection, please don't get an erection, but she did.
- Did you hear about the fat alcoholic transvestite? All he wanted to do was eat, drink and be Mary.

- Two friends are fishing near a bridge. Suddenly a Hearse and two Funeral Cars go over the bridge so one of the men stands up, takes off his cap and bows his head. When the cars have gone he puts his cap back on, sits back down and carries on fishing. His mate turns to him and says, *' Dave, that's one of the nicest most respectful things I've ever seen.'*
  Dave replies, *'Well we were married for nearly 20 years.'*
- Paddy says *' Mick, I'm thinking of buying a Labrador,'*
  'Bugger that' says Mick *'have you seen how many of their owners go blind'*
- Man calls 000 and says *'I think my wife is dead'*
  The operator says, *'How do you know that?'*
  He says *'The sex is still the same but the dishes are piling up on the sink!*
- I was in bed with a blind girl last night and she said that I had the biggest penis she had ever laid her hands on.
  I said *'You're pulling my leg'*
- Spent $140 on eBay last week for a penis enlarger. Just opened it and some smart arse sent me a magnifying glass!!!!

English Signs from Around the World

- In a Bangkok temple: It is forbidden to enter a woman, even a foreigner, if dressed as a man.
- Doctor’s office, Rome: Specialist in women and other diseases.
- Dry cleaners, Bangkok: Drop your trousers here for the best results.
- In a Nairobi restaurant: Customers who find our waitresses rude ought to see the manager.
- On the main road to Mombassa, leaving Nairobi: Take notice: when this sign is under water, this road is impassable.
- On a poster at Kencom: Are you an adult that cannot read? If so we can help.
- In a City restaurant: Open seven days a week and weekends.
- In a cemetery: Persons are prohibited from picking flowers from any but their own graves.
- Tokyo hotel's rules and regulations: Guests are requested not to smoke or do other disgusting behaviours in bed.
- On the menu of a Swiss restaurant: Our wines leave you nothing to hope for.
- In a Tokyo bar: Special cocktails for the ladies with nuts.

- Hotel, Yugoslavia: The flattening of underwear with pleasure is the job of the chambermaid.
- Hotel, Japan: You are invited to take advantage of the chambermaid.
- In the lobby of a Moscow hotel across from a Russian Orthodox monastery: You are welcome to visit the cemetery where famous Russian and soviet composers, artists and writers are buried daily except Thursday.
- A sign posted in Germany's Black Forest: It is strictly forbidden on our black forest camping site that people of different sex, for instance, men and women, live together in one tent unless they are married with each other for this purpose.
- Hotel, Zurich: Because of the impropriety of entertaining guests of the opposite sex in the bedroom, it is suggested that the lobby be used for this purpose.
- Advertisement for donkey rides, Thailand: Would you like to ride on your own ass?
- Airline ticket office, Copenhagen: We take your bags and send them in all directions.

CONCLUSION

I hope you have enjoyed these jokes enough to obtain the other three volumes

Laughter is an essential ingredient to everyday living. If you haven't had a laugh today - you're depriving yourself enjoyment in life. Bring the jokes out when you're having a bad day - that's what I do. You'll find that things just get better.

If you wish to read books on more serious topics, please see the following information about how to order my other paperback, audio and e-books.

www.dealingwithdifficultpeople.info

www.ingramcontent.com/pod-product-compliance
Lightning Source LLC
LaVergne TN
LVHW020711110826
845149LV00012B/2209

9780992357900